The *Prudence* of *Mr* Gordon Brown

Previous works by the author

Consulting Father Wintergreen (1974)
A Real Killing (1976)
Who Runs the Economy? (jointly with Rupert Pennant-Rea) (1978)
Mrs Thatcher's Economic Experiment (1984)
Britain Without Oil (1985)
Mr Lawson's Gamble (1989)
The Spectre of Capitalism (1992)
2066 and All That (2000)

The *Prudence* of *Mr* Gordon Brown

William Keegan

WILEY

Published in 2003 by   John Wiley & Sons, Ltd, The Atrium, Southern Gate
Chichester, West Sussex, PO19 8SQ, England

Phone   (+44) 1243 779777

Email (for orders and customer service enquires): cs-books@wiley.co.uk
Visit our Home Page on www.wiley.co.uk or www.wiley.com

Other Wiley Editorial Offices

John Wiley & Sons, Inc. 111 River Street, Hoboken, NJ 07030, USA

Jossey-Bass, 989 Market Street, San Francisco, CA 94103-1741, USA

Wiley-VCH Verlag GmbH, Pappellaee 3, D-69469 Weinheim, Germany

John Wiley & Sons Australia, Ltd, 33 Park Road, Milton, Queensland, 4064, Australia

John Wiley & Sons (Asia) Pte Ltd, 2 Clementi Loop #02-01, Jin Xing Distripark, Singapore 129809

John Wiley & Sons Canada Ltd, 22 Worcester Road, Etobicoke, Ontario, Canada, M9W 1L1

Wiley also publishes its books in a variety of electronic formats. Some content that appears in print may
not be available in electronic books.

British Library Cataloguing in Publication Data

A catalogue record for this book is available from the British Library

ISBN 0-470-84697-6

Typeset by Mathematical Composition Setters Ltd, Salisbury, Wiltshire.
Printed and bound in Great Britain by T.J. International Ltd, Padstow, Cornwall.
This book is printed on acid-free paper responsibly manufactured from sustainable forestry
in which at least two trees are planted for each one used for paper production.

Dedication

To the memory of Arnold Kemp – 'Confusion to our enemies'

Contents

Preface

The Present does well to profit from the Past, lest Future conduct go astray.

These words, from the Latin inscription on Titian's *Allegory of Prudence*, could well have been the motto for Gordon Brown's Chancellorship. In the late summer of 2002 Brown became Labour's longest-serving Chancellor, beating Denis Healey's record of five years and two months. From the moment he arrived in office, Gordon Brown's watchword was Prudence. If ever a Chancellor wished to profit from studying the past mistakes of governments, both Labour and Conservative, it was Gordon Brown. He had ample opportunity for study because Labour was out of office for eighteen years, from 1979 to 1997, and he was elected to Parliament in 1983, at a very early stage in Labour's 'Wilderness Years'.

Gordon Brown has been an enigmatic Chancellor. On the one hand, he has received widespread praise for granting independence to the Bank of England. This bold move, taken with his fiscal prudence, enabled him to defy the experience of previous Labour Chancellors and avoid a financial crisis for an entire Parliament.

On the other hand, he has been criticised for his caution towards the euro and for the way that under his Chancellorship the Treasury has stretched its tentacles far and wide and become, in the eyes of many, too powerful and a baleful influence on government.

In both political and financial circles there has been much speculation as to whether prudence was a cover for an 'Old' Labour politician – the student 'Red Gordon' of the 1970s waiting to show his true colours – or whether Brown had simply 'sold out' and accepted what many on the left regarded as a Thatcherite agenda.

I attempt to show in this book that the truth is more complicated. Brown accepted much of the 'market' philosophy of the Conservative years, not least the emphasis on promoting competition and 'flexible' labour markets. But he drew the line at competition and privatisation in health, describing his stand as 'an affirmation that duty, obligation, service and not just markets and self-interest, are at the very heart of what it means to be a citizen of Britain.'

The purpose of the prudence was not to gain time before reverting to the kind of 'spendthrift' policies that got Labour into trouble in the 1970s. It was to establish a reputation for financial probity which would enable Labour to embark on a public spending programme which the electorate and the financial markets would regard as sensible and affordable.

But prudence is not necessarily rewarded: having invested less in the public services during the first term than the Conservatives had done in comparable periods, Brown found his prudence was being questioned rather earlier than he had hoped.

Acknowledgements

The author would like to thank the friends, colleagues and contacts who have assisted with the writing of this book. Among those who gave invaluable comments on an earlier version but bear no responsibility for any errors are Anthony Howard, Bill Martin, Ian Gilmour, Alastair Macdonald, Harry Keegan, Michael Coyne, Victor Keegan, Dr Ray Richardson, Adrian Hamilton, Adam Raphael, Nick Mathiason, Simon Holberton and John Llewellyn.

At the *Observer*, Frank Kane, Andy Beven, Andrew Rawnsley and the late Arnold Kemp offered lots of encouragement, while at home my wife Hilary Stonefrost successfully matched full support with a diplomatic silence about the difference between estimated and actual time of completion of THE BOOK.

The gap between my 1960s manual typewriter and modern technology was bridged in the early stages by Jeni Giffen. The lion's share of the work fell to Linda Knights and her computer in Thorpe Bay, ably supported by the faxing and photocopying services of Mary Fulton, Kate Popham and Fiona Laurent at Town House Publicity in Islington.

Paul Anderson generously lent me some of his archive from *Safety First* and *Tribune*; the staff of the House of Commons Treasury Committee were helpful with research; and Michele Wollstonecroft, secretary to *Observer Business*, and assistant Ben Flanagan held the fort on many occasions.

I should like to thank Clive Callow, who introduced me to John Wiley & Sons, my editor Sally Smith, her colleagues Julia Lampam and Tracy Clayton, my copy-editor Lesley Winchester, proofreader Andrew Finch, and of course my agent Gillon Aitken.

Introduction

$\mathcal{I}$ have been interested in the interaction between politics and economics from a disturbingly early age. As someone who grew up during and after the Second World War, I have vivid childhood memories of wartime controls, ration books, and the 'Age of Austerity' presided over by the Attlee governments of 1945–51. For a long time bananas were plastic toys dangling from the ceilings of greengrocers' shops. The most popular pupil in school was the boy who arrived one day at the end of the war with real bananas.

I remember the 1945 general election. On VE Day I had innocently asked my father whether there would be any more news now that the war was over. His firm answer was: Yes, Churchill had done a good job during the war, but he had leant more on Attlee – the Deputy Prime Minister in the coalition government – than people had realised and now it was time to throw out Churchill and the Conservatives and let Labour get on with the job. The job involved not only rebuilding a peacetime economy in which bananas returned to the shops, but also achieving a much fairer society than had characterised prewar Britain; above all, unemployment must be minimised and the balance of power between employers and trade unions redressed.

The wartime economy had been centrally controlled, with the emphasis on defence and 'essential' industries. The transition to a 'normal' peacetime economy absorbed the first Attlee government (1945–50) and the short-lived second Attlee government of 1950–51. Those governments are now fondly remembered for the creation of the Welfare State. 'New' Labour's spin-doctors had not yet been born but would no doubt have christened the era, 'From Warfare to Welfare'. In particular, there was the National Insurance Act 1946, and the National Health Service Act 1948; the attempts to make education available to all had begun with the 1944 'Butler' Education Act under the wartime coalition.

But what stands out most in my memory is the pillorying of the Attlee governments by the press. They were constantly blamed for an era of austerity that was not always their fault. Even legitimate criticism about their commitment to nationalisation seemed over-whelming – anti-government propaganda used to start the day on the breakfast table with the 'Mr Cube' anti-nationalisation campaign run by the sugar company Tate & Lyle.

Peter Hennessy (*Never Again*) paints a broadly sympathetic picture of Labour's attempts to abolish the poverty, the dole queues, the ill-health and the poor sanitation associated with the 1930s. A more sceptical account of the period is *The Lost Victory* by Correlli Barnett, whose message is contained in the sub-title, *British Dreams, British Realities, 1945–1950* (Barnett had also tried to puncture what he regarded as the myths about wartime efficiency in *The Audit of War, The Illusion and Reality of Britain as a Great Nation*). In his memoirs, *Change and Fortune*, Douglas Jay, a Minister in the Attlee governments and the Wilson governments of 1964–70, lamented the degree to which the British press was overwhelmingly anti-Labour throughout his career – a foretaste of New Labour's obsession with trying to control the media and 'spin' the news when it came to power in 1997.

In a sense, there is nothing new about the attempts to 'modernise' the Labour Party under Tony Blair and Gordon Brown. The Party had spent much of the time since the war trying to make itself acceptable to an overwhelmingly conservative country, most of whose press was hostile towards it. Both Attlee and Gaitskell had their tussles with the left.

The persistent ghosts at Labour's planned feast were fear of alienating the country at large by being too left-wing, and fear of being blown off course by financial crisis. The two ghosts were close relations: fear of 'left-wing' policies was seldom far from the minds of those in the City or foreign financial markets – dubbed 'the Gnomes of Zurich' by Harold Wilson in the 1960s – who had the power to withdraw funds from London and cause financial crises.

Ramsay MacDonald, the first Labour Prime Minister briefly in 1924, and then in 1929–31, had hardly been to the left of the Party. Harold Wilson, Prime Minister from 1964 to 1970 and again from 1974 to 1976, disappointed those who looked with favour on his putative 'Bevanite' past, and was very much the pragmatist in office – as was James Callaghan, Prime Minister from 1976 to 1979.

Fighting off pressure from the left traditionally goes with the job of being a Labour Prime Minister or Chancellor of the Exchequer. So does dealing with financial crises. As Gordon Brown prepared for the office of Chancellor, he knew he would have to fight off not only pressure from the left but also pressure from the motivation that had taken him into politics in the first place. As Student Rector of Edinburgh University (in the *Red Paper on Scotland*, 1975), he had complained about Scotland's 'unstable economy and unacceptable level of unemployment, chronic inequalities of wealth and power and inadequate social services'.

Then, the remedy for the ills of society lay in 'the public control of industries essential to the provision of social needs and services, the priorities being building and construction, food and food processing, insurance and pensions'. Also on the list were energy, land, banking and foreign trade, as well as 'the assets of the major British and American multinationals in Scotland' and so on.

It was a manifesto of which Tony Benn would have been proud. Indeed, shortly after it appeared there were fears at the very top of the US government that Britain, during the financial crisis of 1976, might fall prey to a left-wing takeover unless the moderate Callaghan government was given help. While the budding politician sometimes referred to as 'Red Gordon' was developing his political ideas, a Labour government was learning the hard way that the financial markets also had votes and being reminded that they were certainly not left-wing votes.

While financial crises were associated with Labour governments – Labour was in office when Britain was forced off the gold standard in 1931; when the pound was devalued in 1949 (with Sir Stafford Cripps as Chancellor) and 1967 (with James Callaghan as Chancellor); and during the financial crisis of 1976 – on every one of these

3

occasions there were sound *economic* reasons for a devaluation of the pound, irrespective of the colour of the government. The difficulties of conducting economic policy may sometimes have been aggravated by 'left-wing' policies (or sops to the left); but in the end the financial markets decided that the pound was fundamentally overvalued anyway. The fact that these very same financial markets had sometimes contributed to the earlier overvaluation of the pound added a certain piquancy to these crises.

Indeed, notwithstanding the existence of the kind of Labour government (in 1974–75, for instance) to whose policies many operators in the financial markets viscerally objected, those very same markets were driving the pound up and up, in effect preparing it for a hard fall. Such gyrations became all the more destabilising after the breakdown of the Bretton Woods fixed exchange rate system in the early 1970s and the subsequent abolition of capital controls in 1979.

In a sense, idealists in the Labour Party have always been fighting on three fronts: trying to woo the vital middle-class vote in marginal constituencies; attempting to appease the financial markets; and all the while pursuing the goal of what can be broadly described as 'social progress' through a system of government and administration that they felt was Conservative and biased against them. The social progress is the end; the attempt to hold the fort on the other two fronts is the means.

Way back in 1956, Anthony Crosland, in *The Future of Socialism*, had tried to find the appropriate compromise for a Labour Party that did not wish to be in permanent Opposition. *The Future of Socialism* was described by a biographer, David Reisman, as an 'important contribution to the theory of the middle ground'.[1] The German left adopted social democracy at the celebrated Bad Godesberg Conference of 1959. Labour baulked at such a move in 1969, when the Wilson government failed to implement the White Paper, *In Place of Strife*, with its blueprint for the reform of trade unions. Labour also retained Clause Four of its Constitution, committing it to 'common ownership of the means of production, distribution and exchange'.

4

The Wilson governments of 1964–70 attempted to overcome the putative constraints of 'Whitehall and the system' on Labour ideals by instituting the Department of Economic Affairs (DEA). The DEA was supposed to act as a counterweight to the Treasury, focusing on long-term improvements in productivity and raising the economic growth rate. But the long term proved to be a series of short terms and, in effect, the DEA was 'seen off' by the Treasury and by what Harold Macmillan, a decade earlier, had termed 'Events, dear boy, Events'.

Gordon Brown was a schoolboy at the time of the battles between the Treasury and the DEA; but study of that particular episode was to exert a seminal influence on his thinking when, from 1992 onwards, he was Shadow Chancellor preparing for his eventual arrival at the Treasury. If Labour could not beat the Treasury, it would first have to join it and then capture it.

From the point of view of wooing the middle-class vote in marginal constituencies and appeasing the financial markets, the Labour Party of the 1970s and early 1980s had been moving backwards from Crosland. Even Crosland himself, when Secretary of State for the Environment and Local Government, said, of spending by local authorities in the mid-1970s, 'The party is over'.

For many years the Conservatives did not allow Labour to forget that the Callaghan government had had to go cap in hand to borrow from the International Monetary Fund in 1976 in order to restore financial confidence. Yet while that first Thatcher government of 1979–83 was presiding over the worst recession since before the Second World War, the Labour Party was distancing itself from marginal voters and from the financial markets; its 1983 manifesto promised unilateral nuclear disarmament; departure from the European Community; and an 'alternative economic strategy', including import controls. Labour had also distanced itself from some of its own 'modernisers', to the point where Roy Jenkins, former Home Secretary and Chancellor, left Labour to found his own Party, the Social Democrats.

The Labour manifesto of 1983 could have been written by 'Red Gordon'. It was in fact the product of the labyrinthine Labour

Party decision- (and 'resolution'-)making process of the time. Gerald Kaufman, a senior Labour figure, subsequently described it as 'the longest suicide note in history'.

Around that time, Peter Shore, who had been the cabinet minister responsible for the ill-fated DEA just before its demise and who was a former head of the Labour Party Research Department, said to me, 'The Labour Party is like an old baggage train. It keeps taking on additional commitments, but it never sheds any of its load.'

As a prominent opponent of the European Community and an advocate of import controls, Shore was one of the people who piled up that excess baggage, although the most energetic and forceful architect of 'the alternative economic strategy' was Tony Benn. This subversive work had been going on throughout the 1970s. Callaghan, when Prime Minister, gave his officials the impression he was more concerned about the threat from the left than from the Conservatives. A Labour government that believed in workers' rights was reduced to bugging the telephones of prominent left-wing union leaders, long before Mrs Thatcher took on Arthur Scargill.

It was on the 1983 manifesto that both Gordon Brown and Tony Blair were elected to Parliament (and, as Michael Foot reminded his 90th birthday party audience at the Old Labour Party's favourite London restaurant, the Gay Hussar, on 16 July 2003, 'He [Kaufman] got elected on it himself!'). Brown had undoubtedly come from the left; it is said of Blair that he did not know which Party to join. Under the leadership of Neil Kinnock in 1983–92, the Labour Party shed much baggage from its goods train and Tony Blair and Gordon Brown, in close alliance, became important junior members of the 'modernisation' team. Brown was close to John Smith, another Scot, during the latter's short period as leader in 1992–94, after Neil Kinnock resigned on Labour's loss of the 1992 general election.

Under the leadership of Michael Foot (1980–83), Neil Kinnock and John Smith the Labour Party devoted itself to attacking almost everything Mrs Thatcher (Prime Minister 1979–90) and John Major (Prime Minister 1990–97) stood for. Thatcherism and all its works constituted Public Enemy Number One. Although it is the name of Tony Blair that is perhaps most associated in the public mind with New Labour, much of the groundwork was prepared under Kinnock's leadership, with Brown and Blair playing important roles. Nevertheless, while the broad theme was that of making the Labour Party acceptable to middle-class marginal voters and the financial markets, the attack on Thatcherism was maintained; so that, for example, both privatisation and the Conservative government's involvement of the private sector in public projects via the Private Finance Initiative were roundly condemned, in the early stages, by Gordon Brown.

Brown first shone in the public eye as Shadow Chief Secretary to the Treasury in 1987–89. The Chief Secretary is the Number Two minister at the Treasury; it is a Cabinet post with responsibility for the control of public expenditure. The 'shadowing' experience gave Brown his first chance to get to grips with Treasury matters; in particular, he deputised for John Smith as Shadow Chancellor in 1988 after the latter's first heart attack. This brought Brown into direct confrontation with Nigel Lawson, then at the peak of his reputation as a great Chancellor – a reputation that did not endure.

The reason Lawson's reputation descended from its remarkable peak in 1988–89 was, essentially, that the Lawson Boom ended in tears. Brown's superb performance in Parliament contributed to the wearing down of Lawson's morale in 1989, when the latter was also at war with Mrs Thatcher over his policy of intervening in the foreign exchange market – instructing the Bank of England to buy or sell sterling in order to keep it close to the value of the German Deutschmark.

Lawson had adopted a policy of, essentially, trying to tie the British inflation rate to the traditionally low German inflation rate after the Conservative Party's solution to Britain's inflation problem – monetarism – had failed. The Thatcher government had discovered that it was not easy to control the money supply and that, in any case, the forces causing inflation were complex. But Lawson had concluded that the various 'supply-side' reforms introduced during the 1980s (reducing the powers of the trade unions, lower direct taxes, less regulation, privatisation, etc.) had contributed to an 'economic miracle'.

It turned out that productivity (output per worker) had not increased in the way the Chancellor thought, and that the consumer boom revived the inflationary pressures that the Thatcher government had been supposed to repress. Lawson's shadowing of the Deutschmark was a preliminary gambit before what he hoped would be the success of his latest panacea, entry of the pound to the European Exchange Rate Mechanism (ERM).

But Mrs Thatcher's personal economic adviser, Sir Alan Walters, was opposed to this, thus reinforcing her own instincts. Brown in the Commons was able to make a meal of the divisions between the 'neighbours' of Numbers 10 and 11 Downing Street. The Treasury's rashly optimistic forecasts of what the economy could achieve led to a serious overestimation of the strength of the public finances, even to fantasies that the economy was so strong that the entire national debt could be repaid.

The proximate cause of Lawson's resignation was Mrs Thatcher's refusal to sack Walters; but the 'truest' cause was her intransigence over Europe and the ERM. In the light of the evolution of the Conservative Party's subsequent policy towards Europe, it is ironic that Mrs Thatcher should have been fatally weakened in 1990 not only by widespread hostility towards the poll tax but also by her *anti*-Europeanism.

She was gradually being worn down by the pro-Europeans within her Party who, amazingly enough, then predominated at a senior level; and by a collective Whitehall, Confederation of British Industry (CBI) and City view that Lawson had been right and that Britain should put the pound into the ERM. John Major, Lawson's successor as Chancellor, also espoused the ERM cause.

There was a sense in which the British government and the British establishment (financial and otherwise) felt that, to employ a phrase Mrs Thatcher had used in the early 1980s to justify her policies of the time, they had 'no alternative'. Mrs Thatcher's alternative – monetarism – had itself proved a failure. Whatever praise the Thatcher government might, then and afterwards, have attracted for putting the trade unions in their place and introducing the world to 'privatisation', an inflation rate of 9.5% in 1990

(Mrs Thatcher's last year as Prime Minister) was hardly a laudable achievement. Placing the pound in the European exchange rate mechanism might have been seen by the Foreign Office and others as an important step towards an historic union with the rest of Europe, but for the economic establishment it was an acknowledgement of failure.

Predictably, the hoped-for solution proved a failure too. Although only a few of us noted it at the time, the pound entered the ERM at an overvalued exchange rate and the adventure ended in disaster on Black Wednesday, 15 September 1992. In order to sustain the pound within the agreed range, the Treasury and the Bank of England maintained interest rates at a level which threatened to cripple large sections of British industry.

The British recession of 1990–92 was essentially the 'bust' phase of the traditional 'boom-and-bust' business cycle that Gordon Brown vowed to abolish when he became Chancellor, but it was severely aggravated by the high interest rates the Treasury and the Bank of England were forced to offer holders of sterling in order to prevent a run on the pound. In the end, it was obvious to all that the Black Wednesday proposal to raise interest rates to 15% the following day was an empty threat.

Paradoxically, the decline in the pound and the reductions in interest rates that followed the pound's departure from the ERM, while the consequence of a failed political and economic strategy, were the necessary steps towards economic recovery. A lower exchange rate assisted the competitiveness of British industry – by making exports cheaper or more profitable – and lower interest rates helped both industry and the consumer.

But the Major government never recovered from the humiliation of the Black Wednesday fiasco. Meanwhile, however, the Labour Party itself was in a state of shock – not so much for having supported ERM entry too, but over the loss of the 1992 general election, which, on the basis of the subsequent Clinton declaration, 'It's the economy, stupid!', the Opposition should have won handsomely.

After John Smith's convalescence from his first heart attack, Gordon Brown had been Shadow Secretary for Trade and Industry from late 1989 to 1992. Although Smith and Brown worked closely together, it was Smith who bore responsibility for Labour's 'Shadow Budget' in the run-up to the April 1992 general election. The nation was in recession and there was a great deal of evidence to suggest that the electorate had finally become fed up with the Conservatives after their long run. As a very senior Conservative Minister confided to me some years later, '1992 was the election we should have lost.'

Various explanations have been given for Labour's demise after a long period when it was ahead in the opinion polls. There was the reaction to the perceived triumphalism of the Sheffield Rally (although the Labour lead in the polls had already begun to weaken before the rally); it was alleged that some of the electorate were distrustful of the then Labour leader, Neil Kinnock (although Kinnock had also been leader when Labour was way ahead in the polls); and there was panic in middle-class marginal constituencies, and concern in the financial markets, about Labour's tax plans.

It seemed to me then, and still seems now, that the clever exploitation of the threat from 'Labour's Tax Bombshell' by the Conservative Party Chairman Chris Patten, and by much of the press, was the real explanation for the collapse of Labour's lead during the last week of the 1992 campaign.

Neil Kinnock himself was very nervous about John Smith's 'Shadow Budget'. The theory behind the Shadow Budget was attractive: people did not trust Labour with the nation's finances, so a serious effort had to be made to persuade them of Labour's good intent. Labour had spending plans: the marginal voters and the financial markets must be shown that these could be financed. Unfortunately, the financing involved raising tax rates (via higher National Insurance contributions), not just for the rich, nor even for the 'middle classes', but for people earning around £24,000 a year. While this might have seemed a reasonable level at the time for a Shadow Chancellor based in Scotland, it did not go down too well in the Midlands and south-east of England.

Although no doubt constructed with the best of intentions, the Labour Party's 1992 Shadow Budget proved to be a huge political miscalculation. Noting the way the press played up the story, Tony

Blair's 'focus group' adviser, Philip Gould, and the man who became his press secretary, Alastair Campbell (then a columnist on the *Sunday Mirror*), became convinced that the reaction of journalists to the impact of Labour tax plans on themselves had become a major factor in the calculation of what was politically feasible.

It was in 1992 that the three strands of the prudence which was to dominate so much of Gordon Brown's thinking came together. As a 'son of the Manse' he was a naturally prudent and cautious person – even, as we shall see later, in his colourful student days. His long study of the career of his hero, the Clydeside MP James Maxton, had convinced him that principles were not enough if they kept a politician away from the practice of government. After the shock of the April 1992 election defeat, he and others at the top of the Labour Party became almost terrorised by fear of doing anything to offend not just the constituency represented by Middle England – the marginal voters and the *Daily Mail* – but also the ambitious members of the upper working class who had also felt threatened by John Smith's tax plans. It is debatable what impact the front page of *The Sun* on election day actually had (a picture of Neil Kinnock's head inside a light bulb with the headline, 'If Kinnock wins today will the last person in Britain please turn out the lights') but it did not help and, together with prominent front page coverage in *The Times* of the 'tax threat', it made the upper echelons of the Labour leadership prudent to the point of cravenness in their subsequent dealings with the Murdoch press and the *Daily Mail*.

The shock was all the greater because with Neil Kinnock as leader, Labour had already done so much to modernise itself, while John Smith as Shadow Chancellor had for years been trying to develop good relations with the City and business on what he called the 'prawn cocktail circuit'. After the 1992 defeat, Michael Heseltine quipped, 'Never have so many thousands of crustaceans died in vain.'

Gordon Brown came to the fore after the April 1992 defeat, and brought his own natural prudence to the deliberations of a party that, for all its efforts, had not proved prudent enough with its electoral intentions.

After Neil Kinnock's resignation as leader, and John Smith's elevation, Gordon Brown was the natural choice for Shadow Chancellor. In an echo of the interest in American experience that was to form an important part of his economic approach, however, he described himself in *Who's Who* as 'Opposition Treasury Secretary' (they don't have 'Shadow Ministers' in the USA, but they do have Treasury Secretaries).

So an even more prudent Labour Party now had a naturally prudent Shadow Chancellor, who had already been an active 'moderniser' but who would have to re-examine all his beliefs – many of them laid out in public speeches and writings – in the light of the electoral requirement to be more prudent than ever. It would always be prudence for a purpose, although he would have to spend five more years in Opposition and one term as Chancellor before he felt he could fully reveal that purpose.

As we shall see, the years 1992–97 saw meticulous planning by Gordon Brown. He consulted widely, and it is difficult to overestimate the influence of his personal economic adviser for much of that period, and chief economic adviser in office, Ed Balls. Balls was a young leader writer on the *Financial Times* who had studied Labour governments of the past, drawn lessons from the failure of Conservative macroeconomic policies in the 1980s and come under the influence of some of the leading American economists during a postgraduate spell at Harvard. Together with the millionaire Member of Parliament Geoffrey Robinson, who provided them with funds and with useful links to the City and business, Brown and Balls drew up plans for what they termed 'Prudence with a Purpose'.

The essence of their diagnosis was that Labour governments of the past had failed in one way or another with the nation's finances, but that Conservative governments, more trusted in the first instance by the voters and the financial markets, had also failed. The Thatcher/Major period – the formative period for Ed Balls, who was born in 1967 (Brown, born in 1951, had of course been old enough to witness the economic crises of the 1960s and 1970s) – was characterised by a succession of periods of 'boom and bust'.

Monetarism had proved a disaster, but so had the two periods when the exchange rate was chosen as the lodestar (the late 1980s and the early 1990s).

Gordon Brown was the driving force behind the preparation of the economic parts of New Labour's programme and 1997 manifesto but, as leader, Tony Blair would preserve an important veto when it came, for example, to the question of whether they should raise the top rate of tax. Brown and Balls became almost obsessed with the need for financial 'stability'. Past Labour governments had spent too much money in their early years of office and their noble ambitions had ended in tears. Labour was the party of devaluation, and assumed to be the party of inflation too (to prove their point, as the 1997 election approached, bankers and financial advisers in the City were warning their clients that a Labour victory would mean *much* higher mortgage rates).

Balls was influenced by the neo-Keynesian view from the USA that Budget deficits – except as 'automatic stabilisers' in a recession – were not as beneficent as traditional British Keynesians liked to believe, and the important thing for a modern left-wing Party was to establish low inflation and a strong budgetary position. Then traditional Labour goals – a higher growth rate, full employment, a more equitable distribution of income – could be pursued.

'This is the whole point of our emphasis on stability', he said. 'This is why I got involved in politics. If we don't achieve these aims we will have failed.' This was in reply to concerns expressed about the emphasis on 'stability'; an emphasis that could, in the early days, sound like very old-fashioned, pre-Keynesian economics. This firm and well-planned approach was to lead to the strict 'budgetary rules' – introduced by Brown when he became Chancellor – and to that trump card in relations with the financial markets, the surprise announcement within five days of the May 1997 election of independence for the Bank of England in the key area of monetary policy.

The prudence of Gordon Brown and the prudence of the Party that in 1992 had lost its fourth general election in a row were to be reinforced by a very prudent official economic policy machine. For the collapse of the Lawson Boom, the humiliation of the ERM episode, and the ultimate disaster of Black Wednesday had dealt a series of savage blows to the morale and self-confidence of the Treasury itself.

The Treasury had come a cropper. Its economic forecasts in the late 1980s proved wildly optimistic. Its assessment of improvements in productivity and the assumed invulnerability to balance of payments crises were ill-founded. In this it fell prey to a dominant Chancellor in Nigel Lawson. The Treasury admires firm leadership, but this can prove disastrous when that leadership is over-confident and in the wrong direction.

After Black Wednesday the Treasury became very prudent indeed. One could never accuse any Treasury official of becoming 'humble' after the manner of Uriah Heep, but suddenly the Treasury lost its nerve and espoused the newly fashionable virtues of openness, transparency and greater willingness to listen to the advice of independent advisers.

The newly acquired prudence of the Treasury, and sheer necessity, combined to put the public finances on the path to stability well before Gordon Brown arrived. Norman Lamont, the unfortunate Chancellor to the ERM disaster, proceeded with the tax rises and public spending cuts needed to improve the budgetary position. Kenneth Clarke, who succeeded him, meant what he said when claiming, 'good economics is good politics', and handed over a much-improved Exchequer to Brown. After taking a look at the books, Gordon Brown privately expressed satisfaction with the economy he had inherited.

In one of his important early speeches as Shadow Chancellor (August 1993),[2] Gordon Brown had emphasised that Labour 'will not tax for its own sake' and believed in 'creating the necessary wealth to fund the social benefits we demand'. This proved to be more of a 'double' commitment than might have appeared at the time. It was a prelude to the 'low tax' pledges on which Labour was finally elected in 1997, but it was also an advance signal of the 'sequential' approach to policy that Brown was to take in government. Traditional Keynesians believed in using fiscal policy – changes in tax rates and in plans for public spending – to regulate the level of demand for goods and services in the economy. They also knew that, in the long run, public spending could not rise faster than the economic potential of the economy as a whole without 'making room' for it by clamping down on consumer spending; but in general Labour and Keynesian economists had believed that if public spending was deemed necessary, it could be financed one way or another. Gordon Brown's approach was to cut deficits and the interest on them, and build up a kind of war-chest first, which might well mean taking risks with the standard of public services on the way. By 1997 the public sector finances were improving rapidly, but the same could not be said for the public services or the infrastructure. Voters were disenchanted with, and tired of, the Conservatives and concerned about health and education.

Meanwhile, much of the preparatory work for a better monetary policy had been done, so that handing over the setting of interest rates to the Bank of England was described by one official as 'the icing on the cake'. This is not to detract from the historic importance of the decision: fiscal prudence was one important element in Brown's strategy; monetary prudence was the second.

What better way to reassure the financial markets – which were pricing in higher interest rates as an assumed consequence of a Labour government – than to hand counter-inflation policy over to the central bank?

The monthly meetings of what became known as the 'Ken and Eddie Show' in the mid-1990s were part of the more open approach to monetary policy, with the Governor Eddie George being able to publish his previously private advice. The publication of inflation targets, and the innovation of the Bank of England's quarterly *Inflation Report*, were also established practice before Brown arrived at Number 11. The Bank of England had gained in influence from the Treasury's embarrassments over Black Wednesday, but it did not yet have the power. Indeed, one Whitehall official characterised the tone of the meetings in the run-up to 1997 as follows: 'The Ken and Eddie Show is a means whereby the Governor can say why interest rates should rise and the Chancellor can say, "I've listened to you, Eddie, and the answer is NO"'.

It was known that New Labour was considering granting independence to the Bank; but the speed of the decision surprised everyone. What was not known at the time was that, despite refusing to grant independence to the Bank himself, Kenneth Clarke while Chancellor was quite happy for Brown and Eddie George to have a number of secret meetings, during which the form of any future monetary policy committee was discussed.

Caution in fiscal matters and caution in monetary matters were therefore to be the first two prongs of Gordon Brown's prudent approach to the economy – but there was to be a third, and that was Europe. With John Smith, Gordon Brown had been a strong supporter of ERM membership; but after the debacle of 1992 (for which, of course, the Conservative government of the day rightly took the blame) Brown developed a dislike for the ERM. It was noteworthy that he had hired Ed Balls in 1993 as his personal economic adviser when the latter's main claim to fame during his brief career at the *Financial Times* was a *Fabian* pamphlet attacking the ERM and 'Euro-monetarism'.

One of the conditions for eventual adoption of the euro was prior entry to the ERM and the establishment of an independent central bank. But the way in which the Monetary Policy Committee (MPC) was set up was different in key respects from what would be required for entry to the euro. In effect, Brown invented an alternative model to the European Central Bank. Brown was in favour of the single currency for longer than is popularly realised, but after six months at the Treasury, caution with regard to the euro became the third prong of his prudent approach. The MPC (and the fiscal prudence) could be seen as necessary parts of a strategy to ensure that, if and when a positive decision were taken about the euro, the British economy would be strong enough to withstand the loss of the exchange rate flexibility that had been vital in the past, for, on account of relatively low productivity and higher inflation, Britain had required periodic devaluations to restore price competitiveness for its exports (and hence to boost output and employment). Equally, however, if the experiment worked, Britain in the Treasury's view would have established that it did not need to join the euro for defeatist economic reasons. For what drove John Major and the British Establishment in general to embark on the ill-fated ERM venture was in considerable part the belief that other counter-inflation options had been tried and failed.

There were times during Labour's first term (1997–2001) and early in the second term when people began to make comparisons between Gordon Brown and one of his predecessors, Philip Snowden (Chancellor 1924 and 1929–31). Snowden was associated with the disaster of 1931 and had gone down in Labour history as a politician who became in thrall to financial orthodoxy. Had Gordon Brown turned into a Chancellor who was all Prudence and no Purpose?

Brown was certainly being feted as a successful Chancellor by the world at large. There had been no run on the pound during his entire first Chancellorship – unprecedented for a Labour Chancellor! He had proved himself a first-class steward of the nation's finances. But from the Labour Party's point of view, had he not accepted too much of the Thatcherite inheritance? Where *was* that Purpose?

Brown hoped to prove this with his Budget of April 2002, with its open avowal of policies to redistribute income (policies which had been building up slowly but stealthily) and his huge injection of resources into the Health Service. This was more like a 'Labour' Budget than anything he had achieved before. 'Here we see at last the authentic Gordon Brown', said a senior Downing Street adviser.

But the Budget of 2002 came after four years when public sector spending and investment, as a proportion of gross domestic product, had been *lower* than in the previous years of Conservative government – themselves years when public spending had been heavily constrained. While concern grew about the state of the Health Service, the crumbling transport system and the general quality of Britain's public services and infrastructure after 1997, the Chancellor himself persevered with prudence to the point where it could be asked whether, to paraphrase what had once been said about the Conservative politician Iain Macleod – 'too clever by half' – the worry was that Gordon Brown had been 'too prudent by half'.

This criticism might also apply to the perceived success of the independent Bank of England and the Monetary Policy Committee.

Inflation was at this stage well under control, but the Bank's brief was to concentrate almost entirely on achieving an inflation target (2.5%). There was accumulating evidence of a serious trade deficit and a number of members of the MPC were openly concerned that the pound was overvalued, but it was not their job to do anything about this; and ever since the disaster of Black Wednesday, the Treasury and Bank had lost confidence in their ability to influence the exchange rate.

Beneath the apparent success of prudence, there were some long fuses burning away. In his obsession with financial orthodoxy, Gordon Brown had given little weight to the fact that Labour governments in the past had been associated with devaluation primarily because they had presided over long periods of an overvalued currency. Under Gordon Brown, Labour had done so again and all historical experience suggested that trouble lay in store.

We shall examine the 'imprudence' that, ironically, may lie behind the prudence in the following chapters, never forgetting the well-known political overtone – that one of the motives behind Gordon Brown's 'Prudence for a Purpose' was the purpose of eventually becoming Prime Minister.

∞ ∾ ∽

CHAPTER ONE

A prudent background

ordon Brown's father, in common with many members of his generation, had been horrified by the levels of unemployment and the degree of poverty that prevailed in Britain during the 1920s and 1930s. He welcomed the election of the Attlee Labour government in 1945. His second son, James Gordon Brown, was born on 20 February 1951, eight months before the second Attlee government went down to defeat at the October 1951 General Election.

The young Gordon's formative years coincided with what Harold Wilson used to describe as 'thirteen wasted years of Tory misrule'. His father, a Church of Scotland Minister, was not politically active but inculcated into his second son a strong sense of social justice and civic duty.

'He taught me to treat everyone equally, and that is something I have not forgotten,' the future Chancellor observed.[1]

As a son of the manse, Gordon Brown was also brought up with a strong sense of the Protestant work ethic. Many Labour supporters were to be surprised in later years by the impression that, having poured scorn on the Conservatives in opposition, Brown seemed to accept much of the 'Thatcherite Settlement'. The explanation is that, while there was certainly such a thing as 'society' in his Scottish upbringing, there was also an emphasis on those famous Victorian values of self-reliance and self-improvement that were an integral element in what became known as 'Thatcherism'. On Brown's Presbyterian obsession with the work ethic, a biographer has commented, 'He honestly believes that work is good for the soul, which should mean that his own is in no danger.'[2]

In the manse where he was brought up, prudence was indeed celebrated as one of the cardinal virtues. In years to come, those who came into contact professionally with Gordon Brown were to be impressed by the sense of industriousness that accompanied his prudent approach to life. The fact that he himself recalls a somewhat carefree childhood, in which the pursuit of the football ranked higher than the pursuit of his studies, is not inconsistent with his predisposition to hard work. In common with many highly gifted children and teenagers, he seems in those days to have displayed an air of 'effortless superiority' – not, in the pejorative sense, of looking down on lesser mortals, but in the way he could be obsessed by games and still produce first-class results in the examination hall.

While not as precocious as John Stuart Mill – it was children's books that he was memorising at the age of four, rather than Greek or Latin verse – the young Gordon, with his voracious appetite for 'sums', prompted one of his primary school teachers to recall, 'I couldn't keep Gordon in work. I was always having to give him more to do.'[3] He proceeded from Kirkcaldy West (primary school) to Kirkcaldy High School. His academic brilliance coincided with a 'forcing house' experiment in the Scottish education system, which found him having to choose his future specialisation at the age of 12 (history) and going to university at 16, an age that, even at the time, he thought was too young. But the alternative was an extra year at school doing the same syllabus – after two years when he had proved everything he needed to with outstanding examination results.

One of the defining traits of the 'new' Labour government of which Brown was to become such a powerful member was its obsession with 'the media'. Gordon Brown's interest in politics and the media date from his childhood, and in due course his main job before he embarked on a full-time political career was in the media. His own media 'work experience' began when he was nine, as sports reporter for his elder brother John's handwritten *Local News*. At 11 he was 'sports editor' for John Brown's *Gazette*.

The following year politics and the media were merging in the 12 year-old Gordon's life. The enterprising Brown brothers were now calling their very local publication, *Scotland's Only Newspaper in Aid of the Freedom from Hunger Campaign*. The Chancellor-in-the-making wrote an article predicting that 'this year' (1963) might be the Conservatives' 'last in office for a long time'.[4] Harold Macmillan, at 69, was too old for the 'responsible job' of Prime Minister. Then came the 12 year-old's early manifesto: 'We should and must have a strong and reliable government, to promote our interests in Europe and the world. In Britain, too, we must have a less casual government that must take drastic measures in solving our unemployment, economic, transport and local government problems.'[5]

The boy's concern about unemployment was father to the man's obsession with 'Welfare to Work'. There was also an early hint of the concept of 'shared sovereignty' and recognition that Britain needed to be part of a wider group: 'Not long ago we were looked upon as a strong country: now our only hope of survival, in an age dominated by nuclear power, is to link with our stronger Western allies.'[6]

Brown was the undoubted 'success' of the school forcing system, although he said himself that 'at 16 I had more problems than I had years' and he felt a strong sense of unfairness about the way many other 'guinea pigs' fell by the wayside. 'They pushed people too hard,' he said. 'The ignominy and rejection of failure (sic) could have been avoided.' At 16 he was arguing for 'respect for every individual's freedom and identity, and the age-long quality of caring'.[7,8]

But at this stage no one was accusing him of being dour, or obsessed with work to the exclusion of play. A classmate recalled: 'The whole school was an intellectual hot house at that time. But in our class, it was Gordon who set the pace, and the rest of us would do our best to keep up ... socially, as well as academically. He was so sharp. The banter and wisecracking that would go on between the boys was great. Gordon was always the quickest to come out with a funny line and would soon have the rest of us doubled over in laughter.'[9]

As Chancellor, Gordon Brown has persistently given the impression of being a man in a hurry, as well as a man with a mission. He can be impatient to the point of giving offence – a characteristic which, when manifested during meetings in Brussels, can feed suspicions of euroscepticism. But he often metes out the same treatment to his colleagues in the Cabinet, and I have personally seen him occupy himself with something completely different while ostensibly hosting one of his seminars at Number 11 Downing Street.

We shall see later that 'something happened' to him in 1992–94, when the shock of the election defeat of 1992 – the election the Tories should have lost – was followed by the death of John Smith in 1994 and the surge of support for Tony Blair in preference to Brown as Party leader. The darker, more complex Gordon Brown was not much in evidence during what were, at times, his riotous student days at Edinburgh University; neither did he appear to have a reputation for brusqueness in his early days in the Commons, from 1983. But in years to come many people who encountered him were to discover a complicated, brooding, even saturnine figure. His young brother Andrew has described him as having a 'shy' trait. To those with whom he feels relaxed he can be hugely entertaining company; and when he tries he can make very witty speeches to large audiences. But it undoubtedly suited him to cultivate a 'dour' image after 1992.

There were two experiences in his student days that may partly serve to explain characteristics that were magnified by events in the 1990s. The first and most painful experience was his discovery, within days of arriving at Edinburgh University to read history, that a rugby injury earlier that year (1967) was causing him to lose the sight of his left eye. Within the next few years he also suffered a detached retina in his right eye. This eye was saved thanks to the latest laser technology, learnt in America by an Asian eye surgeon, Dr Hector Chowla, head of the eye department at Edinburgh Royal Infirmary. 'The clue to Gordon Brown,' said a Labour Party insider, 'is that he is naturally worried about losing his good eye. He is a politician in a hurry.' James Naughtie has noted: 'Everyone who knows him well recognises that his single-mindedness and relentless determination must in part be attributed to that trial in his late teens. For them, it explains elements in his character which sometimes seem impenetrable to outsiders.'[10] It is interesting to note that his right eye was saved by a union of the health service and American technology. He was to preserve a close interest in the health service, and his Chancellorship was to be marked by a persistent search for new ideas from the USA.

His first (October 1967) term at Edinburgh was dominated by the vain attempts to save his left eye. While the Labour Chancellor of the day, James Callaghan, was fighting to stave off the devaluation of the pound that was eventually forced on him (and prompted his resignation), the 16 year-old Gordon Brown was, according to his memory of it, 'required to lie completely horizontal and virtually stationary for a matter of months' in the misplaced hope that 'if the eye and retina remained completely still they would bond back'.

It was a dispiriting, nay terrifying, time for the young student. Was the psychological impact that some close observers associate with his sense of urgency in later life overcome initially by his youthful spirits? After the first failed operation he bounced back into circulation, beginning his university work in spring 1968. An academic observer says he was 'an important figure, even as an undergraduate. He was hugely popular, a natural politician: totally self-assured. He was good to everybody, and everyone wanted to know Gordon Brown. He was a bit like a Bill Clinton figure'[11] (which was not what Bill Clinton himself was like at Oxford around the same time, from all accounts ...). On the other hand, a flatmate – somewhat closer to home than his politics lecturer – maintains that Brown led 'a quiet life' for the first two years, 'studying hard', while others recall that he could be 'a little dour'.[12]

Certainly, the more flamboyant period of his time at the University – his stint as 'Student Rector' – occurred after he had obtained his first degree in 1972 with flying colours. Brown took the Court of the University by storm. The principal, Michael Swann, had greeted him on his arrival as an undergraduate by proclaiming that he was the youngest Edinburgh student of the postwar era. On experiencing trouble from the student activist, Swann could hardly wait to take up his impending appointment as Chairman of the Governors of the

BBC, leaving Edinburgh within the first year of Brown's three-year term as Student Rector (1972–1975).

The themes of Brown's Rectorship were greater involvement of students in the running of the University and closer association of the University with the town. He defeated Swann's attempt to unseat the Rector as Chairman of Court meetings with an interesting resort to the Royal Prerogative: the Chancellor of the University was the Duke of Edinburgh, and Brown's girlfriend at the time was Princess Margarita of Romania, who happened to be the Duke's goddaughter.

The period spent as Student Rector went down in Brown's mind as a chronicle of wasted time. Reflection on it almost certainly contributed to the subsequent dash for a political career. 'I feel in retrospect I could have done more if I had stood for the local council instead of being Rector. It became a bit of a diversion.'[13]

But it is not entirely clear that the time was wasted: 'It was quite a revelation to me to see how politics was less about ideals and more about manoeuvres.'[14] A certain 'blooding' does seem to have taken place; no student of the former Student Rector's subsequent political career could safely accuse him of knowing nothing about political manoeuvres.

The idea of a Student Rector had been Brown's own, but the first Student Rector stepped down early. What the entire episode showed was Brown's remarkable flair for publicity. Reports of those early efforts of the Brown brothers at 'local' journalism had featured in the Scottish daily press, but one suspects that this was because the press's attention had been drawn to them by the authors.

Student Brown had, early on, embarrassed Principal Swann by revealing that the University had investments in South Africa's mining companies; Swann was a prominent member of the anti-apartheid movement, and a spirited Brownian campaign forced the University to divest itself of the shares. When standing for the Rectorship against the industrialist Sir Fred Catherwood, Brown unearthed undeclared business interests – John Laing, the company for which Catherwood worked, was doing construction work on campus! These were early examples of the 'investigative' approach that the future Chancellor was to perfect on his way up the political

24

ladder. Later, from the Opposition benches, he attracted attention by making capital out of a series of 'leaks' from the civil service.

Having been born shortly before Attlee lost the general election of 1951, Gordon Brown says that his earliest political memory is of being allowed to stay up late for the 1959 election, when the Conservatives under Macmillan retained office and Hugh Gaitskell, that early moderniser, was defeated. That was the 'Never Had It So Good' election. But after that Macmillan and the Conservatives lost their way. It was the Conservatives, under Macmillan, who became concerned about the British economy's relatively poor performance *vis-à-vis* our Continental neighbours in the early 1960s; they tentatively embarked on 'indicative planning' by setting up the National Economic Development Office, with a Council composed of employer, trade union and government representatives.

After Macmillan resigned because of ill-health in 1963, the Tories chose the 14th Earl of Home to succeed him. Home renounced his peerage and fought a by-election in Kinross and West Perthshire (a safe Conservative seat) as Sir Alec Douglas-Home. The 12 year-old Gordon Brown was on a family holiday in the area; he followed Home around and was 'amazed and appalled' that the candidate made 'the same speech everywhere he went. I soon saw through the tricks that the politician got up to. I thought it was awful.'[15]

In those days the big economic issue on the doorstep of the Brown manse in Kirkcaldy, Fife, was the decline of the textile and mining industries and consequent social problems. The National Economic Development Office and Council ('Neddy' as they became known) were supposed to address such issues, and the Department of Economic Affairs, set up by the new Labour government under Harold Wilson in 1964, was intended to take a long-term view of economic decline and try to redress the balance.

As a young teenager Brown was among the millions who were glued to the satirical television programme *That Was The Week That Was* on Saturday nights. 'TW3', as it was known, was part of the culture that helped to destroy faith in the Conservatives' ability to deal with Britain's problems, economic and otherwise. The Macmillan/Home government was tired. It was time for a change.

There was an atmosphere of excitement about the election of the Wilson government, with its promises to modernise the economy.

Brown was hardly alone in being disappointed by the performance of the Labour governments of 1964–70. In 1971 his entry into student politics at Edinburgh was marked by an article for a university newspaper in which he ridiculed 'promises and pledges' made by student politicians, describing them as 'words so devalued by Harold Wilson'.

When one looks back on the British economy's performance in 1964–70, the record does not look so bad, notwithstanding the problems associated with the strength of the trade unions – problems which were exacerbated by the commitment to what some economists described as 'over-full employment'. The principal macroeconomic mistakes were probably, first, to aim, via the various National Plans, at growth targets (4% per year) which were over-ambitious and hence provoked ridicule; and, second, to postpone a necessary devaluation until 1967. After some nervous moments, the November 1967 devaluation delivered the goods (i.e. faster growth of exports, slower growth of imports and a more balanced economy) and Roy Jenkins's brief Chancellorship of 1967–70 is widely considered to have been one of the most successful of the twentieth century.

From the microeconomic point of view, however, new institutions such as the Wilsonian Industrial Reorganisation Corporation did not live up to expectations – although many of its members went on to make names for themselves in other areas of public life; and the government looked problems with the trade unions firmly in the face and blinked.

Harold Wilson was surprised to lose the general election of 1970 and surprised to scrape home in the February election of 1974. The choice of deflationary measures rather than devaluation had been associated with a rise in unemployment from 391,000 to 599,000 between 1966 and 1967 (annual average). But unemployment had fallen in 1969 and Labour had been doing well in the opinion polls early in 1970. In Labour folklore the loss of the spring 1970 election is linked to Roy Jenkins's 'fiscally sound' Budget of 1970. But, as

Jenkins later pointed out, the Budget was popular with the public. It was the freakish impact of two imported 'Jumbo Jets' on the subsequent trade figures that led to headlines such as 'Britain Back in the Red' and put the nail in the coffin of Labour's reputation for economic competence. Subsequent revisions were to show that the trade figures had been in surplus all along – but by the time the statisticians pronounced, the damage had been done and Labour was back in Opposition.[16]

The Conservatives, under Edward Heath, arrived in office aiming to reform the unions, and encourage market forces. They were hoping to avoid having to 'bail out' inefficient companies with taxpayers' money.

Their resolve was severely tested. At one stage they had to announce a rescue package for Rolls-Royce. Unemployment rose from around 600,000 in 1969–70 to 792,000 in 1971 and 875,000 in 1972. But these figures are annual averages. In the winter of 1971–72 unemployment was approaching the 1 million mark – a level at that stage unprecedented in postwar years.

The views of the next Labour Chancellor of the Exchequer but one were not widely sought at the time, but Gordon Brown offered them to Edinburgh student readers. Brown had gone to Glasgow during the 1971 summer vacation to visit the scene of the industrial dispute at Upper Clyde Shipbuilders (UCS). His verdict was ambivalent. Writing several months before the 'U-turn', Brown said, 'Whatever happens, the Clyde workers will have made the point that the right to work forged in Beveridge's time must be restated in Wilson's super-efficient managerial society and Heath's *laissez-faire* individualist nation.'

He said that demanding the right to work was 'a new challenge to the pre-eminence of economic over social planning, and it may lead to a complete rethink of the managerial society with positive policies for workers' control and participation.' But he judged that the 'work-in' was 'doomed to failure ... whatever happens, the old men of Clydeside will look back at the might-have-beens of 1971.'[17]

Ideas about 'workers' control' were prominent on the left at the time, with Yugoslavia seen as a model. When I met Lord Macdonald, a future Minister in Tony Blair's government, way back in those days, his conversation was full of the need for workers' control. After trying to assist UCS, the Conservative Secretary for Trade and Industry, John Davies, lost patience with the firm and decided it should be liquidated. But unemployment rose to over 1 million in the winter of 1972 and the Chief Constable of Glasgow made a telephone call to the Prime Minister, in which he said that if the chaos surrounding UCS continued, he could no longer be responsible for public order in the city, where unemployment was exceptionally high.

That widely proclaimed 'U-turn' was a seminal moment in Britain's postwar economic history. From then on the Heath government tried to cooperate with the unions and to use every weapon in its economic armory to combat unemployment. Fiscal policy was relaxed, so that public spending was encouraged instead of being cut back; the view was taken that, with the floating of the pound after the breakdown of the Bretton Woods system, the balance of payments need no longer be a constraint; and wage agreements were linked to the cost of living index at just the time – the first oil crisis – when inflation was accelerating, thereby aggravating the inflationary spiral. The stage was set for the reaction against consensus politics that took place within the Conservative Party when it went back into Opposition. For, despite his cultivation of the unions, Heath lost the spring election of 1974. The winter of 1973–74 had been a terrible period, with a protracted dispute between the government and the miners over a large wage claim, and industrial trouble that reduced the economy to a three-day week and a period of numerous power cuts. In the words of one senior civil servant, 'We verged on anarchy'. The final straw was the miners' strike, which precipitated the calling of a general election on the issue of 'Who governs the country?' The reaction to the high spending policies of the Heath government (mark two) was seen under the Thatcher governments from 1979 onwards. 'She tries to think what Ted would have done, and does the opposite' was the way one colleague described Mrs Thatcher's approach.

Gordon Brown was going to have to wait until 1983 before entering Parliament and coming to the attention of Party and country as a vigorous opponent of the deflationary policies known as 'monetarism' and of the widening social inequality associated with Thatcherism. But in the second half of the 1970s, while Labour was grappling with the most difficult economic situation since the austerity years after the Second World War, Brown was making his mark in Scottish politics, and attracting the attention of future Labour leaders.

While still an undergraduate, Brown had delivered leaflets for Robin Cook during the 1970 election campaign. Cook had lost Edinburgh North, and in 1974 was contesting Edinburgh Central, which he won. The February election of 1974 brought Labour back to power, but without an overall majority. The October election gave it a small overall majority of four. In both campaigns Gordon Brown canvassed for Cook, who at 28 was five years his senior.

The October 1974 election brought 11 members of the Scottish National Party (SNP) to Westminster. Scottish nationalism was on the rise, and both the SNP and the Liberals were in favour of devolution. In the end, James Callaghan, who took over as Prime Minister after Harold Wilson resigned in March 1976, had to give in to pressure for devolution in order to survive, such was the fragility of his majority.

Callaghan was fighting on many fronts. Labour had inherited a rapidly deteriorating inflationary situation from Heath, and the inflationary trend was severely exacerbated by the 'oil shock' of 1974–75. The financial markets had lost confidence in sterling: Callaghan and his Chancellor Denis Healey were trying in 1976 to negotiate with the International Monetary Fund and to bring inflation (which averaged 24.2% in 1975) and public spending under control.

Although the majority of Labour MPs were against devolution for Scotland, the promise of concessions to the devolutionists was the only way Callaghan could, by pacifying the Liberals and SNP, preserve his majority. In 1975 Gordon Brown had ridden the rising tide of the Scottish devolution movement by editing *The Red Paper on*

Scotland, described by one biographer as 'a collection of essays which was meant to be the socialist prospectus for a new Scotland'.[18] In his introduction, *The Socialist Challenge*, he urged 'the Labour Movement in Scotland' to draw up 'a coherent strategy with rhythm and modality to each reform to cancel the logic of capitalism' (sic). There should be 'phased extension of public control under workers' self-management'. He criticised the SNP for policies that 'reject class warfare'. He complained that it was 'increasingly impossible to manage the economy both for private profit and the needs of society as a whole'.

At this stage in his career he was working on his PhD thesis, *The Labour Party and Political Change in Scotland, 1918–29*, a study that was not completed until 1982 but which was already involving his emotions in the idealism and desire to change society of the early socialists. But he complained in the *Red Paper* that socialism had altered over the years from a 'moral imperative' to a position where 'Today, for many it means little more than a scheme for compensating the least fortunate in an unequal society' – a quotation, ironically, which probably reflected the disappointment of Old or 'real' Labour supporters three decades later with the performance of the Blair/Brown governments.

In 1976, while temporarily lecturing in politics at the University, Brown became prospective Labour candidate for Edinburgh South, at the age of 25. From 1976 to 1980 Gordon Brown commuted between Edinburgh and Glasgow, where he lectured at the Glasgow College of Technology for the Workers' Educational Association. His lectures were on politics and Labour history, dovetailing neatly with his other academic task of those years, the long haul to complete his PhD thesis on the historical relationship between the trade unions and the Scottish Labour Party.

The admirer and student of the 'Clydesiders' of the 1920s and 1930s was now actively becoming a quintessential 'machine' politician himself. One biographer described him as devolution's 'leading advocate',[19] so it was perhaps not surprising that the energetic Scottish champion of the cause that was both constraining the Callaghan government and enabling it to hang on should have been made Chairman of the Scottish Labour Party's Devolution Committee (in 1978).

The man for whom he had campaigned several times, Robin Cook, was against devolution at the time and actively campaigning on the other side. John Smith was the Minister handling the devolution policy for Callaghan from the Cabinet Office in London. As James Naughtie has put it, 'The agonies of the Callaghan government quickly matured Brown and a generation of young Scottish politicians.'[20] And Paul Routledge (Brown's biographer) observes: 'He was only 27, yet here he was in charge of delivering a central plank of Labour government policy for Scotland.'[21]

When the Labour Party returned to office in 1974 it had been against devolution. The rise of the SNP and Labour's knife-edge majority in the Commons had changed the official policy but not the views of all Labour MPs. George Cunningham, MP for Islington South West but a Scot, had successfully inserted into the 1977 Scotland Bill a clause requiring that, in the proposed referendum, 40% of the Scottish *electorate*, not just 40% of those turning out to vote, should approve the plan for a devolved assembly.

The Scottish Labour Party was split and there was much disillusionment with the Callaghan government after the 1978–79 'Winter of Discontent' (involving strikes and the breakdown of a government-imposed incomes policy that had been aimed, with some success, at reducing inflation). Passions ran deep but there was something half-hearted about the campaign, with prominent Labour MPs such as Tam Dalyell and the rising star Neil Kinnock making trips to Scotland to *oppose* devolution.

Brown was on a losing wicket and so was the Callaghan government. Only one-third of the electorate voted for devolution. After the result, the Conservatives, supported by the Liberals and SNP, called a vote of No Confidence in the Callaghan government, which the government lost. Mrs Thatcher and the Conservatives won the consequent general election of 3 May 1979. Thus, the immediate cause of the demise of the Callaghan government was not the 'Winter of Discontent' but the failure of its proposals for devolution. But in popular folklore it has become the former.

Nevertheless, the Opposition was able to capitalise on the economic problems of Labour and to promise lower taxes into the bargain. Despite the fact that it had made serious efforts to come to grips with public expenditure and inflation after the loss of confidence which forced it to borrow from the International Monetary Fund in 1976, the Callaghan government was tired. Indeed, it can be argued that the sheer effort of trying to run the economy in those very difficult times made it almost inevitable that the Labour government would run out of steam.

It is an ill wind that blows no losing politician any good. Labour lost the 1979 election, and Gordon Brown, aged 28 and standing for the first time, failed to win Edinburgh South, but he had already had a walk-on part on the Westminster stage, done his loyal best for the devolution Minister John Smith – who became his mentor – and attracted the attention of the man who was to be a leader when he finally arrived in Parliament in 1983.

Neil Kinnock recalled: 'He was on the other side from me on devolution, but we agreed on all other matters. He was a very bright, very pleasant young chap, with views close to mine on political questions. I would not claim him as a protégé, but I was pretty determined to ensure that I would give him any assistance I could.'[22]

In the *Red Paper* of 1975, Brown had indicated that he was not necessarily averse to the break-up of the UK. Robin Cook subsequently argued that Labour could not counteract the nationalist surge with a kind of 'third-way' solution. A close observer at the time commented that Brown's support for the Callaghan government's compromise devolution proposals showed that 'there is a very, very powerful thread of pragmatism in Gordon Brown's character ... [a] willingness to compromise in pursuit of a bigger objective.' The speaker drew a parallel with the prudent 'fiscal constraints' that Brown adopted 'willingly' in the run-up to the 1997 general election 'to abolish Labour's tax-and-spend image and ensure victory.'[23]

We shall in due course examine whether that later episode of prudent pragmatism was in fact necessary. The pragmatism of the budding machine politician in the 1979 election campaign was shown by the way the young candidate, who was supported by a trade union, went out of his way to dismiss fashionable suggestions for taming the unions. 'What we require is agreement and consultation, not legislative confrontation,' he insisted.[24]

An interesting foretaste of the future Chancellor's prudence was apparent in a statement he made on the eve of the 'No Confidence' vote. At a time when Labour was considered 'soft' on inflation and many non-monetarist economists considered the fight against unemployment to be more important than the fight against inflation, Brown said that a 'No Confidence' vote against the Callaghan government 'would do nothing but harm to the fight against unemployment *and inflation*'[25] (author's Italics).

The Callaghan government had of course been fighting inflation – having reached a terrifying peak of 26.9% in August 1975, the rate fell to around 10% at the time of the 1979 election; but an attempt by Chancellor Denis Healey to impose a 5% ceiling on pay rises had proved too ambitious for the Labour Party's paymasters, the trade unions.

For all the earlier travails with inflation, with excessive public spending and with the financial markets and the IMF, Labour and the economy made a remarkable recovery in 1977 and 1978. Callaghan had hinted that there might be an October election. We shall never know what the result would have been, but many political analysts thought that the government was at least in with a chance. It was downhill all the way after the decision to postpone the election. Commenting on the defeat on 3 May 1979, Callaghan observed, 'I'll tell you what happened. We lost the election because people didn't get their dustbins emptied, because commuters were angry about train disruption and because of too much trade union power. That's all there is to it.'[26]

That had all happened during the so-called 'Winter of Discontent' that followed the October 1978 decision not to call a widely expected election. The myth has grown up that after the Thatcher government was elected on 3 May 1979 the British economy was magically transformed. But if it was indeed transformed – a thesis which is eminently contestable – this was a long time after 1979.

The Conservatives arrived with a naïve belief in the magical powers of monetarism (control of the money supply) to defeat inflation. They took some bizarre decisions, including the near-doubling of VAT (from 8% to 15%), which had an immediate impact on the retail prices index. Within a year the rate of inflation had doubled, to 21.9% in May 1980.

Until the Falklands War of April 1982, Mrs Thatcher was the most unpopular Prime Minister since records began. To double both the rate of inflation *and* the level of unemployment was a difficult achievement, but Mrs Thatcher and her colleagues managed it. This constituted a remarkable rise in what economists call the 'misery index'; and until the Falklands War the economic incompetence of the government exerted a far greater influence on the government's popularity than the leftward march of the Labour Party, which was led by Michael Foot but heavily influenced by the strategy of Tony Benn and other left-wingers. The latter managed to increase the dominance of the extreme left via constitutional and procedural changes at both local and national level. I myself knew of a number of people who tried to enter Labour Party politics at the time but who were driven frantic by the spider's web of arcane procedural rules, which was turning the Party into a kind of *politburo*.

More basic, old-fashioned 'machine' politics were operating north of the border. Gordon Brown had become a member of the Transport and General Workers' Union (TGWU) in 1976; the TGWU was the power behind the Labour organisation in the new constituency of Dunfermline East, and also the biggest union in the local Rosyth dockyard, which was in turn the biggest industrial employer in the whole of Scotland.

Gordon Brown demonstrated all the natural political operator's skills in the way he used his TGWU connections to weave his way into being adopted at the eleventh hour as parliamentary Labour candidate for the safe seat of Dunfermline East. He was good – he had become Chairman of the Scottish Labour Party earlier in 1983 – but safe seats do not descend from Heaven, even for the sons of Presbyterian Ministers. His talent was spotted by the TGWU and he made the most of their discovery. His fellow Scots at the time noted that his approach to politics was becoming increasingly pragmatic – 'He used to vote all over the place as his conscience dictated. Now he votes according to block considerations. He realises you can't operate as an individual, however bright, in the Labour Party,' a colleague observed at the time.[27]

While he was climbing further up the ladder of Scottish politics between the elections of 1979 and 1983, Gordon Brown also worked during most of that period for Scottish Television as a producer, journalist and current affairs editor. These were years when he honed his skills in the 'sound-bites' so beloved of New Labour in power 15 years later. 'Social justice for consumers' would be an apt summary of *What's Your Problem?*, a weekly programme he edited. *Rigs to Riches* was what he called a programme about tax-dodging North Sea oil companies.

On the eve of the 1983 election Brown gave a foretaste of his approach-to-come when he accused the Thatcher government of a 'Watergate-style cover-up', saying that Mrs Thatcher had ordered the destruction of documents outlining plans for cuts in social security benefits. (This concerned a Whitehall study which, based on an unusually low assumption for the economy's trend growth rate, indicated that the burden of future state pensions would be phenomenal. It was 'destroyed' because it offered Labour a chance to say that the welfare state was 'not safe in the Conservative hands'.) But unemployment was the issue that most concerned the Brown family – father and sons: it was on Labour's plans to cut unemployment from 3 million to 1 million in five years that Brown campaigned.

Brownian prudence was seen in the way the candidate promised a 'strong' increase in public spending but also a 'measured' one. The Labour Party manifesto on which he campaigned promised exit from the European Economic Community, unilateral nuclear disarmament (the Rosyth dockyard in Brown's constituency worked on Polaris nuclear submarines), extensive intervention in industry and the imposition of import controls. Intriguingly, Tony Benn, by far the biggest influence on the manifesto, confessed in his diary his view that 'The Shadow Cabinet wouldn't implement it if they were elected.'

As if the manifesto were not bad enough, the Labour Party vote was also seriously eroded by the breakaway Social Democrats (led by Roy Jenkins and David Owen), who took a lot of disaffected Labour supporters with them. But then, it was because of the leftward shift of Labour that the SDP had been formed. Biographer Routledge notes that at a 1981 meeting of the Labour Party's Scottish Executive, 'Brown was the only speaker to state the obvious fact that winning the support of voters must be the overriding priority.' Perhaps this ought to have been an 'obvious fact', but it was not obvious to many of the left-wingers dominating the Labour Party at the time. For them it would have been an important shift in policy.[28]

This was Brown the moderniser speaking. After his personal election victory in June 1983 he could fly down to London and join the effort to rescue the Party. But he could not possibly have known how long that effort would take.

CHAPTER TWO

1983 – 1987

'$\mathcal{R}$oy Jenkins is going to start his own political party' was the remarkable news a friend of mine imparted after staying at a weekend house party in Wiltshire early in 1980. The source was impeccable, but in the *Observer* we reported it discreetly: it was the kind of story that, if too many enquiries were made to make it stand up, would almost certainly have fallen down.

'Own political party' was a slight exaggeration. There was an 'Owen' political party involved too. Jenkins, David Owen, Shirley Williams and William Rodgers met in November 1980 to discuss forming a new 'centre' party in the face of the leftward drift of the Labour Party. For them the crunch issue was the constitution of the new 'electoral college' for choosing Labour Party leaders. First mooted in 1976 by Neil Kinnock after his candidate Michael Foot failed to win the leadership, agreed in principle at the Labour Party Conference of October 1980, the electoral college was born at a special Conference in Wembley in January 1981.

From the left's point of view, the idea of the electoral college had been to broaden the selection process for the leader, in order to embrace as 'electors' not only the parliamentary Labour Party but also the trade unions and the rank and file, in the shape of the constituency parties. As it turned out, Michael Foot himself had not needed the electoral college when becoming the unexpected successor to Callaghan in a Parliamentary Labour Party (PLP) vote in November 1980, between the two conferences.

Even Foot and Kinnock, champions of the electoral college, had hoped that the biggest weight in voting power would remain in the hands of the PLP. But the shock result of the electoral college cup final at Wembley was to give 40% of the votes to the trade unions and 30% each to MPs and constituency parties, where the trend of power was very much to the left.

It has been cynically suggested that forming his own party was primarily a way for Roy Jenkins to return to British politics after his stint as President of the European Commission from 1977 to 1981. He had gone to Brussels in the first place partly out of his genuine enthusiasm for 'Europe', but also because of his disaffection with the Labour Party and his differences with Callaghan over the appropriate job for him (Jenkins) in the Cabinet. No doubt they also had differences about who should be Prime Minister, but that is another story: Jenkins had lost in the PLP leadership election of 1976; he got only 56 votes on the first ballot, well below Foot (90) and Callaghan (84). Jenkins had wanted to be Foreign Secretary in Callaghan's Cabinet, but Callaghan said he was too European for the Labour Party of the time and encouraged him to take up the offer of the Presidency of the European Commission.

The decisive votes in the election of Michael Foot as leader have been attributed to the machiavellian tactics of certain right-wing Labour MPs who wanted an excuse to join a breakaway party and deliberately voted for a left-winger of whom they disapproved. The *casus belli* for Jenkins & Co, who became known as 'the Gang of Four', was the constitution of the electoral college. The following day the defectors came out in public, as it were, to declare: 'The calamitous outcome of the Labour Party Wembley Conference demands a new start in British politics. A handful of trade union leaders can now dictate the choice of a future Prime Minister. The Conference disaster is the culmination of a long process by which the Labour Party has moved steadily away from its roots in the people of this country and its commitment to parliamentary government.'[1]

The result was certainly calamitous for the PLP that Gordon Brown was to join as the newly elected member for Dunfermline East in June 1983. The left was fatally divided for the rest of the decade: 'centre-left' or 'right-wing Labour' politicians who joined the Social Democratic Party (SDP) and, later, the SDP–Liberal Alliance, took a crucial element of the Labour vote with them.

In 1983 the British economy had just been through the worst recession since the Second World War. Yet the Labour share of the vote, at 27.6%, was the lowest since 1918. Having already lost the 1979 election, Labour suffered the sharpest fall (nine points) in voting share between 1979 and 1983 of any party since 1945. With the left of centre so fatally divided – at 25.4% the Liberal-Social Democratic Alliance was only 2.2% behind Labour – it did not matter that the Conservative share of the vote in fact fell between 1979 and 1983. The non-Conservative vote was bigger than the Conservative one but it was definitively split: under the first-past-the-post system, Mrs Thatcher romped home.

Giles Radice, from the right-wing 'Solidarity Group' of the Labour Party, observed, 'The SDP breakaway and the formation of the Alliance was an unmitigated disaster for Labour ... the moderate group inside the party was gravely weakened.'[2] Although Neil Kinnock seems to have been the first to suggest the electoral college, it was the most vociferous and energetic left-winger, Tony Benn, who was usually credited (if that is the word) with having been the driving force behind the series of internal constitutional reforms that included mandatory re-selection of Labour MPs (at the 1979 Party Conference), and the particular form the electoral college took. He believed that the Wilson/Callaghan governments of 1974–79 had betrayed the cause, and that activists outside Parliament had to capture control of the party from Westminster. Again, as Radice has written: 'At its zenith in 1980–81, the Bennite cocktail was a heady brew ... at a time when the voters were shifting to the right, the Labour Party seemed to be lurching irretrievably to the left.'[3]

In 1979–83 the Labour Party should have been pulverising a government whose policies were causing unemployment and hurting the poor and disadvantaged – the very people Labour was supposed to stand up for. Yet the tragedy was that it was locked in internal strife, and the consequence of that strife was that it would be in Opposition for a lot longer than four years, for 1979–83 proved to be merely the first instalment of Labour's years in the wilderness, which were to last until 1997.

Although Michael Foot's decision to resign was announced the weekend after Labour's terrible June 1983 defeat, the new, drawn-out internal electoral process meant that the selection of his successor, Neil Kinnock, was not formally completed until the Labour Party Conference in October. Building on the connection with Kinnock from the devolutionary saga of the late 1970s, Gordon Brown was the only MP from the new intake to be put onto Kinnock's campaign committee.

While 'Red Gordon' had been urging Bennite-style policies from his Edinburgh base in the mid-1970s, Neil Kinnock had been something of a left-wing firebrand in Parliament itself. But Kinnock began gradually to distance himself from the extreme left after Mrs Thatcher's victory of May 1979. Always a member of the democratic socialist Tribune Group, a forum within the PLP for those who tended to be left of the leadership, between 1979 and 1983 Kinnock would be found, in the words of his biographer Martin Westlake, 'fighting alongside the centre and right of the party .... Returning Labour to power became the overriding objective, and certainly took precedence over the intra-party wrangling with which many on the left seemed obsessed.' He was *en route* first to the 'soft-Left' and thence to the 'centre-left'.[4]

As Kinnock put it, 'socialist aspirations had to be meaningful and not just comforting'. He became contemptuous of Benn for trying to have it both ways – serving in the Wilson/Callaghan Cabinets, and then proceeding to try to take the party further leftwards on what another Labour MP, Austin Mitchell, described as the 'Red Titanic'. Westlake neatly summarises the evolving Kinnock position: 'Attributing the failures of Labour governments to the gulf between their promises and their actual record, he increasingly deduced that it was the projected policies that ought to be tempered and formulated in the light of probable circumstances.'[5]

Kinnock was furious about the defection of Jenkins and the others. 'Renouncing a political allegiance is a defensible political act. Making a meal out of the hand that fed them is indefensible political morality' was his scathing verdict.[6] By definition, the immediate effect of the formation of the SDP was to move the centre of gravity of the Labour Party in precisely the wrong direction, and even further away from the centre ground that, in due course, it was going to cultivate heavily – indeed, in years to come under Tony Blair, perhaps too heavily.

Kinnock had been vehemently opposed to Benn's decision in spring 1981 to stand against Denis Healey for the deputy leadership of the Party, under Foot. 'My main objection to Tony's candidature,' he said at the time, 'arises from the belief that it does not appear to take sufficient account of ... the obligation which we have to win support for policies which must be recognised as the Party's policies instead of the property of a faction.'[7] Benn's bid for the deputy leadership in the course of 1981 prolonged the Party's internal conflict and distracted it yet again from the duty of Opposition. Yet with unemployment soaring, the Conservatives ought to have been sitting ducks.

The election for the deputy leadership did not take place until the end of September 1981, affording plenty of adverse publicity about the left and its wranglings. Kinnock was now among the so-called 'soft Left' group, and led some 30 'abstainers'. Benn's bid failed by a mere 0.6% of the total vote. From autumn 1981 onwards, moderates were gaining ground within the PLP and on Labour's National Executive Committee (NEC) and the far left was splintering; urged on by Kinnock, the leadership was isolating the Trotskyist group, the Militant Tendency. But although Kinnock, the future leader, had by now joined the 'centre-left mainstream' of the Labour Party and believed that the first duty of the Labour Party was to get elected, the 1983 'suicide note' manifesto was not the way to appeal to middle England. By the time Gordon Brown got to Westminster and Neil Kinnock became leader, the slow process of reversion to the mean of British politics had begun; unfortunately, the extreme left was to hit back through various forms of extra-parliamentary action.

The 1983–87 Parliament was Mrs Thatcher's second term and Gordon Brown's first. The Falklands War, and the left's attempts to take over the Labour Party, had diverted attention from rising unemployment during her first term. Kinnock's attempts to 'see off' the SDP and make Labour electable in 1983–87 were going to be thwarted, first by the way the left hit back outside Parliament, and second by more favourable economic developments, for after an appalling economic record during its early years, the Conservatives under Nigel Lawson's Chancellorship would ride to another election victory in 1987.

Long before the 'focus group' guru Philip Gould and the 'spin doctor' Peter Mandelson appeared on the scene, Neil Kinnock was learning the lessons of the 1983 election result. On 18 July, while gearing up for the leadership election in the autumn, Kinnock wrote: 'The harsh electoral reality is that Labour cannot rely merely on a combination of the dispossessed, the "traditional" working class and minority groups for the winning of power.'[8] By September 1983 the message had developed into: 'We failed to appreciate that the left can *only* protect the disadvantaged in our society if we appeal to those who are relatively advantaged ... we must have the support of those in more secure social circumstances – the home owner as well as the single parent, the confidently employed as well as the unemployed, the majority as well as the minorities.'[9]

Thus, when Gordon Brown and Tony Blair had only just arrived in the Commons, Kinnock was changing his emphasis 'from issues of unemployment, equality and class to ones of efficiency, individualism and self-interest'.[10] He shifted policy on Europe fast, accepting British membership as a reality – indeed, deciding that since European left-wing parties had fared rather better than Labour, there was something to be said for joining them. In this context, he also recognised that the 'siege economy' alternative strategy was not a vote winner with middle England or with the financial markets, and decided that Keynesian policies of expansionary demand management could better be achieved within the large and safe haven of Europe as a whole.

But although the new leader had embarked on the long process of making Labour electable in a way that former 'Red Gordon' had also come to regard as necessary, the 1983–87 term was overshadowed by the way the left hit back; thus prolonging the period during which the newly modernising Labour Party would suffer 'guilt by association' with the extreme left.

The year from March 1984 to March 1985 was dominated by the miners' strike, and then by Kinnock's struggle against the so-called Militant Tendency extreme left group, whose antics were especially prominent in Liverpool. In the long run, Labour gained from the tough stand taken against the anti-democratic and potentially revolutionary Militant Tendency. But while the battle was raging, it served to remind middle England of the ghosts of Labour's recent past, which the Party was in the process of exorcising. Both episodes were time consuming for a Party that was supposed to be working on its policies, although in the end his biographer concluded: 'Kinnock's dramatic move against the hard left in general, and Militant in particular, was probably the most successful of his career and is certainly the moment best remembered by the general public.'

The miners' strike was excruciatingly difficult for a Labour Party that was trying to modernise itself and appeal to disaffected Labour voters who had either joined the SDP or were among the new breed of affluent workers who now supported the Conservatives. The traditional attachment between Labour and the miners was close: Neil Kinnock's father was a miner; the new young MP Gordon Brown came from a mining area which knew what impact a declining mining industry could have on social conditions.

By calling a strike without a democratic vote, Arthur Scargill, the miners' leader, put Labour in a very difficult position. By falling into the trap set by the Conservatives, who had built up coal stocks for just such an eventuality, and calling the strike in the *spring*, Scargill also showed bad tactics; a strike called in the depths of a bad winter might have met less resistance.

Scargill, who had vehemently disapproved of Kinnock's attack on the Bennites, saw himself as 'taking on' Thatcherism and capitalism. He failed lamentably, gave Mrs Thatcher one of her most famous victories, and caused misery all round.

After the election of Neil Kinnock as leader on 2 October 1983, with Roy Hattersley as his deputy, Labour had painstakingly built up a lead in the opinion polls which it proceeded to lose during the year of the miners' strike. March 1984 to March 1985 was, said Kinnock's office, 'a lost year'. After that the Party took steps to streamline and modernise its organisation, and Philip Gould, the focus group man with a background in advertising, and Peter Mandelson, the supposed master of 'presentation' and 'spin', joined the 'modernising team'. But the economic tide had turned: Nigel Lawson as Chancellor transformed himself from a monetarist into the creator of an old-fashioned consumer boom, and the Thatcher government had little difficulty in retaining a majority of over 100 at the general election of June 1987.

During these difficult four years for a Labour Party that was adapting to reality and doing its best to appear prudent and respectable, Gordon Brown had little more than a bit part at Westminster. But it was a bit part with frequent appearances. He outdid most established MPs in the sheer quantity of his parliamentary questions, and before the summer recess he worked hard and to good effect on his maiden speech in a social security debate on 27 July 1983.

His speech attracted praise from the Conservative benches as well as his own. He got straight down to brass tacks: 'As I represent a constituency in which there are now more men and women without a lasting job than there are people employed in manufacturing industries, and as one in seven of my constituents is dependent on social security, it is appropriate that I should make my maiden speech in a debate on social security.'

Almost immediately Brown staked his claim to be a champion of the unemployed and the poor: 'The greatest threat to the ideals of individual freedom and personal responsibility that the present government so stridently espouses, the grossest affront to human dignity and the gravest assault, on any view of social justice, is mass unemployment and its inevitable consequence, mass poverty.'

The people of Dunfermline East knew about unemployment and poverty, he said. They lived in a constituency which was once at the heart of the mining industry. Yet there was now not one pit in his constituency, and only six in the county of Fife. The new member was particularly scathing about the rise in the number of people having to claim means-tested benefit, and about the government's plans to cut benefits that were already barely adequate.

'It appears that the government are saying that the problem, as they see it, is no longer unemployment but the unemployed. They seem to be suggesting that benefits as low as £26 a week are deterring the unemployed from seeking jobs,' Brown added. 'The debate about the so-called unemployed trap, and the so-called incentives that it is claimed will be needed to get the unemployed back to work, is designed to obscure what everyone knows. If there are no jobs, no amount of poverty and no degree of destitution will create jobs where none exist.'

It was fighting stuff. In making the connection between the government's belief in individual freedom and responsibility and the barriers created by unemployment, Brown was also referring to his own strong, 'Son of the Manse' beliefs. The budding master of the 'New' Labour sound-bite could well have dubbed his message 'employment for a purpose'.

There might seem to be some hostages to fortune in the way, both in his maiden speech and repeatedly afterwards, the new member was going to attack the government about means tests and its obsessions with 'incentives' to work. For when he eventually became Chancellor, means tests and incentives to work were going to bulk large in his own approach, which he christened 'Welfare to Work'. But it is only fair to emphasise that at this stage he was speaking at a time when unemployment was over three million (even on the definition which had been much revised to exclude various categories of unemployed). In many regions there simply *were* no vacancies to speak of.

In his peroration Brown demonstrated a flair for pragmatism and eclecticism that was to be a feature of his Chancellorship. To make his case he quoted a Conservative: 'The state must increasingly and earnestly concern itself with the care of the sick, the aged and the young. The state must increasingly assume the position of the reserve employer of labour.' The Conservative in question was none other than the greatest Englishman of the twentieth century, Sir Winston Churchill.

Brown was now 32. He soon met Tony Blair, the new MP for Sedgefield, who was two years his junior. They got on well, and decided to share offices – it was by all accounts a somewhat inegalitarian form of sharing, with Brown's books and voluminous files scattered all over the place. Both were obviously pleased to be in Westminster and highly ambitious. A veteran Labour MP observed: 'They were young men on the make.'

What lay in the way of 'making it' was the near catastrophic state of the Party. Blair is credited with having forecast: 'This Party has about eighteen months left.'[11] He could well have been wondering, by now, whether he had made the wrong decision in joining the Labour Party (in years to come, that view of Blair's choice was going to be shared by many traditional Labour supporters, for altogether different reasons). Brown, who, unlike Blair, was not a political *ingénue*, immediately became the senior partner in the relationship, and taught his new friend a lot. 'Gordon was in charge ... and Tony was happy with that. It's how he learnt everything,'[12] said Labour MP Martin O'Neill. One of the things he learnt was that Brown was steeped in Labour Party history. He was born and bred in the Labour Party and, while gloomy, was not in despair about its future. The prudent Son of the Manse, who had been taught the importance of goals and objectives in life, was obsessed with the need for the survival and recovery of the Labour Party.

Brown retained his strong Scottish power base – he was Chairman of the Labour Party Scottish Council in 1983–84 – but he deliberately did not aim at a specifically Scottish brief in London. He had early been singled out by Kinnock to be a member of the backbench Commons Select Committee on Employment; and he was put on the Commons committee scrutinising the Thatcher government's Trade Union Bill, which was aimed at curbing trade unionists' rights and restricting (ideally ending) the political levy paid by union members to the Labour Party. But the prudent member for Dunfermline East turned down the first offer of a job as front bench Spokesman, because the brief was Scottish affairs. He seldom missed an opportunity to cite evidence from his constituency when presenting a general case and always nurtured his Scottish power base, but from the point of view of his ambitions, he had to broaden his appeal and the range of his interests.

Both in his many questions (written and oral) and in his speeches, Gordon Brown specialised during those early days in matters concerning employment, poverty, social services and social security, on which he displayed the detailed knowledge coming from assiduous research and unusually good contacts within the Civil Service. The latter enabled him to dramatise 'leaked documents' to great effect, a practice which in turn meant not only that the ambitious young politician was anxious to cultivate the press, but that the press was naturally keen to cultivate him. I recall that few Saturday mornings were complete at the *Observer* during the mid- to late 1980s without the arrival of an indignant press release from Gordon Brown on some issue or another.

During that social security debate in which he had made his maiden speech, Brown had displayed a particular concern for the way benefit cuts were being applied to the 'voluntarily unemployed' – not a category he was unduly sympathetic with in later years. His quizzing of the Minister, Dr Rhodes Boyson – with rapier thrusts such as, 'What definition of hardship was used?' – prompted the latter in his memoirs to single out Brown's debut for special praise.

Gordon Brown's questions displayed an interest in the health service from very early on. He would, for instance, ask for detailed breakdowns of what percentage of planned increases in public spending on health were required simply for demographic reasons, or 'technological changes in requirements for medical equipment' or 'future requirements for nursing and medical staff'.[13] This interest in the nitty gritty was not going to diminish when he became Chancellor – neither, for that matter, was the passionate interest in the health service itself.

Having scored a hit with his neat use of Churchillian dicta as a stick to beat the Tories with, Gordon Brown stuck to a winning formula in his next big contribution to a debate, on the Trade Union Bill (8 November 1983). On what he saw as the blatant aim of the Bill, 'especially in relation to the political representation of trade unions and their financial discretion in political matters', Brown stated: 'The Bill tries to terminate by partisan fiat what Sir Winston Churchill, at the end of a political life during which he had been more involved than most Conservatives in these matters, called "a well-established custom that matters affecting the interests of rival Parties should not be settled by the imposition of the will of the one over the other".'

The government had been attacking the political levy in the guise of being champion of the right of the individual trade unionist to opt out of it. Brown conducted an impressive forensic attack, questioning the government on its grasp of history and turning the emphasis on the dubious basis of corporate contributions to the Conservative Party. The speech was well researched and prepared. Neil Kinnock, who was watching Brown closely, recalled, 'He was always painstaking with articles and speeches, but he didn't think any public speech was complete if it did not raise a few laughs.'

A remarkable episode occurred in March 1984, when Brown, with the help of internal Department of Health and Social Security documents leaked to him, attacked the government for planning a pilot scheme in his constituency to persuade 18–25 year-olds to accept low-paid jobs and to cut benefits for youngsters who refused to accept training places. The charge was: 'Essentially, the papers say that DHSS officers are to inculcate good working habits in the unemployed.' This is precisely what Gordon Brown was to see as his mission at the Treasury some 13 years later ...

During his first year in Parliament Gordon Brown was the joint editor with Robin Cook of *Scotland: The Real Divide*. Using yet another leaked civil service document, he cited chapter and verse for what many had deduced from the Thatcher government's general approach: that redistribution of income towards the poor was 'not among the government's objectives'.

Brown was a student of the works of Tony Crosland. Long before the phrase 'New Labour' had been dreamt up to describe the Party that Kinnock, Blair, John Smith and Brown himself were to modernise, the Croslandite centre-left had placed the emphasis on the fruits of growth to help the poor, rather than on redistribution of existing wealth and income. But – perhaps not surprisingly after a period when the first Thatcher government had presided over the worst recession since the war, and when there had been negligible growth – Brown had concluded that 'the era of automatic growth is not only over but unlikely to return in the near future'; therefore, 'New principles for social security in a low-growth economy are badly needed. The first prerequisite for eradicating poverty is the redistribution of income and wealth from rich to poor.'[14]

Brown believed that changing circumstances meant the left had to reassess its strategy. The gap between rich and poor had manifestly widened since 1979, but Brown reluctantly acknowledged that the new right had got away with it or, in his words, 'consistently won the argument'.[15]

Among other things Brown called for a legal minimum wage, a more generous social 'safety net', more public spending directed at the people and regions most in need, and restoration of a more progressive income tax system.

Further indications of his approach in those days were given by two fairly typical parliamentary questions he asked on 27 June 1984. Of a Social Security Minister, Mrs Edwina Currie, he asked: 'Will the Hon. Lady comment on the fact that Britain still has the most unequal distribution of wealth in Europe and that it has been the least successful economy?' (the listener was of course invited to detect a causal connection). And to Dr Rhodes Boyson, the Minister for Social Security: 'Will the Minister give the House a categorical assurance and an unconditional commitment that the government has no plan to tax or means-test child benefit?'

'Means-test' was still a term of abuse for Gordon Brown. 'Sensible targeting' of benefits, under the overall control of his Treasury, was yet to come.

The publication of *The Real Divide* – which some saw as an update of the *Red Paper* – prompted his sympathetic biographer, Paul Routledge, to complain that it was 'rooted in the Labour Party's tax-and-spend, government-knows-best philosophy'. But Routledge said that Brown's readiness to accept that the new right was winning the argument 'marked him out as a politician ready to inject fresh thinking into the Party's internal dialogue'.[16]

Brown made it clear that he expected things to get a lot worse under Thatcher, and he was certainly right as far as the attack on the unions and the distribution of income and wealth were concerned. Indeed, he was urging a more progressive tax system when the top rate of tax was still 60% and the basic rate 28%. Lawson in 1988 was to establish an even less progressive, two-tier tax system, with a basic rate of 25% and a top rate of 40%. The top rate would still be 40% after what became the Blair/Brown duumvirate's first term in 1997–2001.

Although, as he said in his maiden speech, the mines had vanished from his constituency, there were still mines close at hand; and Brown – like Kinnock, appalled by Scargill's tactics and undemocratic procedures – nevertheless did his best to display solidarity with the miners during the terrible period from March 1984 to March 1985. He was also filled with hope for the Party after Neil Kinnock's well-received attack on Militant Tendency at the Labour Conference of autumn 1985.

His principal theme in *The Real Divide* had been social justice rather than the nationalisation and workers' control highlighted in the *Red Paper*. There was another real divide opening up in Scotland in the 1980s and that was between Brown and Cook themselves. Brown was late for the launch party for the book, and Cook started the revolution without him. Brown had invited Cook to be joint editor of the book of essays, whose common theme was 'the need for redistribution of income and wealth' and that 'taxation should rise progressively with income'. Brown resented the way the launch party (30 October 1983) was 'hijacked' by Cook. Later in the decade Cook was not amused by the way that Brown, who had made his name through showing concern for the poor, was vetoing proposals for extra social spending during his period as Shadow Chief Secretary in 1987–89. Then Cook, who had always taken a strong interest in the economy, was annoyed that Brown and not he was made Shadow Secretary for Industry in 1989. But it was Brown's performance as the 'iron' Shadow Chancellor that Cook found most trying.

In 1995 Brown's 'spin doctor', Charlie Whelan, was portraying him as the very model – indeed modeller – of New Labour, while, when it suited him, emphasising Brown's strong links with the traditional Labour movement. Cook particularly objected to Brown's flirtations in 1995 with US-style 'workfare' schemes and his proposal to remove child benefits from 16–18 year-olds; followers of Cook were convinced that it was at Brown's insistence that Cook was kept well away from economic and social policy after the 1997 Election, having already been 'marginalised' in the run-up. The two also had their differences on the European Single Currency, but before the 1997 Election it was Cook who was the more cautious and insisting on strict conditions.

But back in 1983, when *The Real Divide* was published, Brown's thoughts on the economy were evolving and after 1985, when he finally accepted a front-bench job as a spokesman for Trade and Industry, the future Chancellor had a chance to move into mainstream economic territory.

The shadow Secretary for Trade and Industry was John Smith, who (after working on the devolution proposal) had briefly been Secretary of State for Trade in 1978–79 during the fraught latter days of the Callaghan government. The Scottish connection was of course strong and Smith was an important patron for both Brown and Blair.

Brown sowed the seeds of his future thinking about the economy as early as 7 July 1986, when he delivered a powerful speech in a Commons debate on the future of manufacturing industry. He made some good points about the neglect of manufacturing industry during the Thatcher monetarist experiment, producing devastating statistics to demonstrate that manufacturing output was still some 7% below the level of 1979 and investment was down 20%. The idea that this was somehow an act of God or a world phenomenon was belied by the fact that during the same period manufacturing output had risen 14% in the USA and 10% on average in all the major market economies (nearly 30) that were members of the Organisation for Economic Cooperation and Development.

51

He challenged claims that productivity was rising by pointing out: 'that is a function merely of the fact that employment has been falling faster than output and less is being produced by many fewer people.' To the suggestion that 'sunset' industries were merely giving way to 'sunrise' industries, he had the sharp riposte: 'it is a case, not of the old industries making way for the new, but of the new industries making way for foreign imports.' Sharpening the knife, he went on: 'The government has been stifling the new industries almost as quickly as they have been destroying our traditional industries.'

But he was also constructive, outlining some proposals that were to become a feature of his economic strategy many years later. More resources needed to be devoted to training: there was a 'market failure' in the private sector, so that even where those 'sunrise' industries (information technology, etc.) were in evidence, there were severe shortages of skills. In one sentence he epitomized whole sections of future Budget Reports: 'We must look carefully and pragmatically at how investment in training, science and technology, research and development and plant and equipment can aid an industrial expansion.' This was an area for positive government assistance. Yet the North Sea revenues, instead of being devoted to investment for the future, 'have been wasted on funding ever-rising levels of unemployment.'

Here we see Brown's consistent preoccupation with the unemployment issue, and his particular obsession with the 'waste' caused by unemployment – the waste of human resources, but also the waste of *money* that could be devoted to other, more productive means. His interests and solutions, however, tended to be 'micro'. The all-important role of the overvalued pound in the early 1980s did not figure in this important speech.

As it turned out, even as Brown spoke in that July 1986 debate, the economy was on the turn and, thanks to a shift to a policy of expansion, a pre-election consumer boom was about to appear. The Chancellor, Nigel Lawson, had conducted an unashamed 'U'-turn in economic policy, shifting from a policy of monetarism and disinflation to higher public spending, a lower exchange rate and the active encouragement of a consumer boom. But although manufacturing output and investment recovered from the depths on which Brown's speech focused, his was a valid criticism of the fruits of Thatcher's earlier economic policies.

The years 1983–87 were the years when the close association between Brown and Blair developed; with Peter Mandelson, Director of Communications for the Labour Party from 1985, they almost formed a political *ménage a trois*. Mandelson tried to exploit their potential with the media; and the three were heavily involved in the early 'modernising' discussions that were to lead to 'New Labour'.

One of the most important events for Gordon Brown during his first (1983–87) term as an MP was the publication of his book *Maxton*, the biography of the Clydeside MP James Maxton, in 1986. Maxton was an MP from 1922 until his death in 1946, and Chairman of the Independent Labour Party (ILP) from 1926. He was a big Clydeside figure and also made his mark at Westminster, although his name does not seem to ring many bells south of the border these days.

For Brown his work on Maxton was a labour of love. He confessed that 'this book has been almost twenty years in the making.'[17] Maxton was both a positive and a negative model for the young Gordon Brown. As David Marquand remarked in his biography of Ramsay MacDonald, for the Clydesiders 'the purpose of parliamentary activity was not power, but propaganda: and the propaganda was aimed, not at the uncommitted voter whose support Labour would need ... but at the militant, class-conscious minority who voted Labour already.'

Maxton seems to have attracted Brown as a kind of failed hero. Brown admired his socialist beliefs, and shared the political motivation that comes from disgust at the existence of widespread poverty and mass unemployment, as well as the desire to do something about it. But Maxton the Rebel, the thorn in the side of Ramsay MacDonald during Labour's brief minority government in January–October 1924 and again in 1929–31, would have prompted a parent or teacher to tell the young Gordon, 'let this man's career serve as a warning to you.'

Among Brown's discoveries about Maxton was that the latter had first been attracted to politics in 1904 when hearing a speech by Philip Snowden – a speech that was fired by principles more Socialist than Snowden's eventual performance as a deflationary Chancellor of the Exchequer in 1929–31. But the really interesting thing about the book for students of Brown is the similarity between their interests and views, and the sense that the author is wanting to worship a hero who in the end became too much of a parliamentary 'character' and not the effective politician that lay at the heart of Brown's own ambition.

Brown notes that Maxton's first documented speech on behalf of the Scottish ILP (in 1904) was on a subject close to his (Brown's) own heart, 'a subject which he pursued throughout his subsequent political career – unemployment.' His maiden speech in Parliament in December 1922 contained an implied threat – 'I am as great a constitutionalist as any member on that Front Bench or this Front Bench, but there is a point where constitutionalists have to give way before human necessity ... '[18] Nevertheless, Maxton was generally to be considered more of an agitator than a revolutionary. He most certainly did not have the drive, application or powerful ambition of his biographer, and never progressed beyond the back benches.

Maxton's fiery oratory may have been something of a model for Brown, yet Churchill called him 'the greatest gentleman in the House of Commons'.[19] Brown captured the essence of his hero's career with: 'Maxton never held Government office. No great legislative reforms bear his name. The Independent Labour Party which he dominated for 20 years dwindled eventually to nothing, even as his audiences grew larger. But at the height of his powers, in the 1920s, he threatened to change the whole course of politics by offering British socialism a third way between Labour gradualism and Communism ... a middle way between the views of Ramsay MacDonald and Lenin. Their failure, the failure of the ILP and the Labour Party, foreshadowed the failure of a whole generation of British politicians to solve the problems of unemployment and poverty.'[20]

Unemployment and poverty – the well-springs of Gordon Brown's fascination with politics – figured prominently in a speech by Maxton in March 1933, which Brown covers in a section headed 'Socialism in Retreat'. Maxton in fact introduced an ILP Commons debate on unemployment and poverty, and Brown's description of Maxton's approach – 'he sought to describe the conditions which prevailed in the country and especially in his own constituency'[21] – seems like a brief for the approach Brown took in his own maiden speech in July 1983. As with Brown 50 years later, 'the predominant reason for poverty was rising unemployment'. Maxton went into Dickensian detail about the impact of unemployment, poverty and ill-health on a particular family in his constituency. Brown comments strongly: 'His Labour Party adversary (sic), McNeill Weir, described it as Maxton's best speech and the best attack on the capitalist system he had ever heard in the House of Commons.'[22]

Brown's use of the term 'third way' to describe Maxton's early approach is intriguing (it certainly pre-dates Tony Blair's well-known use of the term). The historian H. A. L. Fisher uses the phrase 'third way' to describe Napoleon III's abortive attempt in 1869 to steer a course between revolution and foreign war by opting for Liberalism. In that case, the newly 'Liberal' government collapsed within months, the third way with it, and war followed.

Pius X, who was Pope from 1903 to 1913, had called for a 'third way' between socialism and communism. The sharp-witted Brown, experienced in the exigencies of brief televisual 'clips', was to become an exponent of the 'sound-bite' in British politics, and Blair was not slow to pick them up from Brown. It is interesting to speculate whether Blair also picked up the term 'third way' from Maxton's biographer, although in Blair's case the third way was some elusive compromise between Old Labour and the capitalist triumphalism that accompanied the fall of the Berlin Wall in 1989 and the collapse of the USSR in 1991.

Just as unemployment and poverty were central to the political interests of Maxton *and* his biographer, so was the subject of mean-tested benefits. Brown notes admiringly that: 'Maxton was at his most masterful as the Member for the Unemployed. He, and others, protested about the inadequate benefits, the reduction of benefits because of war disability pensions [sic], and above all the ubiquitous Means Tests. The unemployed, he said, were being accused of lavish expenditure and blamed for the economic crisis' [this was in 1932–33].[23]

Like his biographer, Maxton found that politics got in the way of courtship, and Brown makes a point of how irregular meetings and broken appointments placed a strain on Maxton's burgeoning relationship with his future wife. Maxton, too, married relatively late but, at 34, somewhat earlier than his biographer, who was to wait almost until his half century.

But it is political lessons for his own political career that Brown draws from his study of Maxton, not marital ones. Maxton – whose slogan was 'Socialism in Our Time' – had set out to transform the ILP from a propaganda society into an instrument for the overthrow of capitalism, yet he 'ended his career as a leader without a Party'. For Brown the moral is that 'a successful socialist politician is one who advances the fortunes of his or her political party and progressively uses political power to transform society.'[24]

CHAPTER THREE

1987–1992

$\mathcal{T}$he 1987–92 Parliament began with Labour, for all Neil Kinnock's efforts at reform, fighting against the odds. The Conservative majority came down from 141 in 1983 to 101, but was still huge. Those veteran students of the British political scene, Dr David Butler and Dennis Kavanagh, concluded that from the start Labour faced an 'electoral Everest' to win an overall majority at the next election.

While Labour had begun to shed some electorally soiled goods from its baggage train of policies, surveys of 'public attitudes' still found it weak on defence, not trusted with the economy and too closely associated with the unions. North of the Wash there had been a 4.5% swing to Labour; but in 'Middle England' – the Midlands and the south – there was hardly any swing at all to Labour between 1983 and 1987.

The so-called 'working class' represented a smaller proportion of the electorate, and the 'new working class' – wooed by privatisation at knock-down prices, by the sale of council houses and by the prosperity associated with the Lawson Boom – were strongly Conservative. This left plenty of scope for the 'modernisers' to work harder, continuing with the switch of emphasis from shop-soiled policies to more appealing ones and from policy 'formation' to 'presentation' and 'continual campaigning'.

Tony Blair has asserted that 'only after 1994 did the modernisation project take a firm grip over Labour.' In fact it began in 1983–87, as we have seen, and continued during the 1987–92 Parliament. Michael Foot, while a strong Keynesian, did not take a detailed interest in economic policy and had tended to leave it to the party machine, which had been heavily infiltrated by the Bennites and their Alternative Economic Strategy (AES). One way in which Neil Kinnock from 1983, and increasingly from 1987, attempted to make the Party more electable was by strengthening the team around him, as for his part did John Smith when he succeeded Roy Hattersley as Shadow Chancellor in 1987.

Hattersley and Smith had worked together on economic and industrial policy in 1983–87. Smith, with the encouragement of Kinnock, had tours of the regions, meeting industrialists and local businessmen, promoting a Jobs and Industry campaign. Labour was shedding its hostility towards the private sector and becoming 'pro-business', although, as Kinnock recalled years later, 'We didn't follow the visits up. We got packed houses, and we banged on about investment, training, the infrastructure, exports and the pound. Industrialists said "What a marvellous set of policies." Then they went home and even if they voted Labour their wives certainly didn't.'[1]

Hattersley, himself no friend of the Alternative Economic Strategists, had had a loosely-knitted group of economic advisers who were not based at the then Labour Party headquarters in Walworth Road. But the Shadow Chancellor was widely criticised for having fallen into what Gordon Brown was later to term 'the tax trap' and ended up shouldering the bulk of the blame for the way the Conservatives were able to scare voters in 1987 with dubious claims that Labour's 'hidden taxes' amounted to £35 billion.

For all its efforts at transformation, Labour had indeed led with its chin over its proposals in the manifesto for tax increases. Its central (economic) electoral promises in 1987 were to alleviate poverty and to reduce unemployment by one million over two years. This would be achieved by increasing pensions and child benefit, and by expanding investment and employment in the public sector. To this end an extra £3 billion would be borrowed for investment; the (March 1987) 2p reduction in income tax (to 27p) would be reversed; and taxes would be raised on those earning more than £26,000 a year. But Labour proceeded to add to the manifesto commitment a proposal to scrap the married man's tax allowance and remove the ceiling on national insurance contributions. The combined effect would be felt by people on close to average earnings.

The Lawson Boom and what Kinnock termed the 'feel-good factor' may well have been more important than Labour's tax proposals in themselves; but the proposals were undoubtedly calculated to diminish the feel-good factor, and the terrible truth was that they were not 'calculated' properly at all. Hence Nigel Lawson the Chancellor, the architect of the 2p tax cut, could talk delightedly of 'a swingeing tax grab' and the Conservatives and the press between them could publicise a grossly exaggerated figure of £35 billion in extra Labour taxes.

Gordon Brown was certainly concerned about Labour's image as a party of taxation. 'We were up-ended by tax ... Labour was supposed to be the Party of aspirations. But it became a Party that put a cap on people's aspirations.'[2] Brown stood for the Shadow Cabinet and was elected. Kinnock made him Shadow Chief Secretary to the Treasury – the person to keep an eye on Labour's spending commitments.

If ever there was an admission of the need for Labour's economic policies to alter it was made by Henry Neuberger, a former Treasury economist who worked for much of the 1980s as full-time Labour economic adviser to both Michael Foot and Neil Kinnock; Kinnock's office was also reinforced by the arrival of John Eatwell from Cambridge, who served from January 1986 until 1992. Neuberger, who had been a fully paid-up advocate of the AES, observed in 1989, 'few of its original adherents would now advance [such measures] without embarrassment.'[3] From believing in extensive intervention in markets, and from displaying open hostility towards the private sector, Labour Party economic advisers became advocates of what Kinnock called 'the enabling state'. Long before Tony Blair assumed the Leadership, Kinnock was talking of the importance of creating wealth as opposed to distributing it; it was now a future Labour government's job to assist the private sector by filling the gaps, assisting through the tax system with investment, education and training, and research and development. Some called this 'supply-side socialism'.

During the 1987–92 period Eatwell worked closely with Kinnock on economic policy and Brown, as Shadow Chief Secretary, with John Smith the Shadow Chancellor. In addition to doing everything possible to adopt a prudent approach to future spending commitments and the implications for taxation, the four of them were going to take economic policy in a distinctly European direction, via strong support for the pound's entry into the European Exchange Rate Mechanism (ERM). Eventually Bryan Gould, the Trade and Industry spokesman in succession to Smith, would feel isolated. Gould had been something of a star performer during the 1987 election campaign, but he was suspicious of Europe and vehemently against any idea of signing up to the ERM, not least because – with good cause – he believed that Britain had suffered from periods of a chronically overvalued exchange rate. But in a letter to Gould early in 1989, Eatwell wrote: 'There is a severe danger of inflation and devaluation being mutually reinforcing.'

I recall a conversation with John Eatwell at about that time in which he appeared to have abandoned faith in devaluation and cited evidence that, although British industry might suffer from periods of a high exchange rate, it did not take advantage and invest sufficiently in new capacity when the pound subsequently fell. Nevertheless, as we shall see, Eatwell was later to accept that a devaluation would be required if Labour won the 1992 election. Eatwell is credited with having contributed to Kinnock's increasing emphasis on the importance of the private sector in promoting economic recovery, and Neuberger with the importance of the need for effective regulation of utilities, as the Party rowed back from the expensive idea of renationalising privatised concerns.

Gordon Brown and his colleagues were lucky that there was then also a 'moderniser' at the TUC in the shape of John Monks, at the time Assistant General Secretary. When Blair was Shadow Secretary for Employment, Monks helped him over the question of the closed shop and European Union legislation. He told him that the TUC would not insist on the return of the closed shop, against which Mrs Thatcher had legislated. On 17 December 1989 Blair announced Labour's support for the law against the closed shop. Impressed by

Monks's help for Blair, Gordon Brown consulted him on how to get off the hook of renationalising the privatised telecoms industry. Monks told him that British Telecom was doing well (at the time) and the unions were happy. This was an important moment in Brown's journey from propagating renationalisation to adopting and introducing the tax on privatised utilities which became a prominent feature of his first 'Welfare to Work' Budget in 1997.

'Privatisation' – selling publicly-owned assets to the private sector – was a policy introduced by Mrs Thatcher in 1982, originally as a diversion from rapidly rising unemployment and the associated unpopularity of the government. It had the advantage of reducing the public sector borrowing requirement while proving popular with those members of the public who were offered shares in public utilities on favourable terms. Labour, in the early days, opposed privatisation every inch of the way.

Essentially, the 1987–92 Parliament saw Labour struggling to gain a reputation for economic competence while the Conservatives were in the process of losing theirs. It is almost comical that Labour was so desperate for respectability, while the Conservatives were handling the economy with such recklessness in the early years that presided over the second biggest recession (1990–92) since the war.

As the economist Mark Wickham-Jones has written, Labour's journey during the 1980s took it 'from a position of advocating the strongly interventionist AES to one of endorsing the ERM as a means of attaining price stability.'[4] The background against which Gordon Brown operated, both as Shadow Chief Secretary (1987–89) and Shadow Secretary for Trade and Industry (1989–92), was one in which the seeds were being sown for some of the 'rules' he was to adopt as Chancellor. Above all, for a politician whose consistent political mission hitherto had been the attack on unemployment and poverty, the Party in whose hierarchy he was rising was now seeking a European solution to such problems, believing that it had limited scope to act independently.

The 1983–87 phase had included 'the abandonment of sweeping intervention, the rejection of far-reaching transformative goals, the advocacy of partnership with the private sector, and the endorsement of the market. All these are to be found at the centre of the economics of New Labour.'[5] When he was Shadow Chancellor from 1987, John Smith's constant theme was 'the Party's commitment to economic stability and the modesty of its objectives.'[6] Even earlier, Roy Hattersley as Shadow Chancellor had, in 1985, singled out one of the indicators for stability that was going to become a favourite of Gordon Brown's – the importance of the 'debt to gross domestic product ratio'.[7] The distinction between government borrowing to invest and borrowing for consumption was also cropping up in internal Party economic documents and speeches during the 1980s.

In the search for prudent economic policies, John Smith called on the experienced Balliol economics don, Andrew Graham, who had held various governmental economic advisory posts under the Wilson governments of the 1960s and who knew many of the pitfalls. Graham was the 'convener' of a group that included Chris Allsopp, an Oxford don who had had OECD experience, David Currie from the London Business School, and leading City economists such as Gavyn Davies of Goldman Sachs, Neil Mackinnon of Yamaichi and Gerald Holtham, subsequently to head the (Kinnockite) Institute for Public Policy Research.

Gavyn Davies had seen the travails of the Callaghan government at close hand, working in Number 10 during the 1970s. The 'City' input from such economists was important for Smith and Brown; Labour had come to terms with the fact that, with the abolition of exchange controls in 1979 and the 'deregulation' of the 1980s, the 'genie had been let out of the bottle', in the phrase of Sir Kit McMahon, a former Deputy Governor of the Bank of England, who was by now Chairman of Midland Bank. The financial markets, more than ever, could vote with their feet. The City economists reinforced the natural caution of John Smith, who often gave the impression that he was less interested in the economics than the politics.

John Smith had of course witnessed the latter days of the Callaghan government from inside the Cabinet. On policy generally – although not, ironically as it turned out, with Labour's next tax package – Smith was caution itself. According to his biographer, as early as 1984 Smith was the author of an anonymous Labour Party memorandum leaked to the *New Statesman* which said, 'People do not believe that our policies will work. The Keynesian argument has been tried and failed ... We should not promise too much too soon. In particular, the term "full employment" may now appear nebulous and over-ambitious.'[8] On the other hand, soon after the 1987 election, Smith as Shadow Chancellor quoted Keynes approvingly and proclaimed that full employment 'must be a fundamental objective of a socially just society.'[9] There were to be many similar twists and turns over the years.

Smith was a superb House of Commons performer, a great debater who visibly enjoyed his tussles with Chancellor Nigel Lawson, as the latter's self-proclaimed 'economic miracle' evaporated in front of his eyes in the course of 1988–89. Smith had specifically chosen Brown for his previous post (1985–87) as spokesman on regional affairs, and it was his senior Scottish colleague who had suggested that Brown should now be Shadow Chief Secretary. This made Brown Number Two in Smith's Treasury team. After the fiasco of Labour's 'hidden £35 billion tax package' during the 1987 election campaign, Gordon Brown's task was 'to excise from policy statements and front-benchers' speeches anything that might be interpreted as an uncosted-but-costable spending pledge.'[10] Smith wanted a tough guy who was prepared to stand up to his colleagues. Brown's credentials as a Tribunite member of the 'soft left' were ideal for this role of poacher turned gamekeeper.

After Gordon Brown eventually became Chancellor, he did so under an agreement with Tony Blair whereby the tentacles of the Treasury stretched into the policy-making of other Whitehall departments as well as over their expenditure control. 'Control freak' was a description frequently to be ascribed to Chancellor Brown. One may detect the origins of this, or at least the political development of characteristics that went further back in his life, in the crucial role he played as Shadow Chief Secretary, saying 'No' to potential commitments in the policy review ordered by Neil Kinnock in 1987 and completed in spring 1989.

But this was not work that hit the national headlines. Brown came into the public spotlight more through his parliamentary performances in the late 1980s, before there was a determined attempt by Peter Mandelson, as Director of Communications, to raise his public profile even further in the 1990s.

The year 1988 was an outstanding parliamentary year for Brown. He began on good form on 14 January, during the debate on the previous November's Autumn Statement, with one of his favourite tricks: quoting prominent Conservatives back at the government. This time it was not Winston Churchill, but John Biffen, a former monetarist member of Mrs Thatcher's Cabinet, who had long since declared 'enough is enough' when it came to public spending cuts. Referring to one of his pet subjects, the health service, Brown pointed out that Biffen, earlier in the debate, had suggested that £2.5 billion would have been better spent on the NHS than on Lawsonian tax cuts of 2p. Brown said that Biffen 'has done more in a few minutes to speak up for the traditions of one-nation Toryism than the Chancellor has done in eight long years as a member of the Conservative government.'

But the man who was to gain a reputation as an Iron Chancellor with the severity of his public spending freeze after 1997 castigated such behaviour in Lawson: 'The government refuse to spend enough on Britain. Money that was once withheld on grounds of financial prudence is now withheld for reasons that can only be described as ideological. Again and again in the last eight years they have said that they would spend if they could. Now they can, and they will not.'

The key phrase, of course, was 'grounds of financial prudence'. The future Chancellor would regard his own behaviour as 'Prudence for a Purpose' and was to relax his constraints during the second Blair term. The question is: was it necessary to be quite so prudent for so long? There were certainly those in Whitehall and Westminster, not to say the country at large, who were to wonder whether, during the first 1997–2001 Blair term, Brownian prudence was not becoming an ideology in itself.

In the debate on the 1988 Autumn Statement, Brown continued to harp on such favourite themes as the need for 'higher levels of investment in research, development and training, as well as on fixed capital' – a quote he happily attributed to the CBI.

The consistency of his interests is illustrated by the way he referred in this speech to aspects of health spending about which he had first asked parliamentary questions (as we saw earlier) in 1983. His point was that, after what was needed to keep pace with demographic and technological change, and shortfalls in nursing staff, the NHS needed an increase in real spending (above inflation) of 3% merely to stand still. Lawson was proposing a mere 0.7%. Such considerations were going to be raised by Brown's critics many years later, when the 2002 'Health Budget' would be examined as to how much real extra spending there would be – although no one could seriously argue that, by 2002–3, policy was as stringent as the Lawsonian attitude to health in the 1980s.

In years to come the prudence of Gordon Brown and the sheer defensiveness that paralysed Labour after so many electoral defeats was going to wreak havoc with the prose style of public speeches and statements. But in these early days of opposition Brown continually scored points with a clarity, incisiveness and wit that few could equal. 'Does closing schools in the inner cities provide the opportunity to be self-reliant?' he asked rhetorically. 'Does cutting the number of beds and wards in hospitals give patients the opportunity to be self-reliant?' he mocked.

Brown's passionate belief in the NHS is abundantly evident from these early parliamentary speeches. It was 'more efficient, less administratively expensive to run' (than the private sector alternative) and 'in a unique way it combines economy with equity.'

This was to be the essential message of a lecture Brown gave to the Social Market Foundation some 14 years later, in justification for the huge injection of resources he put into the NHS in the 2002 Budget. The disappointing thing was that, after 1997, he waited so long to do so.

In a foretaste of the disillusionment that was to set in about the state of the public services during the Blair government, Brown asked in the Commons, some two months before Lawson's seminal tax-cutting Budget of March 1988: 'Is it not clear to the Chancellor that the wish of the country and of the vast majority of its people is that, instead of tax cuts to make the rich few who will benefit from them richer, the money should be spent on our Health Service, public investment and the expansion of our public services?'[11]

Alas, this was not a message that Nigel Lawson wished to hear. Lawson was at the height of his popularity, even being talked about, for a brief moment, as a possible successor to Margaret Thatcher. On the very day Brown spoke, calling in evidence John Biffen's view that public services were now a greater priority than further tax cuts, Lawson was already planning a Budget in which the basic rate of income tax would be reduced by a further 2p to 25p, and the top rate slashed from 60p to 40p. The tax trap for Labour was getting tighter and tighter, making future planning of policy ever more difficult.

Lawson, who could on occasion outdo the famous comedian Max Miller with his own 'cheeky chappie' approach, was not beyond claiming that tax cuts for higher earners would pay for themselves in terms of the 'incentive effect' they would have on entrepreneurship. Evidence for such claims was, not surprisingly, rather thin on the ground, and even Lawson's own budgetary arithmetic showed, quite simply, that lower taxes meant less revenue.

Gordon Brown, with his head for figures, revelled in the detail. In the Budget debate on 21 March 1988 the Shadow Chief Secretary rose to his feet at 9.30 pm and rammed home the point. 'As my right honourable friends and honourable friends have said during this debate, indeed as many Conservative Members have said, the final effect of the Budget will be to transfer £2000 million to the 5% at the top who are already extremely rich.'

Having pointed out that there would be various tax reliefs for business, including relief from capital gains tax liabilities – one would not have thought from the tone that in due course Brown himself would be introducing such tax reliefs for 'entrepreneurship' – he emphasised: 'yet 95% of the population will make no cash gain from the changes.'

It was obvious that the reduction in the top rate would only benefit a small section of the population. But the basic rate? Brown pointed out: 'The tax cuts are taking place against the background of social security changes and the introduction, next month, of the social fund.' From April, child benefit for seven million mothers was going to be frozen, a million men and women would lose their housing benefit, and four million of the poorest households would have to pay rates at 20% for the first time 'no matter how poor they are'.

The Shadow Chief Secretary expanded on the mind-boggling detail of the social security changes, concluding: 'I estimate that nine million people will be worse off as a combined result of the tax and social security changes.' The tax cuts at the top were to be paid for by the withdrawal of benefits and the misery that would cause to the poorest. This was certainly not 'redistribution of income' after the traditional Labour manner.

It was not tax cuts that would promote economic efficiency or competitiveness, but 'investment in training and education, investment to effect the use of the resources of our regions and inner cities, investment in personal security and investment in the health service,' argued Brown. These were the policies Brown then believed were necessary to bring about growth in living standards and improvements in the quality of life, and he was to persist with such themes in speeches and articles right up to, and during his Chancellorship. His Budgets from 1997 onwards involved endless tinkering with the tax and social security system, but they were all largely justified in the context of beliefs he had long and firmly held.

He went on and on about low levels of manufacturing investment, too, emphasising the way that North Sea Oil revenues seemed to be doing precious little for the manufacturing base of the economy. Earlier in the year he had asked rhetorically in the Commons: 'If the Germans discovered oil, would they have closed down the Ruhr and invested all the money abroad?'[12]

In that March 1988 Budget debate Brown was prescient about the rocks that lay ahead. 'Our objection to the Chancellor's statement is that, although he may claim to have balanced the Budget, just about everything else in the economy and society was left unbalanced,' he warned. This may have been a slight exaggeration, but the Lawson

Boom was to prove unsustainable; Lawson had stoked up the inflationary fire and set off an incipient balance of payments crisis. 'Never, until this government came to power, did we import more manufactured goods than we exported,' Brown reminded the insouciant Chancellor, whose line was that the private sector would happily finance trade deficits. In those days Brown was a strong advocate of manufacturing. He invoked another great Conservative name: 'It is often said we must export or die. I would add: we must manufacture or die even more quickly' (the words of Mrs Thatcher when leader of the Opposition).

It is interesting that in that early Budget speech Brown referred several times to the health service as the victim of Lawson's preference for tax cuts, even claiming 'the £2 billion that will go to the very rich could have rescued the NHS.'

It was certainly a remarkable Budget, for its impact on British politics and the international debate about taxation policy. Lawson had 'simplified' the tax system, reducing the number of tax rates at that time to no more than two – the basic rate of 25p and the top rate of 40p, but he had also been unashamedly 'redistributive' towards the upper income brackets. 'No Budget this century has seen such a huge redistribution of wealth from poor to rich,' said Brown. He might also have added: 'No Budget this century has made life more difficult for a Labour Party obsessed by its image as "The Party of Taxation"'. Because this was undoubtedly the second most important Budget of the Thatcher years, the one that built on Sir Geoffrey Howe's first Budget of June 1979, when the top rate was brought down from 83% to 60%, and the basic rate from 33% to 30% (albeit largely financed by a near-doubling of VAT).

Whatever the Thatcher revolution had done to the economy – and the collapse of the 'Lawson Miracle' was to demonstrate that there was a significant element of myth behind the putative achievements of Thatcherism – the Chancellorships of Howe (1979–83) and Lawson (1983–89) indubitably 'changed the mould' of the British approach to direct taxation. In his peroration, Brown described the 1988 Budget as 'an epitaph for social justice and an obituary for the fairness and decency that should lie at the centre of our social arrangements.'

Implied in his attack was, of course, the view that by so blatantly favouring private consumption as opposed to investment in public services, the Conservative government was storing up trouble for the future – trouble for what would at some stage (always getting later) be a Labour government, with Brown playing a prominent part.

Thus Brown qualified his observation about the Budget's being 'an epitaph for social justice' etc. by saying, 'as long as this government are in power'. It was to be an awful lot longer. Brown prefaced his judgement by saying that the Budget was, however, 'not [to be seen] as an epitaph for socialism in this country.' One wonders, at this distance, whether there might not have been a powerful element of wishful thinking in that judgement. Certainly, it was Lawson's unashamed intention that his Budget would be such an epitaph.

In a strange way, that Budget, while the apotheosis of Thatcherism, was also the high point of Lawson's career and the beginning of his descent from grace. Having tried monetarism and failed, Lawson had become obsessed with achieving control over inflation by 'shadowing' the Deutschmark; in this way he hoped he would induce the kind of counter-inflation discipline on Britain that the Bundesbank was famous for: indeed, from spring 1987 to spring 1988 he had been stealthily conducting monetary policy so as to stabilise the sterling/Deutschmark rate. It took a long time for the Pfennig to drop on Mrs Thatcher (she evidently did not read the *Observer*, which broke the story that the pound was 'shadowing' the Deutschmark) but when it did, she was furious. His remarkable Budget was not, for Lawson, his finest hour. He was deep in conflict with his Prime Minister over the related issues of the shadowing of the Deutschmark and entry to the ERM, which he wanted but Mrs Thatcher was passionately against.

These issues were related because Lawson had hoped to prove to Mrs Thatcher that a successful 'shadowing' of the Deutschmark (DM) would lead to entry to the ERM as a natural next step. But he was having great difficulty in holding the pound at around DM 3.00, and having to reduce interest rates in order to steady it; for sterling was going through one of its phases as a fashionable currency in which to invest. Lower interest rates were designed, other things being equal, to make London a less attractive place to invest. But they were also fuelling the consumer boom, which the Budget's tax cuts had also done nothing to cool.

In the end Lawson would have to take action in the 1989 Budget and, through interest rate policy, to counteract the inflation and balance of payments pressures that were building up. Meanwhile, in 1988–89 his life was made miserable by disputes with Mrs Thatcher over the ERM issue, which he and Sir Geoffrey Howe, the Foreign Secretary, were pressing. What was to bring things to a head was the return of Sir Alan Walters as the Prime Minister's economic adviser, and the battle between Walters and Lawson for the Prime Minister's ear. Both Gordon Brown and John Smith were to have a hand in wearing down Lawson's morale to the point where the latter resigned in exasperation in the autumn of 1989. But first Brown was to have an unexpected chance to appear on the national stage; early in October 1988 his revered senior, John Smith, suffered his first heart attack, and did not reappear on the Westminster scene until January 1989. Brown kept closely in touch with Smith, visiting him frequently, and displaying genuine concern for the latter's well-being. At the same time, however, he deputised as Shadow Chancellor, putting in a display of magnificent pyrotechnics in the parliamentary debate on the Treasury's traditional Autumn Statement.

Brown was so impressive in the debate that it was difficult to believe that it was Lawson who was the Chancellor and Brown merely the (Deputy) Shadow Chancellor. He was confident, relaxed and witty in a way that did not detract from the seriousness and the passion of his message. *The Times*, not disposed in those days to dish out compliments to Kinnock's team, decided that Brown was 'good looking and an accomplished television performer' and the *Guardian* declared that he was 'already talked of as Neil Kinnock's successor'. Newspaper profiles are two-a-penny these days, but it was quite something for the 'high-flying Son of the Manse' to become the subject of the *Observer* profile at that time.

It can have been no accident that a mere two days after what Paul Anderson of *Tribune* referred to as 'this *tour de force*', Gordon Brown came top of the poll in the elections for the Shadow Cabinet. His parliamentary speech on 25 October had been the most important of his career to date, and had an unmistakable impact on the rest of his career. In it he had the opportunity to build on the foundations of the critique he had laid earlier in the year during the Budget debate. On the first occasion he had been addressing a depleted House, well into the evening. This time it was a packed House at peak parliamentary viewing time. It is important to note that after the tax-cutting Budget of March 1988, the Chancellor had been forced to raise interest rates eight times between May (when they were 7.5%) and August (when they reached 12%), in an effort to cool inflationary pressures in the economy.

Brown began his speech to maximum effect: 'It is now seven months since the Chancellor came to the House at the end of the Budget debate in March and told us that he was presiding over an economic miracle. These have been seven months during which, with real interest rates among the highest in Europe and inflation rising to the highest in Europe, every major forecast and assessment that the Chancellor had made has been proved wrong.'

Lawson had said in March that inflation would be 4%. It was now nearly 6%. He had said imports would rise by 7% – they were rising by 15%; the trade deficit would be £4 billion – it was £10 billion. Savings would rise because of the tax cuts – they had fallen. Unemployment would fall – it had begun to rise. Interest rates had been 'just about right' – they had risen eight times to 12%. Having been wrong about all these things, Lawson was now preaching self-discipline – 'not from him, but from everyone else who borrows and spends. These problems could have been averted if the Chancellor had practised some self-discipline himself ...'

At which point Brown was interrupted by a Conservative who could not resist a reference to the £35 billion tag which had hurt Labour during the 1987 election campaign. 'The honourable gentleman talks of the need for self-discipline. In view of his Party's wild promises to spend money, will he say how much more than £38 billion [sic] his Party would now spend?'

This was a timely reminder to the man who, as Shadow Chief Secretary, had to keep a firm grip on potential spending commitments. 'There are no such commitments!' he said firmly.

Brown maintained that 'what people had gained in tax cuts they have now lost in price rises and mortgage increases.' The House knew there had been overheating and overspending, a credit explosion and a consumer boom, and about the economic imbalances that had resulted, but: 'There has been no overheating in the health service, no overspending on our schools and no explosion of credit for hospital or other community building. There is no consumer boom among pensioners and low-income families.'

Brown said the economic imbalances arose not from an excess of public spending on those who needed it and were entitled to it, but from the extravagances of unnecessary tax cuts for the well-off. 'The Chancellor is prepared to give people at the top or on unearned income rises of 30%, 40% or 50%, but is not prepared to up rate child benefit even by 45p a week in line with inflation.'

There were some hostages to fortune in the future Chancellor's most successful Commons speech so far. In castigating Lawson over his meanness with regard to child benefit, Brown derided, because of the poor take-up, the so-called 'family credit'. Yet as Chancellor he was to build on the social security approach of the Conservatives, and face similar criticisms about 'take-up' and complexity.

Again, Gordon Brown was scathing about the fact that some years earlier the Tories had broken the link between pensions and average earnings. This, he said, had been a 'vindictive decision' and he added the £18 billion that the government had saved from this measure so far to a list that included the advantages the government had gained from £120 billion of North Sea Oil revenues and £40 billion from asset sales. 'That is £180 billion available to this country that has never been available under any other government, yet no government have invested such a small share of our national income in our future.'

While Gordon Brown was making his name in the Labour Party hierarchy, the Party itself was being hemmed in by Conservative advances, as is well illustrated by what happened with policy on pensions and the top rate of tax. In the speech that made his name he contrasted the generosity of the previous Labour government – 'they linked pensions to earnings. They raised pensions in line with earnings' – with the results of that 'vindictive decision' made by the Conservatives: 'When the Chancellor boasts about the fiscal surplus, let him remember that it has been attained on the backs of the pensioners.' Years later there was to be another Chancellor, with another fiscal surplus, who was not going to restore the formal link between earnings and pensions, and who was to be accused of being mean with increases in pensions. Again, one would have thought from the way Brown fulminated about Lawson's reduction in the top rate of income tax from 60p to 40p that he might have wanted to reverse it – 'We are calling for an Autumn Statement about investment and, if necessary, that would have to be paid for by withdrawing the top rate tax cuts,' he said in November 1988.

Lawson was sufficiently riled by the pensions point that early on in his reply to Brown he accused the young 'shadow' Shadow Chancellor of 'impertinence'. By 12 January 1989 – still in the debate on the Autumn Statement – Lawson (with John Smith not yet back) was chiding Brown: 'In spite of all his very frequent speeches, letters to me and television appearances, the House, I have to say, is little clearer than it has ever been on what Labour's policy on the economy actually is.' By this time Brown had also rowed back from calling for complete withdrawal of the top rate tax cuts (for diversion to investment); with an eye on the coming 1989 Budget, Brown referred to a report that Lawson was planning to ease the tax burden of the lower-paid, and urged him to do even more: 'Would not the Chancellor be doing better if he took back *at least part* [my italics] of the top rate tax cuts that he gave to people who did not need them ... in that way, he could take many thousands more out of tax.'

It is interesting that, while Brown chided Lawson for his imprudence in stoking up the boom with tax cuts, he was very much opposed to the Lawsonian prudence with public expenditure in general and public investment in particular. Brown complained of a doctrinaire obsession with reducing public spending below a notional and arbitrary mark of 40% of national income. It became widely acknowledged in the early years of the new century that the nation was suffering from 'decades of under-investment' in the infrastructure and public services. The 1980s was probably the most significant decade of all in this respect. As Brown pointed out, was it not a damning comment on the Thatcher/Lawson government that 'they should congratulate themselves on bringing public expenditure below 40% of GDP, even though that means that public investment in our future has fallen?'

For Brown on 12 January 1989 it was important to assure the Chancellor 'that we believe in more public investment'. He insisted that 'to make that possible we would have a different fiscal strategy from the strategy that the Chancellor is pursuing.' This point was to be hammered away in speeches, broadcasts and articles – not least for the 'soft' left *Tribune*, for which Brown wrote frequently in the early 1990s in an assiduous effort to cultivate his left-wing credentials. Who would have thought that during the entire four years of his first Chancellorship, the man who believed so passionately in investment was going to preside over some of the lowest figures on recent record for public sector investment as a proportion of GDP? Again, who would have thought that he would allow investment in the London Underground to be held up by protracted disputes over his obsession that public investment required not just a different fiscal strategy but also private finance?

What was to go horribly wrong was not only the then Conservative government's fiscal position but the next (1992) general election. For all the prudent efforts of the Shadow Chief Secretary in 1987–89, ensuring a very strict limit on Labour's plans for increases in spending (largely confined to pensions and child benefit), Labour was once again going to become ensnared in the 'tax trap' that Conservative General Office and the press were so adroit at exploiting.

Both Brown and his successor as Shadow Chief Secretary, Margaret Beckett, adhered strictly to the formula that, apart from a few strictly costed commitments – pledges to raise pensions and child benefit, and a promise of a national minimum wage of £2.80 an hour – other spending would only take place 'as resources allow'. Indeed, the 'Shadow Budget' which John Smith unveiled shortly before the 1992 election was largely based on work done under a review ordered by Neil Kinnock in 1987 and completed while Brown was still Shadow Chief Secretary in spring 1989. As Paul Anderson of *Tribune* noted, the detailed documents were 'most of them stuffed with policy ideas that meant increased public spending'. But Brown 'simply removed every proposal from them that could be said to carry a cost'[13] (apart, that is, from the pledges mentioned above).

When the real Chief Secretary of the time, John Major, asked his civil servants to cost the Labour proposals in the hope of opening that famous 'tax trap', the Permanent Secretary at the Department of the Environment, Sir Terry Heiser, wrote in an internal memorandum: 'The review document has been drafted much more carefully than on previous occasions. The promises do not readily lend themselves to precise costings. And in most cases the assumptions you have asked us to cost are vulnerable to counter-attack from the Opposition.'[14]

This memorandum was leaked to Gordon Brown, who made great play with it. Indeed, Brown's remarkable ability to acquire leaked documents from Whitehall sources while in Opposition may have been an advantage to him and to the cause of (reluctantly) open government at the time, but the experience was undoubtedly going to affect his method of operation in government in two ways, neither of them necessarily healthy for the cause of good governance. One was the way that he himself became obsessively secretive when in office, and not terribly keen on leaks that were not authorised by him or his entourage. The second was the way in which he and New Labour generally would 'spin' the news.

While Gordon Brown was making his parliamentary name with searching criticisms of the uses to which Nigel Lawson was putting fiscal policy, Lawson himself made some remarkable boasts about his own achievements. In the light of subsequent developments,

Lawson's view is worth recording. In January 1989 Lawson felt able to claim that his monetary policy was 'buttressed by the firmest fiscal stance of any government since the war: for the first time for at least half a century we have a government in this country that are engaged in repaying the national debt and will continue to do so next year too.'[15]

Repaying the national debt, rather than immediate action to deal with the run-down of the public services of which he had long complained, was also to become a Brownian obsession, with the intention of spending more on the public services in due course. Lawson went so far as to claim that the 'immensely strong fiscal position ... guarantees that the historic tax reform and tax reductions in last year's Budget – for which I make no apology whatever – will remain fully in place, to the immense benefit of the British economy in years to come.'[16]

He was right about the tax reductions, which survived the whole of Labour's first term in 1997–2001 and had not been rescinded well into the second term. Lawson said he fully understood that the Opposition did not like his tax reform. 'What they want – what they have always wanted – is to see income tax put up. That is why they voted against each and every reduction in income tax – each and every one of them.'[17]

'Voted against', or abstained, but accepted in practice on arrival in office. Unfortunately for the Labour Party, that was still going to be a very long time indeed. Despite the prudence of Shadow Chief Secretary Gordon Brown in 1987–89 in excising many a wished-for policy from Labour's commitment, Labour was once again going to fall foul of what it came to regard as a conspiracy between a ruthless Conservative Central Office and a largely hostile press. John Smith's 'Shadow Budget' of spring 1992, the basis of Labour's tax and spending promises during the election campaign of that year, was carefully costed, with the principal commitments (dating back to the earlier policy review) amounting to no more than £3.5 billion for higher pensions and child benefit payments.

Even in those days Labour was promising to stabilise public spending as a proportion of GDP. At first the 'careful costing' approach seemed to go down well, and those closely associated with the Shadow Budget, not least Margaret Beckett, who was then Shadow Chief Secretary, subsequently argued that people had been unfair to blame it for Labour's fourth consecutive election defeat.

The problem was that there was a delayed reaction to the Shadow Budget. The careful costings involved a rise in the top rate of tax to 50%, and higher national insurance contributions for people earning more than £21,000 a year as a result of the proposed abolition of the earnings ceiling on which national insurance contributions were paid.

Not only did the Conservatives manage to turn the £3.5 billion of spending commitments into a ten times larger sum – so that the familiar £35 billion scare figure used in the 1987 election campaign surfaced once again – but economic and political journalists suddenly noticed that they personally would have to pay higher taxes and gave prominent coverage to 'Labour's Tax Bombshell'.

There were differences within the Labour camp about the wisdom of the Shadow Budget; Neil Kinnock himself was unhappy about it, not least with the national insurance plan which, he repeated at a pre-election dinner with journalists (at Luigi's restaurant in London), might be 'phased in'. One way or another there was an atmosphere of panic in the Labour ranks, a panic which was cleverly exploited by Conservative Party Chairman Chris Patten and played up in the press. Despite doing well in the opinion polls until close to the election, Labour lost in a last-minute swing, a swing that just preceded whatever reaction there was to the apparent triumphalism of the Sheffield Rally.

Butler and Kavanagh concluded in their book on the 1992 election: 'In spite of what the public polls were saying until election day, the 1992 election seems to reflect – however furtively and reluctantly – a classic pocket-book outcome in the classic mould.'[18] The Conservatives had presided over the second major recession of their years in office (1990–92 as well as 1980–82); but Labour was once again ensnared in the 'tax trap'.

The day after the 1992 election, Tony Blair and Gordon Brown met in Blair's constituency and decided they had to plan 'New Labour'.

CHAPTER FOUR

Labour and the ERM

Labour's problem on 9 April 1992 was that it was distrusted on the economy more than the Conservatives, notwithstanding the collapse of the Lawson Boom and the serious recession of 1990–92. It was Labour's bad luck that the Conservatives did not finally lose their reputation for economic competence until five months later, on Black Wednesday, 16 September 1992. This was the day when the Major government finally gave up trying to maintain the pound's value within the exchange rate mechanism, in the face of overwhelming speculation against it.

There had been a conspiracy of silence about the European exchange rate mechanism during the 1992 election campaign. Membership of the ERM had become a bi-partisan policy, and there were not enough differences between the parties – or rather, differences that could be admitted openly – to be exploited by either side, or by the media, during the campaign.

Labour was in office during the late 1970s when the European Monetary System (EMS) was conceived. Despite his very good relationship with West German Chancellor Helmut Schmidt, one of the architects of the EMS, the Prime Minister James Callaghan baulked at putting the pound into the exchange rate mechanism for both political and economic reasons. The 1975 referendum on whether Britain should remain in the European Economic Community had been a wearing affair for Labour. As one Minister subsequently wrote, 'The politics of the question were clear enough. Joining the EMS would divide the party and the government. It could not afford to be divided once again on a European issue at such a time.'[1] Also, the Treasury had advised strongly against putting the pound into a fixed exchange rate system, even if it was 'fixed but adjustable'. The Treasury believed that, even with possession of North Sea Oil, the pound would have to decline over the years in order to maintain competitiveness. Given how 'political' decisions about devaluation had proved in the past, involving damaged prestige and loss of face, the Treasury's considered view was that it was better to stay out.

Harold Lever, the Prime Minister's special economic adviser (and a Cabinet member), was concerned about Britain being isolated from the EMS and losing power to influence economic decisions within the EEC. Denis Healey, the Chancellor, devised a wonderfully jesuitical compromise, whereby Britain would formally join the European Monetary System, thereby participating in meetings and having a say in policy, without putting the pound into the principal manifestation of the EMS, namely the exchange rate mechanism (it was only quite late in the 1980s that the arrangement came to be referred to as the ERM; for years the government and media called it the EMS).

Ironically, the decision not to join the ERM was the prelude to a major shock to the British economy. The Treasury had sought the freedom for the pound to depreciate; instead it became hugely overvalued, contributing to the serious recession of 1980–81. This was the period when the Thatcher government was pursuing a policy of trying to conquer inflation by controlling the money supply, and failing dismally. Lawson, then Financial Secretary to the Treasury, had propagated monetarism for a while, and was to support it publicly for some years; but as early as June 1981 he was raising the question of whether the Government might not be able to enforce and maintain a greater degree of financial discipline if it were to embrace the exchange rate discipline.[2] This was at a time when the pound was so overvalued that tying it to the Deutschmark would have been insane.

During his Chancellorship (1983–89) Lawson tried in vain at various times and at various exchange rates to persuade Mrs Thatcher of the wisdom of entry to the ERM. He and Sir Geoffrey

Howe (then Foreign Secretary) eventually persuaded her in June 1989 to make a commitment, but only by threatening their joint resignations; in return Thatcher – advised by Sir Alan Walters – insisted on a strict *quid pro quo*, which became known as the Madrid Conditions. These conditions included clear evidence that other European countries were dismantling exchange controls as part of the move towards the European Single Market, and that the British inflation rate was heading downwards again after the upward spiral set off by the Lawson Boom.

Lawson's obsession with joining the ERM was a reflection of his own search for a 'credible' economic policy, while the Labour Party was itself desperately trying to devise policies that would persuade the public to trust it. Both Lawson and Labour ended up putting their trust in the ERM and Gordon Brown, while still Shadow Chief Secretary with principal responsibility for keeping spending commitments under control, was a key member of the inner circle which collectively decided that Labour's economic salvation lay within the ERM. But it was the Conservatives who were in office at the time; it was the Conservatives who eventually took the decision to join the ERM in October 1990. And it was the Conservatives who lost their reputation for economic competence as a result of the way they handled a policy to which Labour, too, had been converted. The episode was going to make Gordon Brown deeply suspicious of the ERM cause which he had happily espoused in the late 1980s: he would end up hiring as his Chief Economic Adviser, both in opposition and in government, a man, Ed Balls, who scathingly denounced the ERM mechanism as an example of 'Euro-Monetarism'.

But first it will be useful to make a brief diversion to France. Michael Foot had failed to win the 1983 British election on a left-wing economic programme; François Mitterrand, in France, had campaigned and won on a 'socialist' and 'growth' agenda in 1981 but ran into trouble with the financial markets. Jacques Delors, as Finance Minister, then embarked on a (*franc fort*) policy of disinflation and a stable franc in March 1983, but only after the franc had been devalued three times within the EMS. Delors became President of the

European Commission in January 1985 and served two terms. He presided over the formation of the European Single Market (the '1992' programme) which gradually dissolved internal trade and financial barriers, and indeed Delors was the political father of that programme, seeing it as a means of dynamising the European economy and preventing Europe from turning into an economic 'museum'. He was also the driving force behind the eponymous *Delors Report* (1989), which prepared the way for the single currency and European economic and monetary union (EMU); but he always wanted a strong 'social dimension' to the single market and EMU, with an emphasis on workers' rights.

Delors and many on the left regarded the failure of the 1981–83 experiment with 'Keynesianism in one country' as a sign that Socialism needed to be rethought in a broader European context. They hoped that a single currency would provide collective protection for individual economies whose currencies were vulnerable on their own to the vagaries of the financial markets. Delors saw the EMU project as more expansionary and socially-minded than it subsequently became.

Delors became the *bête noire* of Mrs Thatcher and the Conservative press for being a 'Federalist'. Delors was the embodiment of the French version of a socialist 'moderniser'; as his biographer notes, his speech to the 1988 TUC Conference in Bournemouth 'helped to banish the British Labour movement's Euroscepticism'.[3] Mrs Thatcher had seen the European Single Market as a way of exporting Thatcherism to the Continent; but she seriously underestimated the extent to which, by signing the Single European Act (in 1986), she was giving the go-ahead to the single currency as well. Delors – Frère Jacques – so won round TUC leaders with his reassurances about 'Social Europe' that he received a standing ovation and the TUC passed a resolution in favour of the Single Market. Delors emphasised that, as he saw it, the Single Market would be beneficial to social welfare and workers' rights. Of course, by giving the European Commission a mildly socialist image – and indeed by addressing the TUC at all – Delors antagonised Mrs Thatcher and the right, a position he cultivated by not concealing his ambitions for European political as well as monetary union. Both the unions and the Labour Party generally now saw Brussels as a kind of countervailing power against Thatcherism, thinking there must be something good about an institution towards which Mrs Thatcher was so vehemently opposed.

Delors's TUC appearance took place only a few months after what Neil Kinnock's biographer regards as 'the crucial turning point' in Labour's thinking on the Single Market. Kinnock had been taking the Party in a more pro-European direction from 1983 – provided, in keeping with the de Gaulle approach of old, that it could be shown that this was in his country's interest – and saw policies of economic expansion as more feasible within a European context. But he was initially suspicious of the Single Market, until a paper presented to a meeting of the Shadow Cabinet's economic sub-committee in May 1988 by the Cambridge economist Iain Begg persuaded him that Labour should not stand back from the process but ought instead, *à la* Delors, to become actively engaged in promoting a 'Social Europe'.

The Single Market was going ahead. Labour had to become involved, and Labour leaders were deliberately engaging with their Continental counterparts at various international meetings. 'If,' said Neil Kinnock on 7 September 1988, just before Delors's visit to the TUC, 'the Single Market was to mean nothing other than a Big Finance free-for-all it would be a social, industrial and environmental catastrophe.'[4] The market must serve the people, not the people the market.

It was the following year, 1989, that the Labour leadership developed its cooperative attitude towards the Single Market into a major pro-European platform with adoption of the ERM as the main feature of macroeconomic policy. The key politicians involved in the pro-ERM move were Kinnock, Smith and Brown. All three enjoyed a year during which they ruthlessly played on the divisiveness of Mrs Thatcher's decision to invite Sir Alan Walters back to Downing Street as her economic adviser, and the embarrassing impact they hoped this would have on Lawson's position and the government's European policy. Gordon Brown was an active matador, putting down a well-informed parliamentary question on 10 January 1989

'To ask the Prime Minister when Sir Alan Walters will resume his duties as her economic adviser', to which the answer was 'around the middle of this year'. As the day approached, Brown was mischievously asking the Prime Minister 'if she will publish a list of Sir Alan Walters's outside interests' and 'the salary of Sir Alan Walters on appointment' (3 May 1989).

John Smith told me around this time that if there was one thing that made him pro-ERM it was the embarrassment of the Tories, who were 'all over the place' on this issue. The issue had to be finessed within the Labour Party because the main policy review group on the economy was under the Chairmanship of Bryan Gould, who was anti-ERM and strongly in favour of retaining the flexibility to devalue when necessary. However, John Eatwell, Kinnock's economic adviser, was favouring the ERM as a way of associating Labour with financial and exchange rate stability rather than with devaluation. For Kinnock and Gordon Brown the counterpart was that, if it bound its hands in this way, a future Labour government must nevertheless be committed to higher public investment. For Eatwell, the ERM was a route to lower interest rates and an active fiscal policy.

'For me the whole ERM episode was, with "no new taxes", part of the business of building up Labour's credibility,' said Eatwell. 'We had to look credible. I have always believed in a passive, low interest rate policy and an active fiscal policy.'[5]

But, mindful of the failure of the Mitterrand experiment of 1981–83, and of the punishment meted out to governments by the financial markets, Eatwell associated floating rates, which Bryan Gould preferred, with 'financial instability and the need for higher interest rates'. Eatwell stated in 1992 that one of the main developments in Labour economic policy while he was there was 'abandonment of the idea that short-term macroeconomic management is the key to the maintenance of full employment. It is argued in effect that it is no longer possible to have Keynesianism in one country.'

This was perhaps the nadir of the hopes of economists like Eatwell, who had been brought up in the Cambridge tradition of Keynesian economic policies. Keynesians believed, essentially, that if you were in a hole you did not dig deeper (unless you paid people for doing so ...) and that the way to full employment was to unbalance the Budget temporarily, via lower taxes and higher public spending. The combination of the inflationary problems of the 1970s – associated with trade unions flexing their muscles over wage claims, and a quintupling of oil prices – had made life difficult for Keynesians, and led to the ascendancy of monetarists. But while the beliefs of the monetarists that they could solve Britain's inflation problem by controlling the money supply were soon shattered (even the arch-monetarist guru, Milton Friedman, ultimately recanted), economists such as Eatwell had, especially after the failed Mitterrand experiment with 'Keynesianism in one country', become nervous about the ability of left-wing governments to stray from financial orthodoxy without being punished by the financial markets.

As we shall see, Gordon Brown as Chancellor was going to preach the virtues of 'stability' until he was blue in the face. But the same message was already being preached by those around him, Kinnock and Smith in the late 1980s. Thus Eatwell wrote of his advice at the time: 'Fine-tuning [short-term changes in fiscal policy to manage demand in the economy] should be replaced by a search for macroeconomic stability as a framework for long-term investment.'[6]

Eatwell defined stability as 'a stable exchange rate, stable interest rates at levels no higher than those of Britain's competitors, and low inflation.' This was of course precisely what was on offer from the European exchange rate system, and, *a fortiori*, from the then distant prospect of a single currency, which was also beginning to attract senior Labour politicians.

Labour's economic advisers – including Eatwell, Gavyn Davies and Meghnad Desai, who advised John Smith – convinced themselves that a Europe which, taken as a whole, was the economic equal of the USA (or on some definitions greater) could offer a stable background for policies of expansion that one country alone dare not risk. But this belief was always subject to the way the rules for policy within the ERM and the greater goal of the single currency actually evolved. The French, in particular, were concerned about the dominance of the Bundesbank in European monetary policy, and wanted to dilute the Bundesbank's influence by subsuming it in a more growth-orientated European Central Bank. But the fact of the matter was that the central bankers (and the German Finance Ministry, fearful of 'Latins' who might misbehave under a single currency) insisted both in the *Delors Report* and the *Maastricht Treaty* (negotiated in December 1991 and signed in spring 1992) on tough conditions that made 'Keynesianism in Europe' not as easy to achieve as the left, including Delors, had hoped. Years later Eatwell himself was to complain in a public lecture that most of the high unemployment in the European Community was not the result, as fashionably argued, of 'structural rigidities', and could be cured by Keynesian policies specifically designed to achieve full employment.[7]

There was a now largely forgotten but important event at the time, for a 'modernising' Labour Party hierarchy that was beginning to see macroeconomic policy in a European context: the European elections of June 1989. As Kinnock's biographer records, the outcome of these elections was 'a triumph for Labour, providing the Party with its first national victory over the Conservatives since 1974. Kinnock later admitted that the hours he spent watching the results come through late into the night of Sunday 18 June were the best of his entire period as Labour leader.'

Labour won 45 seats in the European Parliament, the Conservatives 32 and the Liberal Democrats none. The years 1989–90 saw the demise of the SDP, not least because the 'modernising' Labour Party had moved into social democratic territory the way the old German left did after the 1959 Bad Godesberg Conference. Although this was a 'European' election it was inevitably fought largely on domestic issues. The Lawson Boom was evaporating, interest rates were on the way up, Lawson's 1989 Budget had taken some of the gloss off the wonders of his 1988 tax 'giveaway', and Mrs Thatcher was determined to introduce the poll tax. Labour captured the high tide of pro-Europeanism – at the time 55% of the electorate said membership of the European Community was a 'good thing' and only 18% a 'bad thing'.

Always remembering that Labour's economic policy review under Bryan Gould was about to produce an anti-ERM document, one cannot but admire the way the Labour leadership campaigned in the June European election on a platform of the wonders of a 'Social Europe' (*au* Delors). On the ERM the compromise with Gould was that Labour was not prepared to enter unless the exchange rate was 'realistic and competitive' and European economic policy was sufficiently expansionary. As this stage Labour was still opposed to the single currency, but things were moving fast.

Around this time (1987) a new think-tank was set up to foster debate. Although the Institute for Public Policy Research (IPPR) was officially described as 'independent', it was very much in the 'modernising' Labour camp. Gordon Brown spoke enthusiastically and hopefully about it at a small inaugural dinner, after which one of the financial sponsors commented to me, 'they may call it independent but I am backing it because I want a Labour government.'

The first pamphlet produced under the auspices of the IPPR was by the economist Gavyn Davies, who had been in Number 10 during Callaghan's premiership and had since become a prominent economist in the City. His wife Sue Nye was Neil Kinnock's executive secretary and subsequently Gordon Brown's. John Eatwell and Patricia Hewitt (Kinnock's former Press Secretary, later to be in the Blair Cabinet) were also involved with the IPPR and with the first pamphlet. It called for early entry of the pound into the ERM.

So the situation in the summer of 1989 was that the Kinnock camp and the academic and City advisers around John Smith (chaired by Andrew Graham of Balliol) were desperately seeking stability – or rather a reputation for it, via the ERM and the acceptance of the economic orthodoxy of the day – while Bryan Gould had chaired the key group that influenced the economic policy conclusions of the document *Meet the Challenge, Make the Change*. This document had been published in May but was discussed at the Labour Conference in October where, as Paul Anderson observes, 'it was passed with minimal dissent'.

Gould, a New Zealander, had been consistently anti-ERM. While a moderniser who was happy to emphasise consumer sovereignty and the 'supply side' socialism programme of measures to encourage training and investment, Gould managed to produce a document that highlighted the deflationary aspects of the ERM and which was more positively and openly Keynesian than Eatwell and Smith were prepared to stomach at the time. There was also a proposal for a strong, interventionist Department of Trade and Industry, run on Japanese lines, and new official financial institutions as a counterweight to the putative 'short-termism' of the City of London.

Some of this would have appealed to the 'Red Gordon' of the mid-1970s but not necessarily to the modernising one. It is therefore interesting that Gordon Brown was on the Gould Committee, as indeed was Eatwell. Brown was by all accounts an 'irregular attender' at the meetings, which absorbed his and Eatwell's 'supply side' socialism but not their burgeoning enthusiasm for the ERM. The document was a long time in the making, and in his memoirs Gould reveals that, for all his irregular attendance, Gordon Brown had the opportunity to influence the policy but did not take it. According to Gould, Brown played 'virtually no part in the work of my policy review committee. He attended only rarely, and spoke, as I recall, on only one occasion.' Indeed, Gould is rather scathing: 'Nevertheless, I somehow gained the impression that he was not fully supportive of the line that the committee was taking on various issues but that he either did not dare or did not know how to put a contrary view.'[8]

The first version of Gould's economic document had been ready in May the previous year (1988) and Gould recalls that 'a delegation' turned up at his office to object to some of its contents. The delegation comprised Eatwell, Gordon Brown and Tony Blair. 'They left empty-handed, but no doubt, as subsequent events have demonstrated, unconvinced.'[9]

Gould had also detected the imminent embrace of the ERM by the Party at a meeting of the Shadow Cabinet economic committee on 27 June 1988. In an interesting foretaste of what Labour was eventually going to do in a different way in 1997 (i.e. via an independent central bank, not ERM membership), Gould records Eatwell as wanting 'in effect to reassure the City and other critics that they need have no fears about inflation under a Labour government, since monetary policy would no longer be under the control of government *but would be contracted out to an independent mechanism'* (my italics). Gould warned that if Labour committed itself to the ERM, 'we would not be waiting for the City to shackle us. We would in effect be offering up our wrists in advance for the application of the handcuffs.'[10]

Gould maintains that none of those who were about to embrace the ERM – namely Kinnock, Smith and Brown – was prepared to take him on in argument 'since, I assume, they realised they would not get the better of it.' He acknowledges that Eatwell would have been capable of arguing the contrary case but, as he was only an adviser, was not qualified to speak at a Shadow Cabinet meeting.

The move towards the ERM was part of an effort by the inner core of Labour's economic policy team – Kinnock, Smith and Brown – to shake off the label of the 'Party of Devaluation'. Yet the history of Labour – the 1931 departure from the gold standard; the 1949 devaluation; the 1967 devaluation; the 1976 crisis at the hands of the financial markets and the International Monetary Fund – suggested that it only acquired the 'devaluation' label because it adhered for too long on each occasion to an overvalued exchange rate, with inevitable and often politically disastrous consequences. Gould tried to warn Kinnock in a paper in 1988 (*Why we can't afford a blind spot on the exchange rate*). In it Gould recalled the spikes on which Ramsay MacDonald (in 1929–31), Harold Wilson (in 1964–67) and James Callaghan (in 1976) had allowed their policies to be impaled. They were all 'hooked on the primacy of some monetary measure, and as a consequence finding themselves defending the financial establishment rather than their own electorate.'

At all events, in the month (October 1989) when the document expressing caution about the ERM was being passed by the Labour Party's annual Conference, those with the real influence on economic policy were about to stage a major shift and Bryan Gould, who had been joint convener of the committee that drew up macroeconomic policy in 1987–89, was about to be shifted to another job; Kinnock wanted him to take on 'the biggest issue of all at the time', the poll tax as Shadow Secretary for the Environment. Gould's opposition to the ERM move has been presented by his enemies as an integral part of his anti-Europeanism; it was in fact entirely the result of his own economic assessment. Whatever his earlier views about 'the Common Market', Gould had long since accepted that Britain would remain in 'Europe' and was motivated more by the desire for what he saw as enlightened macroeconomic policies.

The section in *Meet the Challenge, Make the Change* referring to the ERM, drafted by Gould, was demanding. It said that the EMS 'suffers from too great an emphasis on deflationary measures as a means of achieving monetary targets and it imposes obligations which are not symmetrical.' Substantial changes would be required before the next Labour government could take sterling into the ERM. It implied that central banks should intervene more to stabilise currencies, rather than relying on changes in interest rates. 'There must be a coordinated EC-wide growth policy. The pound would have to enter at a rate and on conditions which ensured that British goods became and remained competitive.'

Although Gould was vilified for insisting on these provisions, they were not unreasonable and, indeed, some of the key reservations were going to survive. But the tone seems to have irritated Kinnock, Smith, Brown and Eatwell at a time when they were undoubtedly warming to the EMS in a way Gould certainly was not.

Neil Kinnock himself had decided, after the publication of the government's 'Madrid Conditions' for joining the ERM, that Labour should have its own conditions, and the kind of points made by Gould were relevant to this. Eatwell, Smith, Brown and other Labour advisers discussed this over the summer, and in October 1989, a few days after the Labour Conference had approved *Meet the Challenge, Make the Change*, Smith and Brown began a tour of European capitals to discuss the ERM and plans for European Monetary Union with Delors in Brussels, senior German and French politicians and Karl Otto Pohl, President of the Bundesbank.

On the flight to Brussels (18 October) Gordon Brown drew to Smith's attention an article in the *Financial Times* in which Sir Alan Walters, on the eve of his reappointment as Mrs Thatcher's economic adviser, described the ERM as 'half-baked'. Egged on by Brown, Smith used a parliamentary debate the following Tuesday to probe the divisions on the ERM between Thatcher and Walters on the one hand, and Lawson on the other. Smith's punchline was: 'I advise the Chancellor to make an early decision on the important question of whether he will jump or be pushed.' In the wind-up speech, Brown himself goaded Lawson further by saying: 'Many lonely, sad and embattled people labour under the delusion that their thoughts are being influenced by the Moonies next door. I assure the Right Honourable Gentleman that he is not paranoid. They really are out to get him.'

Smith's biographer plausibly argues that by exploiting the divisions over the ERM within the government, Labour leaders were able to finesse their own transition from suspicion of the ERM to support, not only for the ERM itself but also for prospective European monetary union. According to one backbench fan of theirs, the team of Smith and Brown were 'like the grandmasters of political strategy, capable of seeing fifteen moves ahead.' In the speech during which he chided Lawson, Smith made a casual reference to Labour's 'prudent' conditions for entering the ERM. These were: entry at an 'effective' rate; adequate central bank arrangements to ward off speculative attacks; and a growth-orientated macroeconomic strategy (not too different from Gould's!). On 5 November 1989, in a newspaper article, he added 'increased support for regional policy' to the list.

The word 'effective' was deliberately used, in accordance with the decision the inner group had taken to avoid association with Labour's history as the Party of devaluation. It was delightfully vague; and, as a matter of fact, the phrase 'effective rate' is in common official use to describe the average value of the pound against a basket of other key currencies. In this sense, *any* rate is an 'effective' rate.

John Smith had always been a strong pro-European. He was impressed by the way the European left was signing up to the ERM and the prospect of the single currency, but also wanted to exploit the divisions within the Tory Party. Gordon Brown encouraged him. Smith told a meeting of Euro MPs: 'We are keen to play a full and constructive part in the debate on progress towards monetary union.' Gould's document had stated: 'We oppose moves towards a European Monetary Union.'[11]

The Walters article in the *Financial Times* was an old one, and ironically Walters seems to have offered it to one of the paper's correspondents, Simon Holberton, in a conscious effort not to say anything new or additionally controversial when they asked him to write. But Lawson blamed Walters. In a debate on 24 October, Smith administered more salt to Lawson's wounds by provocatively saying that he should ask Thatcher to 'Back me or sack me.' Lawson had made resignation threats before, but on Thursday 26 October 1989 he finally did the deed. The timing surprised his senior officials, who thought their Chancellor was safely away on a scheduled trip to Germany. When the news of Lawson's resignation came out, Treasury Permanent Secretary Sir Peter Middleton was having his hair cut, and Chief Economic Adviser Sir Terence Burns was on the golf course. Walters, too, resigned within hours.

In an economic debate on 31 October 1989, Gordon Brown teased Mrs Thatcher, saying she did not seem to realise why Lawson had resigned. 'It was not a personality clash ... it was a fundamental question of exchange rate policy, right at the heart of government economic strategy, a matter that has not yet been resolved.' Behind this rather mischievous afterthought was the full knowledge that Thatcher was adamantly opposed to the ERM, while Labour had only just resolved its own position, with at least part of its motivation being to capitalise on Conservative divisions.

Lawson was succeeded as Chancellor by John Major, who had had experience of the Treasury as Chief Secretary but who had only a few months earlier been made Foreign Secretary. When senior officials in the Treasury were told by the Cabinet Office that it was to be 'JM', they immediately assumed it would be John MacGregor, a Conservative with considerable financial experience who to many seemed a more plausible candidate than Major, who was still finding his feet in the Foreign Office. On top form, and on the eve of topping the Shadow Cabinet elections for the second time in a row (his patron John Smith was only second), Gordon Brown went on to tease Major: if he had been truly ambitious, surely he would have preferred Walters's job, which had been 'the most damaging appointment of an adviser by a head of government since – I was going to say, since Caligula's horse, but at least the horse stayed in Rome and worked full-time.'

Two events which were important factors in the development of both Conservative and Labour policy towards the ERM and the single currency also occurred in 1989. The *Delors Report*, on what the road to monetary union might look like if European leaders decided to go ahead, had been published on 17 April 1989, suggesting (as duly happened) that 'stage one' should begin on 1 July 1990. Among other things, stage one would see the completion of the single market; also, prospective members of the proposed monetary union would have to join the ERM if, like Britain, they were still outside. At the Madrid Summit in June 1989 – the summit that gave its name to Mrs Thatcher's 'Madrid Conditions' for British membership of the ERM – the Delors proposal for 1 July 1990 as the starting date was accepted by European leaders.

The second, very significant event occurred within weeks of Lawson's resignation and Major's appointment as Chancellor: the Fall of the Berlin Wall on 9 November 1989. From the point of view of this narrative, there were two especially relevant aspects of that event: first, the French President Francois Mitterrand was so concerned about the impact a unified and possibly 'resurgent' Germany might have on Europe that he became determined to extract a firm date from Germany for economic and monetary union; and second, German unification itself was to put such inflationary strains on the German economy in the early 1990s that it would radically affect the workings of the ERM: not to put too fine a point upon it, the counter-inflationary anchor sought in their different ways by both major British political parties would become dislodged.

With Gould moved to be Kinnock's 'big hitter' against the poll tax, Labour's key economic policy-making committees were now chaired by Smith and Brown. In the course of spring 1990, Neil Kinnock, encouraged by Smith and Brown, began to favour making a firm commitment to join the ERM. Gould got the impression that 'it was almost as though he believed that if Mrs Thatcher was against our membership, it must be a good thing'[12] (just as I myself got the impression from John Smith that this was an important influence on him). At a parliamentary Labour Party meeting in the summer of 1990, Gordon Brown presented the ERM as a means of disarming the speculators and warding off the sterling crises that had plagued previous Labour governments. Gould recalls Brown suggesting 'that by fixing the parity within the ERM, we would somehow be applying a form of socialist planning of the economy, rather than leaving such important issues to market forces'. The idea of Gordon Brown as the man who would disarm the speculators went down well with the MPs. Gould noted ruefully: 'He, and they, seemed unaware of the fact that the only thing which gave speculators their chance was if governments were foolish enough to defend a parity which was seen by traders to be out of line with a currency's real value.'[13]

Gould complains of 'an astonishing ignorance of economic history' all round. 'People like John Major and Gordon Brown truly believed, I think, that the ERM was a new and magic device which would somehow insulate their decisions about the currency against reality.' Essentially the ERM was an attempt to use the reserves of one or more countries in order to defy the market – an attempt that failed lamentably, with deep ill-feeling all round, on Black Wednesday, 16 September 1992.

But first Britain had to join. It was not just the Labour Party that was keen on the ERM. By summer 1990 the conventional wisdom in Whitehall, the City and among CBI and trade union leaders was that the ERM offered the best hope at a time when the Lawson Boom had ended in tears, interest rates had been raised to 15% for almost a year, and the rate of inflation was rising. Ironically, although Lawson had been reduced to resignation by Mrs Thatcher's intransigence over the ERM, his successor John Major – much less of a political heavyweight – eventually wore her down, with the aid of heavy pressure from her officials. As Philip Stephens has observed: 'Among Treasury officials the economic case for the ERM was obvious, too obvious.'[14]

The Lawson Boom had destroyed the Conservative government's anti-inflation strategy. Monetarism had been tried and failed. The Treasury had run out of options. The announcement that the pound was entering the ERM was made on Friday 5 October 1990 in the afternoon, upstaging the last day of the Labour Party Conference in Blackpool. The pill for Mrs Thatcher was sweetened by accession to her demand for a 1% cut in interest rates to 14% – a help for the Conservative Conference the following week. Within a fortnight the Treasury admitted that growth in domestic demand in 1988 had been, at 8%, double what it expected at the time of the Budget. Officials later claimed that their original economic forecasts had indeed indicated such a rate of expansion but that they seemed too implausible, and were revised.

Few complaints were made in London about the rate – DM 2.95 – at which the pound was put into the ERM. Labour supported the move publicly, although Neil Kinnock had severe reservations about the rate – as did the Bundesbank and the European Commission (Mrs Thatcher had wanted an even higher rate). It was a botched affair, without proper consultation with our European counterparts, who were simply informed of the rate at which we were going in; this left bad blood which had most certainly not disappeared when the time came for understanding from our partners in the run-up to Black Wednesday. Among other things, with inflation running at 10.9% a year – i.e. the rate had been rising, not falling – the Madrid Terms had been softened or 'seasonally adjusted'.

After the British decision about DM 2.95, a senior member of Jacques Delors's staff in Brussels produced a paper warning the Commission that it would not be long before Britain would have to devalue within the ERM. 'We did not think the accompanying interest rate cut was the greatest sign of firmness of purpose,' said the Brussels official. Although no other country was consulted about the rate, and the Germans certainly thought at the time that it was too high and unsustainable, the French did not object because they thought a lower pound would, in the words of the official, 'disrupt the system'.[15]

In the closing months of 1990 Labour was coming close to giving support 'in principle' to the concept of the single currency, while other EEC leaders, at a summit in Rome in late October, were firming up their plans, with a date, 1 January 1994, for the preparations to set up what eventually became the European Central Bank. But, having been browbeaten over the ERM, Mrs Thatcher made her opposition to the single currency perfectly plain when she returned from Rome, and this was the last straw for her Deputy Prime Minister Sir Geoffrey Howe, who resigned from the Cabinet; his resignation speech so wounded Mrs Thatcher that by November 1990 she herself had been forced to resign as leader.

High interest rates aimed at cooling inflation had already contrived the onset of recession, and the poll tax was proving deeply unpopular – criticised even by Donald Trump for the insistence that 'the rich man in his castle should pay the same as the poor man at his gate'. But it was her anti-Europeanism, and her insistence that joining the single currency was not on, that riled Howe and other Cabinet Ministers most. The issue of the single currency was going to bulk large in Gordon Brown's eventual Chancellorship, and the Conservative Party was to become very anti-European. In November 1990 the Conservative Party discarded Mrs Thatcher. She had become a liability and one of the reasons, as far as the most senior members of the Cabinet were concerned, was that she was not European enough.

During 1991 and early 1992 the British recession deepened. While Kinnock, Smith and Brown were working on Labour's image as a party that could be considered economically responsible, the Conservatives were losing their reputation for economic competence. Black Wednesday would be the final nadir. The issue of 'Europe' was ever-present. At Maastricht in December 1991, John Major, Prime Minister after Mrs Thatcher, negotiated his famous 'opt-out' from the Social Charter and monetary union (a senior Whitehall official said, after the arrival of Gordon Brown in 1997, 'I prefer to regard it as an "opt-in"'). British politics under both

Major and Blair/Brown were going to be influenced by the fact that no time-limit was placed on the opt-out from EMU. Equally, however, they would be affected by President Mitterrand's insistence that Chancellor Helmut Kohl of Germany give a firm date for the formation of EMU – provided that the economic 'convergence criteria' were met. The dates were 1997 – or 1999 at the latest. Kohl was as concerned as Mitterrand about the possibility of German 'resurgence' after unification; he and the German Establishment were always aiming at a 'European Germany' not a 'German Europe'. Economic and monetary union – the sacrifice of the almighty Deutschmark – were seen as the essential means.

John Major's Chancellorship of just over a year – October 1989 to November 1990 – was memorable for two things: interest rates were maintained at 15% for eleven months in the long wait for the monetary squeeze to bring inflation down; and the pound finally entered the ERM. Norman Lamont's Chancellorship was memorable for the onset of the severe recession of 1990 to 1992 – the second major recession under the Tories' reign since 1979; for a politically adroit Budget in spring 1992 which upstaged Labour's plans for a 20p starting tax rate (thereby helping the Conservatives' election victory of April 1992); and for Black Wednesday later that year.

But one of the most interesting things about Lamont's Chancellorship before Black Wednesday (he was to begin the improvements in fiscal and monetary policy afterwards, which Kenneth Clarke built on) was that he had no faith in the ERM policy itself. 'Why are we doing this?' he would ask senior officials such as Sir Terence Burns. After European finance ministers' lunches, Sir Nigel Wicks, the senior Treasury official for international matters, would ask members of Jacques Delors's Cabinet what had occurred and what Lamont had said. The verdict of one such official was, 'Norman Lamont was clearly euro-sceptic and wobbly, while defending the policy in public.'

The Treasury had not covered itself in glory during the Lawson Boom, when it miscalculated the impact of financial deregulation on consumer (and business) spending. Neither did it come well out of the ERM episode. Eddie George, then Deputy Governor of the

Bank of England, while unhappy about ERM entry, had acquiesced for a time simply because of the counter-inflationary effect of the high interest rates dictated by the requirements of the ERM. But even George, once memorably described by a member of the parliamentary Treasury Committee (Labour MP Brian Sedgemore) as an 'inflation nutter', thought that the ERM-induced squeeze was by 1992 too tight. It was not just that the entry rate for the pound had been set high; the 'inflation anchor' was now being cast adrift by the inflationary impact of German unification and interest rates were correspondingly higher than they would otherwise have been. George himself was not critical of the DM 2.95 exchange rate but of the interest rates made necessary by the ERM commitment to hold it.

The Treasury's response was effectively one of 'double or quits'. A senior official at the heart of the ERM affair in 1992 said of his institution's stubborn adherence to the policy, 'We had already lost one Chancellor. We could not afford to lose another.' As 1992 progressed, the Treasury view on the need to stay within the ERM hardened. Shortly before the April 1992 election, the Bank of England considered advising an incoming Labour government to devalue within the ERM but decided that this would not deal with the most pressing problem, the high level of interest rates placing a crippling burden on British industry and consumers.

Nevertheless, the Bank was prepared for action should Labour actually win the election, for notwithstanding all their disavowals of devaluation and their criticism, indeed isolation, of Gould, Labour's leadership had taken on board the difference between being the party of devaluation and the party of the high exchange rate.

Kinnock recalled: 'If I'd given support for the step of ERM entry while simultaneously complaining about the rate ... I would have been accused of "carping" and "inconsistency" and – much worse – given sustenance to the claims that Labour was "the party of devaluation".' Nevertheless, he felt that the rate was too high, and so did advisers such as Eatwell, Andrew Graham and Meghnad Desai.[16]

There was a well-attested edginess in the relationship between Kinnock and Smith and a strong impression that, although credited as one of the 'architects' of Labour's ERM policy, Smith at times complained that Kinnock was pushing him on the issue. Nevertheless, there appeared to be a consistent approach by Kinnock, Smith and Brown towards the status of sterling within the ERM. What this approach boiled down to was that, in order not to upset the electors or the financial markets, they would dismiss in public any suggestions that the pound needed to be devalued. But there was in fact a secret plan to cut interest rates and seek a devaluation.

Rather as with Brown's immediate move to offer independence to the Bank in 1997, a devaluation within the ERM would have had to be sought immediately, otherwise history suggests they would never have got round to it until forced, and then in humiliating circumstances.

The economic advisers who played an important role in the secret plan for a devaluation were known as 'The Ten to Three Club' because they envisaged a devaluation to a central rate of DM 2.50, as opposed to the DM 2.95 at which the Conservatives had put the pound into the ERM. They appeared to have something of the sort in mind for a good 18 months before the April 1992 election, i.e. from shortly after the UK had entered the ERM arrangement. The idea was that interest rates would be raised the morning after the election, and negotiations over a devaluation of sterling, as part of a 'general realignment', would take place over the weekend.

While negotiating a press release with the Treasury saying they would stick with the existing ERM exchange rate, Labour had secretly agreed with senior Bank of England officials on the need for a realignment. And the CBI, by now regretting its strong backing in 1990 for entering the ERM at DM 2.95, was independently preparing in the last days of the April election campaign to call upon Labour, if elected, to devalue the pound.

Several months later Neil Kinnock dropped a hint about this when writing to the *Financial Times* on 16 July 1992, on the eve of standing down formally as leader: 'This morning I can write without having my words treated as formal Labour Party policy,' he said, going on to urge that the Major government 'takes a real lead among the ERM countries in pressing for an immediate revaluation of the Deutschmark.'

By now Shadow Chancellor, Gordon Brown was generally considered by his colleagues to be implacably opposed to devaluation. Six days before Black Wednesday, on 10 September, Brown was asked by Bryan Gould, David Blunkett and Michael Meacher to consider urging an ERM realignment. He replied, 'Our policy is not one of devaluation, nor is it one of revaluation or realignment ... One of the things the Germans may wish to propose is whether a realignment of the currencies will bring interest rates down. There is no guarantee that that would happen, and it is not our policy.'[17] On 15 September, the very eve of Black Wednesday, Brown dismissed devaluation but did call for a pan-European reflationary package. 'Quite overwhelmingly, the recession had made the case for intervention,' he wrote.

Bryan Gould recalled: 'I had watched aghast as the Party, and particularly our Shadow Chancellor Gordon Brown, had maintained an even more intransigent line than the Tories throughout the ERM crisis. Gordon had even gone so far as to say that if the Germans had revalued the mark as a means of stabilising the ERM ... he would want to see the pound revalued in line with the mark.' Gould, who had stood against John Smith for the leadership after Neil Kinnock resigned, was positively venomous about Brown: 'It has always been a puzzle to me that people who make mistakes of such magnitude and reveal such a total inability to understand the issues of which they are supposed to be masters nevertheless sail serenely on, unscathed by any suggestion that they might not be up to the job.'[18]

Brown was haunted by Labour's past association with devaluation. He subsequently recalled: 'I walked into a big storm. I said devaluation should not be the way that we should be judged.' He certainly did not want to be attacked by the government for having 'talked the pound down' – an accusation he most certainly avoided. According to a biographer, Brown's tough stance 'created friction with John Smith', by now the leader of the Labour Party. Yet Smith himself had been just as intransigent on the issue when Shadow Chancellor.

Brown appeared over that summer to be inconsistent, even confused, for on 29 July he had called on European finance ministers to consider 'collective action' – action which he hoped would involve a revaluation of the Deutschmark, a counterpart of which would have been a sterling devaluation against the Deutschmark. But he no doubt hoped that, presentationally, the emphasis on a revaluation of the Deutschmark would not lay Labour open to charges of being 'the party of devaluation'. An overwhelming consideration was that he did not want Labour at any stage to be seen to be 'rocking the boat'.

Brown later told *Tribune*: 'It is now quite clear that the government could have asked the German authorities in particular to consider a realignment. All the information that has now become available shows that there was a far more comprehensive realignment possible and that the government ruled it out without discussing it in detail. Faced with the choice between realignment within the ERM and leaving the ERM in order to devalue, many of the difficulties could have been avoided with a realignment' (*Tribune*, 1 January 1993).

At all events the Conservatives, egged on by the Treasury, spent the summer digging themselves further into a hole. A speech delivered by Norman Lamont to the European Policy Forum on 10 July 1992 ruled out all options other than trying to see the current policy through. As a matter of pride the government was not prepared to take part in a realignment that did not involve the French, and the French were not budging. At the Bath meeting of finance ministers on 4–5 September, Norman Lamont annoyed the Germans by using his position as Chairman to attempt to bully them into reducing interest rates. The Bundesbank President Helmut Schlesinger had to be physically restrained from walking out. The British government took exception to statements made by the Bundesbank on the eve of Black Wednesday and recriminations went on for years. John Major, the Prime Minister, in his own words 'went for broke' in a speech to the Scottish CBI the week after the Bath meeting, rejecting 'the soft option, the devaluer's option, the inflationary option', which would be 'a betrayal of our future'.

Probably the worst aspect of Black Wednesday was the slow-motion way in which, all day, the Cabinet was seen to be ineffectual and powerless in the face of a run on the pound that cost the British taxpayer upwards of £3 billion. That was the exchange rate loss on the official currency reserves, as the government spent most of the day defending the pound against a massive speculative attack. Yet one of the officials most closely involved said: 'We knew the game was up at 8.05 a.m.'

There are those in Whitehall and the City who believe that the problems facing an incoming Labour government in April 1992 were such that they would have suffered another great historical disaster and lasted only one term. They would have been handed a 'poisoned chalice'. According to this view, the 1992 result afforded the Conservatives five years in which to destroy themselves, while Labour was able, finally, to make itself electable again. Perhaps this was what the senior Conservative quoted earlier really had in mind when he said, 'It was time for a change in 1992.'

But it is interesting to speculate what would have happened if the plan to devalue to DM 2.50 immediately had been implemented. The associated aim was to ease the pressure on interest rates. Kinnock wanted them down but his hard-line advisors expected that interest rates might have to go up first before coming down.

One very well-informed source insisted that a 'general' or 'comprehensive' realignment was never on the cards in September because 'the Dutch, the Belgians, the Danes and the French all saw themselves as *virilely* following the Deutschmark, so it wasn't possible.'[19]

But Labour believed that it would have been possible in April if it had won the election to devalue within the ERM and get the necessary adjustment of the exchange rate out of the way at once, as well as political embarrassment. It had sounded out the Bundesbank. Neil Kinnock thought that John Smith would probably have accepted that the circumstances justified going back on his own 'no devaluation' promises – it is widely accepted in the financial markets that finance ministers, let alone 'aspirant' ones, cannot be expected to tell the truth about devaluation plans. But if Smith had refused, Kinnock was prepared to offer the Chancellorship, that April 1992 weekend, to Gordon Brown. That was how highly Brown was rated by his leader and how certain Kinnock was that devaluation had to be achieved there and then.[20]

∽∾ ∾∽

CHAPTER FIVE

From Black Wednesday to the Granita restaurant

One of the unsung heroes behind Gordon Brown's rise to the job of Shadow Chancellor in 1992 had been his younger brother Andrew, then a television programme editor at ITN. The Browns are a close family, and the moral support given to their middle son and his choice of career by his parents was vitally important to him. So was that from his two brothers. John, who had been the senior partner in those early journalistic exercises when young Gordon was barely out of short trousers, remained in Scotland, working for Glasgow City Council, but always on hand on the telephone; moreover, Gordon Brown's practice has been to spend as many weekends back in Scotland as he can.

But Andrew had been closer on hand in London when Gordon came to the Commons in 1983 and seems, out of manifest brotherly love, to have given his elder brother vital practical assistance during that first parliamentary term. Such assistance took the general form of helping to bring order into his brother's notoriously chaotic working habits, with Andrew performing the role of everything from *aide de camp* to research assistant. And the specific task had been to lend a firm helping hand to the work on Gordon's biography of Maxton, a project that could well have turned into the future Chancellor's King Charles's head.

The bond was such that Gordon, closer in age to Andrew, was the youngest brother's natural choice as best man. As it happened, Andrew and his bride Clare were due to get married in Spain on

Saturday 19 September 1992, three days after Black Wednesday. Gordon had been up to his neck in the decision-making and political manoeuvrings that led to Labour's support for membership of the ERM, and much of his subsequent behaviour in office over the euro can be traced back to the fact that, as events turned out, he had been wrong and Bryan Gould, the man he had effectively supplanted, had been right in his caution about the ERM.

Nevertheless, it was of course the Conservative government that deservedly shouldered the blame for entering at what the conventional wisdom eventually dictated was 'the wrong time, the wrong date, and for the wrong reasons' (at the time, the conventional wisdom had been overwhelmingly in favour of entry). And it was the Conservative government that was going to suffer.

Brown immediately appreciated the potential for a sustained campaign embarrassing the Tories on the Black Wednesday issue. Parliament was in recess at the time, but Brown became involved in intense discussions with John Smith, now of course his leader, and other associates about how to handle the issue. And, apart from anything else, he was also busy following the day-to-day, indeed hour-to-hour, progress of the pound on the exchange markets after it had been pulled ignominiously out of the ERM, and enjoying the political recriminations, both national and international, that followed. Culprit Number One for John Major's government was the Bundesbank, which it felt had contributed to the crisis, first with indiscreet press interviews and second by not employing sufficient financial resources to come to the pound's rescue when the crisis happened.

But the scope for embarrassing the government was almost limitless, and Smith and Brown immediately grasped the significance of the event for the Conservatives' reputation for economic competence. It is an ill financial wind that blows nobody any political good, and this national humiliation was a present bestowed by the gods as compensation for Labour's historical embarrassments of 1931, 1949, 1967 and 1976.

The immediate question for the Brown family was: would family duty triumph over Gordon's natural tendency towards a workaholic way of life and his obsessiveness with every minute political and financial detail of Black Wednesday? Not to put too fine a point on it, where did his priorities lie? Would he get to his own brother's wedding, at which he was supposed to be best man?

Three flights were booked, and three flights were cancelled. Eventually Gordon took time off from the minutiae of Black Wednesday and embarrassing the Tories to fly out to Andrew's wedding and perform to perfection the vital role of best man. A contingency plan to ask elder brother John to deputise as best man did not have to be put into operation. But, just to reassure those many politicians and officials who have formed the view that Gordon Brown is an incurable workaholic, eyewitnesses (and earwitnesses) recall that, having performed his ceremonial duties, the Shadow Chancellor was then on the phone from Madrid to London for most of the rest of the trip and that his telephone bill easily exceeded the cost of his hotel room.

Such was the assiduous devotion to duty that the Shadow Chancellor was going to demonstrate throughout the last period of Labour's long uphill struggle to regain office. And he was in fine and well-prepared form at the emergency debate on the government's economic policy called the week after Black Wednesday, on Thursday 24 September 1992.

The government was easy meat. John Major had been Chancellor when the country joined the ERM and was Prime Minister when it departed. He had, as he later admitted in his memoirs, gambled and failed, digging in his heels at his end of the tug-of-war to preserve the pound's value. There had been absolutely no chance of the French agreeing to a revaluation of the Deutschmark before the French referendum on Maastricht; this took place the weekend after Black Wednesday, was won by the narrowest of margins and would almost certainly have been lost had the French opponents of Maastricht been able to point to the embarrassment of a French devaluation on the eve of the vote. Major thought of resigning but was dissuaded by family and officials. Lamont's position – although Black Wednesday's outcome allowed him to take some sensible decisions on economic policy – was politically fragile. He too thought of resigning but was dissuaded by officials and by Major, who told him, 'You are a lightning conductor for me.'

Lamont had been a believer in floating rates, was against the economic policy for which he was responsible and was anti-European into the bargain. By contrast, Gordon Brown was pro-European and pro-ERM. Yet it was Brown who ultimately profited from the episode, even if it left scars. The job of Chancellor was probably one step above Lamont's political station in life, and he got it largely as a reward for being John Major's successful campaign manager in 1990. But it was a mistake for Lamont not to resign immediately after Black Wednesday, even if he rationalised the position by saying, 'Now I have got the economic policy I want, I don't see why I should resign' and by the following Sunday, at an IMF meeting in Washington, was declaring to an amazed BBC correspondent, 'My wife said she heard me singing in the bath this morning'[1] (he had certainly not sung in Bath).

By agreeing to be Major's lightning conductor, Lamont laid himself open to being sacked at the Prime Minister's pleasure during any forthcoming storm. Senior civil servants had no doubt that Major kept Lamont in place to save his own skin. And when Lamont was dismissed from the Treasury the following spring, it was so long before the election of 1997 that nearly all the credit for economic policy changes made after Black Wednesday went to Kenneth Clarke. Much of this was deserved, but it was under Lamont that the important innovations of an inflation target and the publication of the Bank of England's quarterly inflation report took place. These were to become incorporated into Gordon Brown's own economic strategy in 1997, although one further Conservative innovation, the Treasury's new Panel of Independent Economic Advisers, did not stay the distance.

One of the many difficulties for the Major government of 1992–97 was the growing euro-scepticism on its backbenches and indeed within the Cabinet itself. This presented a continual threat to Major's authority, which in any case never recovered from the Black Wednesday episode. The irony was that, by dropping out of the ERM and contributing to the avoidance of a realignment between the Deutschmark and the franc, the Conservative government of John Major had probably saved the entire Maastricht process, because the French vote was perilously close. But the ERM episode certainly hardened anti-European attitudes within the Conservative Party, making it easy for Labour – the Party that used to be divided over Europe – to play upon Conservative divisions as an effective electoral card, especially in the election of 2001.

A largely unappreciated aspect of the ERM fiasco and its aftermath was that John Major himself was privately convinced that he, as Chairman, could have achieved a much more constructive result at the Bath meeting of finance ministers that preceded Black Wednesday and ended in disaster. The conviction that Lamont had ruined any chance he (Major) had of salvaging his (Major's) ERM policy continued to gnaw away at the Conservative Prime Minister and certainly did not help Lamont's medium-term chances of political survival.

Even without knowing this, the team of John Smith and Gordon Brown, which had so successfully contributed to the wearing-down of Nigel Lawson's morale as Chancellor in 1988–89, now embarked shamelessly on exploiting the government's embarrassment over the collapse of an ERM policy that they had so passionately supported themselves.

In the debate on Thursday 24 September the motion, somewhat paradoxically, was to the effect that 'This House expresses its support for the economic policy of the government'. John Smith pointed to 'a certain vacuity about such a motion', since no one now knew what the government's economic policy was. Norman Lamont was sufficiently impressed by Smith and Brown's assault to cite them in his memoirs. He blithely quotes Brown's pungent comment: 'The Chancellor is entirely consistent. We can rely on him always to get it wrong. There are two possible explanations for the Chancellor's behaviour. The Chancellor can choose between them. He has been seriously wrong for the past two years or he has been seriously wrong for the past two weeks.' The pound, of course, had now been devalued – it was already down about 12% and some critics were to rechristen September 16 as 'Golden Wednesday' or

'White Wednesday' because of the boost devaluation gave to the economy. But Gordon Brown, with an insouciant disregard for the scorn he had poured on Bryan Gould and other Labour proponents of devaluation, reminded Lamont of the latter's July description of devaluation as 'fool's gold' and added, 'The Chancellor has no shame, makes no apology and gives no hint of remorse for damaging the stability of people's lives.'

Lamont hit back by citing what he described as Smith and Brown's 'endless calls for faster and deeper interest rate cuts coupled with simultaneous calls for us to remain in the ERM', a combination of policies that the market had proved was impossible.

The 'stability' of people's lives had certainly been affected by the way that, in order to preserve the pound's position in the ERM, the government had been forced to keep interest rates too high. Starting at 14% on entry in October 1990, rates were still 10% on the eve of Black Wednesday. This was prolonging recession well after inflation had been brought down from 9.5% in 1990 to 3.5% early in 1992. This sort of inflation rate was very satisfactory by post-war standards, at a time when few people had dreamed that an inflation target of 2.5% might be achieved for more than a short period. But the 'stability' of some people's lives had threatened to come to an end on Black Wednesday, when interest rates were first raised to 12% and then it was announced that they would go to 15% the following day – a rise that never took place, because of sterling's withdrawal from the ERM that afternoon. I know of people in the City who were opening bottles of champagne on the evening of Black Wednesday because they knew that their entire livelihoods would collapse on the altar of 15% interest rates. It was a case of 'tomorrow we die'.

Gordon Brown's coruscating attack on Lamont and the failure of the ERM policy was his first parliamentary speech in his new role as Shadow Chancellor, the summer holidays having intervened after the leadership election in which John Smith triumphed easily over Bryan Gould, the most vigorous opponent of the ERM. In one sense it was the perfect occasion on which to inaugurate Brown's new role in Parliament – he was, after all, kicking into a very open goal. In another sense it was of course awkward because of his own commitment to the ERM. But it was nonetheless a vintage Brownian speech, as always well prepared; his speeches in those days were still quite a contrast with some he was to deliver after becoming Chancellor, when parroted repetition of 'sound-bite' phrases and clichéd concepts gave the impression that, as was said of the American novelist William Burroughs, the author merely shuffled the pages.

This important speech gave plenty of opportunity for displays of Brown's withering wit: 'Our argument is that economies do not weaken in a single morning,' and again, 'There is no point in the Chancellor setting monetary targets other than in negotiations with the publishers of his memoirs.' For Brown knew, as he said, that with regard to Lamont's eventual demise it was 'not a question now of "whether" but "when".'

The speech was also interesting for the clues it gave to a certain confusion at the heart of Brown's own policies at the time, as well as offering a pithy summary of the direction in which Labour's broad economic strategy was now moving.

The Shadow Chancellor no doubt felt he had to threaten dire things from the failure of the government's policies, and to a large extent he was uttering some of the orthodoxies of the time when predicting that 'millions of home owners' were 'about to suffer higher inflation as a result'. Brown seemed to believe that the devaluation would inevitably be inflationary and asked, 'Will there not always be a credibility premium now, which will have to be paid, whether in interest rates or in something else ...?'

He was certainly right about the fact that a Conservative Party that had run a general election campaign on the slogan 'You can't trust Labour' had 'shown itself completely unworthy of trust itself'. He was also justified in charging: 'They may hold office for five years, but even after five months they have lost all authority to govern.' Again: 'They have lost all claim to economic competence and credibility.'

Given this assessment, which proved remarkably astute, it seems a pity that in subsequent years Labour itself redoubled its own efforts to win trust, when to a large extent the job had been done for them. The extra caution built into Labour's efforts was undoubtedly going to aggravate the problems they inherited.

As it turned out, a devaluation taking place against the background of one of the worst recessions since the war did not produce the inflationary consequences that might have taken place at full employment. The country's good luck in this respect was assisted by the impact of the generally disinflationary climate in the wider world, partly the result of ultra-cautious economic policies in mainland Europe in the run-up to the single currency, and partly attributable to the price competition associated with the phenomenon known as globalisation.

But some credit must also be due to the policy framework which, having made a complete mess of things in the run-up to Black Wednesday, Lamont introduced and Clarke subsequently built upon. For the moment it was noteworthy that Gordon Brown laid great emphasis in his speech on 24 September on the importance of the supply side of the economy – a theme he was to develop further in due course. Thus, he complained that the Conservatives had compounded the recession 'by applying a one-club policy of high interest rates without an underlying plan to improve the real economy.' He called for 'a national recovery programme ... a new industrial policy ... [and] an emergency employment programme.'

The new Shadow Chancellor was emphatic about the difference between the two parties that had both hitherto supported ERM membership. 'The Chancellor cannot even tell us – nor could the Prime Minister – whether they support floating or managed exchange rates.' For Labour, however, the position was now: 'We believe that any membership of the exchange rate mechanism must be accompanied by an industrial policy for Britain' but, quite explicitly, 'our policy is for managed exchange rates.'

Although Lamont was on a hiding to nothing in that debate, he did manage to highlight the contradiction in Brown's own position. Why 'just two days before the lira was devalued' (the weekend before Black Wednesday) Brown had written 'Our policy is not one of devaluation, nor is it one of revaluation or realignment ...'

Lamont began to unveil the first tentative signs of the new monetary policy that was going to assist a remarkable period of recovery and indeed sustained growth for the British economy in the run-up to the 1997 election. He had already been able to *reduce* interest rates from 10% to 9% that Tuesday, and 'in setting interest rates over the period ahead I shall be guided by a range of indicators. We shall maintain our current target of 0–4% for narrow money. We shall follow broad money and asset prices, as well as the exchange rate itself.' And he reminded the House that in the early 1980s, 'we showed with a floating regime that it was possible to reduce inflation,' adding, 'I am determined that we shall achieve that success again.' Indeed, the inflation rate remained low for the rest of the 1992–97 Parliament, notwithstanding the devaluation, which brought the average level of the pound down from DM 2.75 in 1992 to DM 2.26 in 1995.

The Shadow Chancellor had an early stab at trying to dwell on the inflationary consequences, with a parliamentary question to Lamont on 12 November 1992 asking why, in the month after devaluation, 'input prices for manufacturers rose by 2.5% in only four weeks.' But the fact of the matter was that in 1992 as a whole input prices fell slightly, and rises in some later years of the Parliament did not feed through to cause any embarrassing impact on the politically sensitive retail prices index.

This question was asked on the same day as the Autumn Statement, in which it was the practice for the Chancellor to give a progress report and perhaps some indication of his intentions for the spring Budget. But the principal policy statement had been made shortly after Black Wednesday, in the midst of an embarrassed Conservative Party Annual Conference in Brighton, in the form of a letter from Norman Lamont to the Chairman of the parliamentary Select Committee on the Treasury. In it the Chancellor unveiled the basis of the counter-inflation policy that Gordon Brown would build on in 1997 by granting the Bank independence. Successive Conservative governments since 1979 had tried and failed to conquer inflation by aiming at intermediate targets such as the money supply and the exchange rate, latterly by locking the pound (albeit briefly) into the ERM. Now they would aim directly at controlling inflation, by using a mix of monetary and fiscal policies to keep it within a certain range. Given its fears about the inflationary consequences of the post-ERM devaluation, the Treasury wanted a range of 1–5%. Lamont himself opted for 1–4%. This meant that the middle of the range was 2.5% – the very figure Brown himself was to settle for later. It was hoped that by the end of the Parliament inflation would be 2.5% or less.

With the Treasury thoroughly demoralised by the failure of its 'last throw' (the ERM policy), 1992 marked the beginning of the ascendancy of the Bank of England. In the 29 October Mansion House speech, Lamont announced that the monthly meeting of the Chancellor and the Governor would be followed by the publication of a regular report explaining the background to interest rate decisions (or non-decisions) and the Bank would monitor the government's progress on the inflation front in a quarterly *Inflation Report*, to be published with its customary *Quarterly Bulletin*. Lamont also announced the setting up of the Panel of Independent Forecasters – the Seven Wise Men – whose brief was to report 'three times a year on the current position of and future prospects for the UK economy'.

Having moved from the fixed exchange rate regime of the ERM to a more flexible policy, Lamont made an important point in his letter to the House of Commons Treasury Committee about the limits to the advantages of floating exchange rates: 'The lesson from the 1980s is that exchange rates can move a long way, upwards or downwards, if markets come to believe the authorities do not care.' The pound must be watched to see if falls, especially rapid ones, threatened the achievement of the inflation objective. Interestingly, even the Bank of England was not too concerned about the immediate impact of the pound's devaluation. Although the pound had dropped from DM 2.75 on Black Wednesday to DM 2.43 by 12 November, such had been the severity of the 1990–92 recession that the Bank was more concerned about deflation than inflation. There was so much spare capacity in the economy – unemployment was high, output was depressed – that the kind of inflationary consequences feared by the Treasury and by Gordon Brown were conspicuous by their absence for several years.

Even if it was a necessary devaluation – and the inflationary consequences did not prove to be dire – Gordon Brown as Shadow Chancellor was acutely aware of Labour's history as 'the party of devaluation'. While taking full advantage of Tory embarrassment over Black Wednesday, he carried on fighting the 'devaluationists' within his own Party and ruled out any suggestion that Labour should welcome the devaluation. It was left to Labour sympathisers in the press to point out that Black Wednesday marked the beginning of the recovery of the British economy from its second-worst recession since the war, and that the Bundesbank and others had done the UK a good turn by not going to the limit to support sterling at the penal interest rates then ruling.

In a highly significant move, Brown wrote an article for *Tribune* (25 September 1992) whose headline proclaimed, 'Europe still the answer'. He managed to square the circle of Conservative embarrassment over the ERM fiasco and his own position by stating, 'Measures to combat unemployment and for industrial policy are most effectively to be taken through European action' while, as far as the government was concerned, 'Having promised that they would oppose devaluation, stay within the exchange rate mechanism ... and make it the basis of their counter-inflationary policy, the Tories have now abandoned every central economic policy pledge on which they fought the election.'

Although Gordon Brown and his Labour colleagues had supported the ERM, we also know (see Chapter Four) that Kinnock had had a plan for a devaluation that, had history turned out very differently, might even have been managed by Brown himself. From Black Wednesday onwards the pound was to float freely. After suffering £3 billion of exchange rate losses on Black Wednesday itself, when almost all the official reserves were devoted to the losing battle, the UK monetary authorities reacted by ceasing to intervene to steady the market at all. Towards the latter part of his 1993–1997 Chancellorship, Kenneth Clarke, who hailed from the industrial Midlands, would show concern for the competitiveness of industry by refusing to raise interest rates so as to avoid adding to what was by then *upward* pressure on sterling. But even he, battle-scarred by witnessing the impotence of the government on Black Wednesday itself, was set against intervening directly in the foreign exchange market – even for the easier option of preventing the pound from rising.

From 1997 Brown was to continue this 'hands-off' attitude to sterling. When asked, he would say – at whatever level the pound happened to be – that he believed it should be 'stable and competitive'.[2] But as Shadow Chancellor, even after Black Wednesday, his view was very different. 'Labour rejects the notion that a free-market approach to currency markets will bring lasting benefits to the British economy,' he wrote. Labour continued to believe that 'a managed and stable exchange rate is essential for sustainable growth'. Brown was also against the practice of relying on what Sir Edward Heath, in a golfing analogy, had termed the 'one-club' approach to curbing a consumer boom. As far as he was concerned, the root of the problems the Tories had run into was that there had been no industrial policy to prepare and underpin the supply side of the economy for the earlier consumer boom. Brown's opposition to the 'one-club' (reliance on interest rates) approach implied a readiness to use fiscal policy, or even perhaps direct controls on credit, to control the growth of consumption; but again, this was a belief he was to discard in office.

Writing almost five years before the time when, as Chancellor, he would impose a two-year freeze on public spending, Brown was giving the impression that Labour would 'tackle the backlog of repairs in our houses, school, roads and hospitals' as a matter of urgency. He actually attacked Norman Lamont for having promised 'a new rigorous approach to public spending'.[3]

On 28 September 1992 Brown's position in the Labour Party was strengthened further when he was elected in the constituency vote to the Labour Party's National Executive Committee at the annual Conference in Blackpool. His election was presented very much as an example of the way the new leader, John Smith, was strengthening his grip on the Party machine, with the election of what Michael White in the *The Guardian* called his 'two key lieutenants' – the other being Tony Blair. Smith also made good use of the union block vote to reject calls that Labour should demand a referendum on the Maastricht Treaty.

Both Smith and Neil Kinnock said the pro-Maastricht position demonstrated that Labour was rejecting the isolationism of the past. In a variation on the fashionable left-wing theme of the time, that it was difficult (*au* Mitterrand) to achieve 'Keynesianism in one country', Gordon Brown in his own Conference speech chided the Conservative Prime Minister, John Major: 'I challenge him to tell the truth, that he has retreated from the challenge of Europe to the squalid pursuit of Thatcherism in one country.'

In a foretaste of his 'Welfare to Work' programme during the 1997–2001 first Labour term, Brown began to use the Roosevelt phrase 'New Deal' from about this time, employing it in *Tribune* and in his 1992 Conference speech. There were also very strong hints of the highly activist approach to social and industrial problems that he would adopt when Chancellor. In a Fabian article he called for '... an intellectual debate which will encompass the new public interest economics ... [and] the opening up of our public services'. 'Enabling' and 'empowerment' became favourite Brownian words, implying active intervention to encourage research and investment in industry and 'individual development' for the people at large.[4]

Brown's interest in 'public–private partnership' also dates from this period. Launching Labour's 'Campaign for Recovery' on 9 November 1992, he called for a 'private–public task force' to consider and implement infrastructure projects.

This was a period when Brown and his colleagues lost no opportunity to oppose and mock Conservative privatisations. Brown's burgeoning interest in 'public–private partnership' stemmed partly from the continuing process in which Labour modernisers had been discarding old and unfashionable goods from what Peter Shore had once described as its ideological 'baggage train'. Modern socialism was not about ownership but about 'what worked'. In office, Brown's enthusiastic adoption of such Conservative devices as the Private Finance Initiative was going to lead to all manner of problems, raising questions about whether, in certain areas previously the preserve of the public sector, the private sector approach did work. But right from the start, the predominant motive in Brown's mind was that, if he was going initially to adopt a hostile approach to policies of 'tax and spend' in order to secure Labour's election, private finance would be a way, he hoped, of doing *something* to boost the public sector without antagonising those 'Middle English' taxpayers.

The problem, however, with being Shadow Chancellor of a Labour Party whose tax-and-spend policies were so distrusted by the voters was that one became vulnerable to the age-old practice of 'shooting the messenger'. Gordon Brown and Tony Blair were very much the 'coming men' in the modernising Labour Party of 1992. Had John Smith not been standing for the leadership in summer 1992 and the contest been between those two great political friends Brown and Blair, Brown would almost certainly have coasted home. Brown was so popular that he was approached by some colleagues and urged to stand against his friend and mentor Smith; but he refused. Blair only contemplated standing for the deputy leadership in the summer of 1992. Kinnock believed Gould should have stood for the deputy leadership.

Some Party sources say that senior Labour figures had picked Blair out as a leader before 1992, and varying accounts suggest that at different times John Smith favoured Brown and Blair as his successor. What is abundantly clear is that in the roughly two years between Labour's loss of the 1992 election and the traumatic event of John Smith's death in May 1994, Gordon Brown lost considerable ground in the potential leadership stakes. He might have been impressive at lambasting Norman Lamont and the government after Black Wednesday, but his own previous espousal of the failed ERM cause contributed to a loss of support for him on the left. Then, after Lamont's Chancellorship went the predictable way of all flesh in May 1993, Brown found he had a much more formidable opponent in the redoubtable Kenneth Clarke. Brown could no longer count on superiority in the regular parliamentary jousts with the new Chancellor and, for all his diligence in attacking 'Tory sleaze', 'fat cats' and the excesses of privatisation, Brown was batting on a sticky wicket when it came to the economy generally. This was because, freed from the constraints of the ERM and the accompanying monetary strait-jacket, the economy, from the second half of 1992 onwards, embarked on an impressive recovery of output and employment – right up to 1997. The country might have been 'falling apart' from another perspective, in that public spending was tightly constrained and manifest problems were developing with the health service, the rail network and the transport and social infrastructure generally, but the jovial Ken Clarke was presiding over a spurt of growth that rendered earlier Brownian criticisms (of high unemployment, etc.) somewhat less potent.

Until 1992 Brown had been a fairly popular figure within the Party. But his lot as the man who felt he had to say 'No' to most if not all of his Shadow Cabinet colleagues' spending requests was not a happy one. He did not get on with Mo Mowlam, who handled City matters in the Shadow Treasury team, and she became an enemy when she was moved. Other colleagues were rubbed up the wrong way too. Nevertheless, in the view of Neil Kinnock – who was still an MP, had an office down the corridor from his two protégés and saw a lot of them in 1992–94 – 'If John Smith had died a year before,' i.e. in 1993, 'Tony would have said 'yes' to Gordon.' The two had had an understanding, dating from the July 1992 leadership election, not to stand against each other.[5]

Neil Kinnock says support for Blair 'surged – in six months' before Smith's death. While Brown was suffering the unpopularity of the iron Shadow Chancellor in the cause of making Labour 'electable', Blair was riding high in both Parliament and Middle England with his 'tough on crime, tough on the causes of crime' approach. Ironically, this remarkably successful sound-bite has been attributed to Brown, the man who eventually chose to stand down in Blair's favour at the subsequent leadership election. Until this period, the 'deal' of 1992 had stood; in the words of James Naughtie: 'Brown was clearly the more powerful figure. Therefore the deal was simple: Blair would defer to Brown.'[6]

Kinnock recalls that Blair and Brown were frequently 'popping into' his office; 'They probably thought I was too old to walk down the corridor.' In a further twist, Kinnock says: ' "Tough on causes" was my phrase, although it could equally have been Gordon's. Tony stuck it in his pocket. There was no resentment, but a real team spirit. The two had extremely healthy relations, there was no doubt about that. Then out of nowhere came the sudden surge in support for Tony Blair. It numbed Gordon Brown more than anything else.'[7]

The sphere in which relations had not been so healthy was in the attitude of the two young turks, Brown and Blair, towards their patron John Smith. The two were concerned in 1993 and early 1994 that the 'modernising' movement begun by their first patron, Neil Kinnock, was losing momentum. Smith won a famous victory, with considerable effort, in the move towards 'one member, one vote' (OMOV) for the selection by Party members of parliamentary candidates. This was at the 1993 annual Labour Party Conference in Brighton in October (OMOV was also meant to apply to the selection of the Party leader, but does so in a very 'Labour' sort of way: the leader is selected by an electoral college, with the parliamentary Party, the trade unions and constituency members each accounting for one-third of the 'one member, one vote' total).

Kinnock, Brown and Blair had all campaigned actively for OMOV, and a famous speech by John Prescott was considered crucial in persuading reluctant 'block vote' trade unionists to change their minds. In fact, the unions had been 'squared' earlier in the day.

But John Smith, a strong trade union man, felt there was a limit to the need for further 'modernisation'. He was firmly of the view that, from Black Wednesday onwards, the Conservatives had lost their reputation for economic competence. 'Governments lose elections,' he once told the author, 'and my job is to let John Major do so without making commitments I might come to regret.'

A phrase used by a number of close observers of John Smith in the months leading up to his death on 12 May 1994 was 'masterly inactivity'. This was valid up to a point. He set up the Commission on Social Justice under Sir Gordon (now Lord) Borrie towards the end of 1993; and Gordon Brown himself was to head an economic commission, to develop economic policy. Smith was a passionate believer in 'social justice' and deeply loathed the Thatcherite line that there was 'no such thing as society'. Unlike modernisers such as Brown and Blair, however, he was not prepared to move away from the strong Labour Party belief – once held passionately by Brown himself, but probably never by Blair – that pensions and child benefits should be paid universally, as of right (a view also shared by traditional 'paternalist' Conservatives such as Lord Gilmour). Smith seems to have upset the embryonic 'New Labour' approach of Brown and Blair by publicly reiterating his view on the day he set up the Borrie Commission.

In a sense, the setting up of commissions such as Borrie could be seen as 'masterly inactivity' and kicking policy problems into touch. Smith himself was hardly inactive personally and had won a popular place in the hearts and minds of the British electorate, as was made clear by the spontaneous outburst of affection after his death. Moreover, his death took place the morning after a very active evening, when he had been in fine form at a Labour fund-raising dinner in a Park Lane hotel (it is a sign of the times that the news of Smith's death the following morning was broken to his private office via a telephone call from the *Sun* newspaper).

Given the public's reaction in the years 1994–97 to 'Tory sleaze' and the state of the public services, it is by no means certain that Smith's policy of 'masterly inactivity' was the incorrect one. Nevertheless it frustrated Brown and Blair. 'Both were immensely restless about John,' said a source close to each of them at the time. News of this restlessness began to seep out. Neil Kinnock said, 'It was a cloud no bigger than a man's hand, but they did articulate their frustrations to me. I said "you can say that here, but nowhere else, because it is hugely damaging".' Kinnock, who had achieved so much to make the Labour Party almost electable and who had reason to believe there were times when Smith himself had in his past expressed his own feelings of frustration about *his* (Kinnock's) leadership, decided to speak to Smith. 'I saw him in April and told him "you must take the initiative to start the march".' In retrospect, Kinnock believes that the delay may have been caused by Smith's physical condition.[8]

Brown and Blair believed in a Labour Party that was much more 'European' than the Conservatives, that was the equal of the Tories on 'law and order', that promised electoral reform and was committed to traditional social welfare goals, but not at the cost of excessive taxation. Smith was not so keen on this last point and was biding his time.

Both Brown and Blair must have felt some guilt that their leader and mentor John Smith died at a time when they had been criticising him behind his back. Nevertheless, it seems that Smith's death had a greater impact on Gordon Brown than it did on Blair. He had not only lost a close friend, political master and ally; he had lost him in circumstances where a human being of his sometimes tortured personality was almost bound to feel terrible that he had been privately critical of his now lost leader.

The Brown family and his close political circle feel to this day that the Blair camp acted with unseemly haste in rallying its troops to fight for the succession even while the dead leader's body was warm. The role of Peter Mandelson, who had championed the cause of Brown and Blair since his days as Director of Labour Party Communications in the 1980s, in switching sides from Brown to Blair, was enough to make some of Brown's acolytes regard Mandelson from then on as 'pure poison'.

Nevertheless, it is difficult to accept that the in-fighting after Smith's death made a substantive difference to the outcome of the leadership election. Blair was 'the man of the moment'. In the eyes of those who mattered, the junior partner of what subsequently became the duumvirate that was to run the government from 1997 had become the senior partner. An ICM poll showed that 31% of the country supported Blair, 22% Prescott and that Brown's support was an unlucky 13%.

The Labour Conference elects National, Executive members from the Constituency section of membership and, in October, Brown had come seventh (bottom) in the elections to the National Executive Committee and Blair sixth. It was evident that the inevitable unpopularity of (Shadow) Iron Chancellorship had begun to take its toll. In the words of one long-serving backbench MP who was close to both: 'Tony Blair was the man of the moment. Gordon Brown was of the Party, Blair wasn't. Blair could only have been picked after four election losses in a row. He was the man to appeal to Middle England. We could not have another Scot.'[9]

The dispute over who said what to whom when, and who behaved badly during the run-up to the leadership election is a diversion – no doubt painful in Brown's case – from the 'truest cause': Blair had already been on what was known colloquially as 'a wave', and in the weeks after John Smith's death that wave turned into a veritable tide of support for the man who, in the words of another veteran MP, 'can reach out and communicate in a way Gordon can't.' The author recalls being one of no doubt hundreds who encountered Gordon Brown at the time and told him, 'Gordon, you should stand', only to see a pained look on his face and to become aware that it was more complicated than that.

It was more complicated not just because the two had agreed not to stand against each other but because as a strong Labour Party man, Brown, although seething with personal ambition, did not wish to damage the Party in general and the modernisers' cause in particular by splitting the latter's vote. As a student of Labour Party history, he had seen what the rivalry of Roy Jenkins, Tony Crosland and Denis Healey had done to the earlier 'Gaitskellite' modernising cause (as it happened, Denis, by now Lord, Healey was among the powerful voices proclaiming, 'it has to be Tony Blair').

But that pained expression on Gordon Brown's face also suggested, which other sources have borne out, that he was badly affected by John Smith's death and, dour fighter though he is on most occasions, found the whole business of the leadership contest distasteful. The reaction of seasoned observers in this matter is a cynical 'That's politics'.

The 'Granita Dinner' in Islington on Tuesday 31 May 1994 is celebrated for two things. It is popularly supposed to have been the first occasion on which Brown told Blair he would not stand against him; and in the course of the dinner Blair, apparently on the advice of the very Peter Mandelson whom the Brown camp regarded suspiciously, gave Brown to understand that he (Blair) saw him (Brown) as his natural successor. In a difficult and fraught situation Blair wished to offer his friend 'hope'.

Brown had told his immediate entourage the previous evening that he had finally decided against standing, and had discussed the situation with Blair a few days earlier on a private visit to Blair in his constituency. Some sources believe he even gave an indication to Blair on this occasion.

For all the speculation about that dinner, people very close to the two camps have not (as yet) found circumstantial evidence that a 'deal' was done over the timing of a handover. And apart from anything else, while the preference of a retiring Prime Minister can be expected to carry enormous weight, the election of the successor still depends on votes of Labour's electoral college of MPs, trade unionists and constituency members.

The deal that was most certainly done was that under which Blair agreed to make Brown a very powerful Chancellor, with a remit covering not only the economy but also large areas of welfare and social policy. This involved agreement not only on Brown's control over policy but the nomination of key Brownian allies to strategic ministerial positions.

A copy of the 'background' notes confirming the existence of this deal fell into the hands of Michael White, Political Editor of the *Guardian*, nine years later (*Guardian*, Friday 6 June 2003). A key sentence stated that in two recent speeches (after John Smith's death), 'Gordon has spelled out the fairness agenda – social justice, employment opportunities and skills – which he believed should be the centrepiece of Labour's programme and Tony is in full agreement with this and that [sic] the Party's economic and social policies should be further developed on this basis.' On White's copy the words 'in full agreement with' had been deleted by Brown and replaced with 'has guaranteed that this will be pursued'.[10]

The then proprietress of Granita told the author, some years later: 'I am sick and tired of being asked at which table they sat, but I can tell you it looked like a really boring occasion. The two of them spent most of the time poring over spreadsheets.' The acoustics at Granita were not good, prompting one official to joke that the controversy surrounding what was or was not agreed at the notorious dinner might have stemmed from the participants' difficulty in hearing one another. But I was told: 'No – it was a very quiet night.'[11]

∞ ∞

CHAPTER SIX

From Granita to government: the advent of Mr Balls

$\mathcal{I}$t has been put to me by one of his colleagues that one motive Gordon Brown had for not standing against Blair was not just that the Party might be damaged, but that he too would have been damaged in some way. This is debatable: Healey, Crosland and Jenkins may have damaged the Party through their rivalry but they preserved their personal reputations. Opinion polls and soundings among MPs suggested that Brown would probably have lost a contest against Blair in 1994. But he could not help feeling resentment anyway, and this resentment was a factor in their relationship that became obvious to all who dealt with them from then on, both in opposition and in office. His most public comment was, 'Nothing was to be gained by me standing against my friend Tony Blair.'[1]

One of the points against Brown, in the real world of politics, was that he was unmarried. Brown told the BBC interviewer Sue Lawley in 1996 that the question had not arisen during the leadership election. Brown had always had girl friends, including one long relationship with a lawyer, Marion Caldwell, that lasted thirteen years and broke up in 1994, the year of the leadership election. He then resumed an old relationship with a broadcaster, Sheena Macdonald, before meeting Sarah Macaulay in February 1994, a few months before the leadership election. He also remained in touch with the girl friend of his Edinburgh student days, Princess Margarita of Romania, who was one of the friends he consulted during the difficult decision-making days before the Granita dinner.

Gordon Brown is an intensely private man, and comes from a certain breed of Celt who find it difficult to tell their parents that they are having a relationship. Rumours about his putative 'gayness' led to Sue Lawley's raising the issue in her *Desert Island Discs* programme. Brown could easily have denied that he was homosexual but did not like the intrusive nature of Ms Lawley's questions and honourably decided that it was no business of hers. As Paul Routledge has pointed out, if Lawley was *that* interested, her researchers could have uncovered 'a fascinating world of [heterosexual] relationships down the years'.[2]

Brown is a man with deep moral convictions; he is also someone whose sense of duty and practice of industriousness would have made Adam Smith proud. In modern parlance he is a 'workaholic'. We have already seen how the combination of his association with the failed exchange rate mechanism policy and his dourly negative approach to his would-be spending colleagues contributed to his yielding ground to Tony Blair in the 1992–93 popularity stakes. 1994 was the year when, according to close colleagues and in the immortal words of Joseph Heller, 'Something Happened'.

This was the year when he lost the close friendship of John Smith; yielded to pressure not to stand against Tony Blair for the leadership election; and met the woman who was going to become his wife. His devotion to work and Party, and reluctance to marry and have children at that stage, had led to the breakdown of his relationship with Sheena Macdonald. Neil Kinnock recalls saying to Brown, only half-jokingly: 'Listen pal, if you want to go where *you* think you ought to go and *I* think you ought to go you should fall in love a bit faster.'[3]

'Something happened' in the sense that in response to all these changes in his life Brown seems to have made a conscious decision to become more serious and to wear the burdens of the Shadow Chancellorship even more heavily. He decided that a great deal of what he did constituted a diversion from the main job, and it was the impression of many who came into contact with him during the 1994–97 period that he was in a constant hurry, arriving late and leaving early, and having rather less time for people than in the past.

Gordon Brown was widely known in the Party as someone who could be charming, brilliantly funny and self-deprecating. But he seems to have rubbed quite a lot of colleagues up the wrong way – unnecessarily, in the view of those who bore this 'with a patient shrug'. And, while being a quintessentially modern politician when it came to handling the media and offering press and broadcasters the sound-bites they required, Brown came over publicly as tediously repetitive, often looking rather sour-faced and sullen. Peter Hobday, the *Today Programme* interviewer whose intelligent and urbane technique Brown greatly admired, recalls the way the Shadow Chancellor drew in on himself, hunched in his seat, repeating the 'mantra' and not even looking at his interlocutor.

It was during these years that television comedians such as Rory Bremner began to poke fun at Brown's facial expressions; the public received an image of a dour, dull, unfriendly man. Nothing could be further from the truth about the natural, private behaviour of the real Brown. Occasionally the old flashes of wit would appear in small gatherings. For instance, in some remarks to a small reception after the John Smith Lecture of 1995 Brown was in excellent form, quipping: 'The first privatised train didn't run. The second was a bus. And the third is helping police with their inquiries' (all three of which assertions were based on recent news stories that had embarrassed the government).

But more often what the public heard were the repetitive statements about his opposition to 'the economics of tax and spend', his determination to avoid 'boom and bust' and perhaps the phrase that in garbled form is the most remembered by the public – his reference to the putative importance of 'neo-classical endogenous growth theory and a symbiotic relationship between investment in people and infrastructure'.[4]

'It's not Brown's at all, it's Balls,'[5] said Michael Heseltine to a delighted Conservative audience. The phrase had been contained in a speech Brown delivered during one of New Labour's seemingly endless 'relaunches' of its policies, at the National Film Theatre on London's South Bank in 1994. At least, it had been in the text of the handout but was passed over by the Shadow Chancellor when he reached it. Brown was recovering from 'flu and assured the author at the time that, great though his respect for his relatively new economic adviser was, if he had been in better physical shape he would have excised the passage from the draft text.

Ed Balls had been Gordon Brown's official economic adviser since the autumn of 1993 but had been in touch with him for about a year before that. After Black Wednesday Brown, while capitalising on the Conservatives' political humiliation, nevertheless felt bruised himself by the collapse of the ERM he had also espoused. The left did not hesitate to encourage the wound to fester.

Brown felt the need for a new adviser, and consulted widely. Gavyn Davies of the BBC, then at Goldman Sachs (and husband of Brown's secretary, Sue Nye), was involved in the deliberations; so were Geoff Mulgan of the think-tank Demos and Richard Lambert, Editor of the *Financial Times*. Another important influence was Lord Paul of St Marylebone, the Indian-born Labour Peer and industrialist, who gave Brown's office financial support. Lord Paul had become convinced that under Blair and Brown, Labour was 'entrepreneur-friendly and very supportive of free enterprise'. Paul believed Brown had 'three qualities that I have not often seen combined in any statesman – an extraordinary appetite for work, a constant desire to do what is right for the country and a willingness to learn.'[6]

Neo-classical endogenous growth theory was not the only thing Brown was to learn from Ed Balls. The first thing he learnt was that Balls thoroughly disapproved of the way Labour under Kinnock, Smith and Brown had made such a strong pitch for the ERM. In October 1992, shortly after Black Wednesday, Balls was doing some routine photocopying in the *Financial Times* building, where he was the youngest (at 25) of the paper's leader writers. Lambert told Balls that Gordon Brown wished to see him. The *Financial Times*, under Lambert, had rather surprisingly opposed the Conservatives in its pre-election leader and got egg on its face not least because the money-men (and money-women) who buy the *Financial Times* do not like their paper to back a loser. Also, most *Financial Times* readers were probably Conservative supporters anyway.

A critical group of F.T. leader writers, including deputy editor Ian Hargreaves, Andrew Adonis, Philip Stephens and Ed Balls himself had persuaded Lambert not to support the Tories. Now, some months later in the same year, here was Balls – himself most certainly a Labour Party supporter – being approached by the Shadow Chancellor for a key position. Indeed, at that meeting in October 1992 neither Brown nor Balls probably realised just how important the latter was going to become in the scheme of things.

At this first meeting Balls told Brown he ought to be aware that he (Balls) was working on a Fabian pamphlet which was going to be strongly critical of the ERM. Much of the pamphlet, which was published in December 1992 and entitled *Euro-Monetarism: Why Britain Was Ensnared and How It Should Escape*, could have been written by Bryan Gould. (But Gould, feeling sidelined – wrongly in Kinnock's opinion – departed from the political scene, a sad loss to Labour's future cabinet material.)

Balls had been strongly recommended as an up-and-coming star and Brown was not at all put off. Indeed, the episode became part of the process by which Brown reacted against the ERM he had so strongly supported and became virulently opposed to any suggestion that Britain should ever rejoin the mechanism – a formal requirement for any country proposing to sign up for the euro.

Balls told Brown: 'In order to do what a Labour government should do, you've got to earn credibility first.' It was clear that Brown had all sorts of ideas for improving the supply side of the economy and for a modernised version of 'social justice'. But in Balls's view all previous Labour governments had eventually fallen foul of the financial markets, and Brown needed a policy anchor to which all his other ropes could be attached.[7]

Much has been made in the press since May 1997 of the remarkable influence exercised by Ed Balls once he got to the Treasury. But it is fascinating to note the enormous contribution to Gordon Brown's subsequent strategy that was contained in Balls's Fabian Society *Discussion Paper* of December 1992. He began by noting the failure of Britain's economic institutions 'to provide a credible policy framework' – a vacuum that had been exposed by the pound's suspension from the ERM. Balls dismissed 'a monetarist policy of trying to pursue low inflation through high interest rates and an overvalued exchange rate, without regard for the economic costs of reducing inflation' as 'economically destabilising and politically unsustainable'.[8]

The ERM had been the last throw of the Thatcher government as its various monetarist panaceas – control of monetary indicators sounding like motorways (M1, M3, M4) – had failed lamentably and Nigel Lawson's policy of 'shadowing the Deutschmark' had led to a damaging, indeed terminal, row between Prime Minister and Chancellor. In the end, having failed to control inflation itself, the Conservative government had tried, via the ERM, to attach itself to the better-behaved German rate of inflation. But as we have seen, it chose the wrong time – German unification, when even German inflation took off – to conduct the experiment.

In 1992 Balls stated, in a sentence that was to be a guide to much of what Gordon Brown attempted to do as Chancellor: 'ERM membership cannot provide, but instead requires, a credible, flexible and transparent domestic macroeconomic policy framework and a medium-term strategy for industrial regeneration.' He added: 'European integration can only foster economic growth and low unemployment if it puts political and social integration before fixed monetary rules.'[9]

Most observers interpret the Maastricht Treaty as laying down that countries signing up for the euro should first ensure that their currencies enjoy a period of two years of stability within the ERM. Sir Edward George, as Governor, was of the view that a period of stability would be enough, within or outside the ERM. But Gordon Brown, since becoming Chancellor in 1997, has been consistently hostile to the idea of rejoining the ERM whenever the subject has arisen.

In 1992, when Balls's pamphlet appeared, the Maastricht Treaty was still in the process of being ratified by member governments and it was not at all certain – at least in the eyes of the British – that the euro would go ahead as planned. But one can reasonably interpret his point as applying to Britain's preparations for the euro, irrespective of what might happen on the ERM front. The essence of the argument was that the British economy had to be in the right shape for joining the ERM or signing up for the euro. The word 'stability', which was subsequently used by Gordon Brown on countless occasions before and after May 1997, was right there in Balls's paper.

He urged 'a credible and predictable macroeconomic policy framework which can deliver *economic stability* combined with active government measures to promote growth and full employment. Only then will sterling be able to re-enter the ERM in a sustainable way.'[10]

Another phrase that was going to recur time and time again in the Brownian mantra also came from Balls, for he added: 'Only then can the UK hope to avoid a third, destructive, *boom–bust cycle* ... Only then can public and international confidence in British policy-making be restored.'[11]

When examining Brown's subsequent approach in office, it is important to bear in mind the concerns of the young adviser whose Fabian pamphlet so impressed him. What concerned Balls about the 1990–92 recession was similar to the concerns he shared with others about the 1980–81 recession, when he was a young grammar schoolboy reading the newspapers: high interest rates and an overvalued exchange rate being used to bear down on inflation at the price of 'high and persistent unemployment and a further damaging loss of industrial capacity'.[12]

During that first of many discussions between the ambitious Shadow Chancellor and his prospective adviser, Brown told Balls he had had to be supportive of the ERM because he could not possibly associate the Labour Party with devaluation.

After Black Wednesday Labour was still committed to an early return to the ERM. But Balls argued: 'Before it can define itself as a credible Party of stability, growth and full employment, Labour must first confront the fact that its European commitments may well conflict with these goals.'[13]

Brown and Balls were both portrayed after 1997 as 'anti-European' because of their extreme caution over the European issue, which was by now the question of joining a monetary union that from 1 January 1999 would be a reality – at least for the financial markets. Euro notes and coins were to begin circulating in January 2002. Balls's view was: 'Labour rightly wants to define itself as the Party of Europe. The logic of British and European politics has effectively made a vote for the Maastricht Treaty a vote for Europe.' But he warned: 'The economic implications of the Maastricht Treaty are dangerous and unworkable.' Labour's current policy – early ERM re-entry and support for a single currency by 1997 or 1999 – risked being in conflict with what ought to be Labour's (and Europe's) aim: 'a stable, growing, low unemployment community'.[14]

The message was something of a blow to the Shadow Chancellor, who had spent a lot of time fighting the anti-ERM faction within his own Party. Balls was also scathing on the economics of the single currency, pointing out – as Sir Donald MacDougall had done in an important report in 1978 – that vast inter-state migration, and the federal tax and transfer system, greatly eased the pain of a 'one-size-fits-all' economic policy in a currency union such as the USA. As far as Balls was concerned, monetary union à la Maastricht was economically and politically misconceived. 'The mistake is to let economic schemes run ahead of political realities,' he wrote. The Maastricht Treaty's inflation and fiscal 'convergence criteria' were rigid, over-ambitious and likely to produce slow growth and high unemployment. The persistence of four million (over 10%) unemployment in Germany ten years later in 2002 showed how prescient Balls was, although he was not alone in such a diagnosis. To work, the proposed Eurozone required 'a much closer degree of social and political cohesion and integration than Europe was likely to achieve in the 1990s, and probably in the next decade too.'[15]

Gordon Brown was not then, nor seems since, especially interested in the subject of macroeconomic policy but was – and is – fascinated by a whole range of 'micro' issues. What he was searching for was someone who could offer him a macroeconomic policy that left him free to pursue his other interests. Ed Balls offered him this – on what he hoped would be a sustainable basis.

But what Balls proposed was something different from past interpretations of macroeconomic policy. He believed that, for all his disavowal of Keynesian-style macroeconomic policy in his famous Mais Lecture (of 1984), Nigel Lawson, in his latter days, had been an active 'macro-manager' and had given demand management a bad name. For Balls, active macroeconomic management was necessary and desirable when economies were stuck in recession and confidence was low. But 'old style Keynesianism, pursued for too long, simply leads to high and rising inflation, unwieldy fiscal policies and, finally, damaging recessions.' This, concluded Balls, was 'the stuff of which *boom and bust* [author's italics] cycles are made'.[16]

The monetarist Conservative governments since 1979, said Balls, had only brought periods of low inflation at the expense of persistently high unemployment. 'When times are good, it [monetarism] has required unemployment to stay higher than it need be in order to keep wage inflation under control. Then, when boom turns to bust, it has required a high price in terms of unemployment in order to bring inflation down again.'[17] Norman Lamont had notoriously referred to high unemployment, in the cause of reducing inflation, as 'a price well worth paying'. This was one of the most injudicious and insensitive remarks made by a Conservative Minister throughout the period 1979–97, rivalled perhaps only by Norman Tebbit's injunction to the unemployed to 'get on your bike'.

But Balls maintained, on a subject close to Gordon Brown's heart, that such 'boom–bust' cycles added to the pool of long-term unemployed 'who find it harder to re-enter employment when the recovery eventually arrives'. This problem had grown enormously during the 1980s and early 1990s. When he eventually came into office, Brown was going to adopt a stern 'deserving poor'-style attitude towards the unemployed – a far cry from his earlier speeches in the Commons, when he castigated the Conservatives for penalising the unemployed.

Balls's message was that governments could not achieve economic salvation by relying on macroeconomic instruments alone and that, in the wider public interest, governments had to be constrained. He was reflecting not only on his observations of the 1980s but also the trend of some of the academic economic literature of the time, in leaning towards 'rules' rather than 'discretion' and questioning the efficiency of decisions made with the short-term political timetable in mind. There was a 'credibility gap' between 'politicians' short-term desire to stimulate the economy' and 'the public interest in medium-term stability'. No one, he charged, had mastered the art of 'boom–bust economies' better than the British Treasury.[18]

It was at this point in his argument that Balls offered the solution that Brown was eventually to seize on, a solution that was to become the most significant move of his entire Chancellorship – the granting of independence in setting interest rates to the Bank of England. But the prudent Mr Brown would take nearly five years to be fully convinced.

Interestingly, the master of 'boom–bust' economics himself, Nigel Lawson, had been reduced to advocating an independent Bank of England when all else had failed him. He revealed this in his resignation speech in (November) 1989. There was a sense in which serious politicians were beginning to feel their hands needed to be tied. Geoffrey Howe (Chancellor 1979–83) had come out in favour, as Kenneth Clarke was also to do after his 1993–97 Chancellorship. Indeed, Norman Lamont revealed, after he was sacked in (May) 1993, that he too had urged Bank independence on the Prime Minister John Major, but the latter was vehemently against such a loss of democratic control. Balls cited both major parties' belief in the ERM (at least until 16 September 1992) as evidence that politicians were beginning to realise that they needed to tie their hands.

We shall discuss the details of Balls's proposal in the next chapter. Suffice it to note at this stage that, as early as 1992, Balls was arguing that an independent Bank of England would 'strengthen and not weaken the hand of a Labour government.' As he saw it: 'Freed from debilitating market doubts about the government's anti-inflationary resolve, a Labour Chancellor would be free to concentrate on the many other aspects of policy, including fiscal policy, which are more important in determining whether the UK can build and sustain an economic recovery.'[19]

Another aspect of Balls's 1992 paper was the emphasis he put on the importance of manufacturing and of a competitive exchange rate. But he rightly contrasted the experience of the UK with that of the USA and Australia during the 1980s, to show that not enough of the competitive edge provided by devaluation in this country went into profits and hence investment and productivity. This led to the need for both the government and central bank keeping a weather eye on the growth of earnings and wages – a focus which was certainly emphasised by the Bank of England's monetary policy committee when it came into being in 1997. It should be noted that there had seldom been a period when the Treasury and Bank were *not* concerned about growth of earnings.

In becoming an advocate of an independent central bank, Balls was to some extent showing the influence of his time at Harvard as a Kennedy scholar, working under the guidance of Lawrence ('Larry') Summers, who left Harvard to become Deputy Secretary to the US Treasury in the Clinton administration, later Treasury Secretary, and then returned as President (of Harvard). Summers's research (with A. Alesina) entitled *Central Bank Independence and Macroeconomic Performance: Some Comparative Evidence* figured prominently in Balls's paper.

Balls and Summers cooperated on a paper about unemployment in Britain, prompting a senior Treasury official to joke years later: 'Gordon Brown and Ed Balls are eclectic. They imported ideas to try here which North American economists could not get through Congress.' Within a few months of meeting Balls, Gordon Brown had flown to Washington in January 1993 with Tony Blair for what was to become an obsessive study of 'things American'. They were interested in both the US economic model, with its 'workfare' approach to unemployment, and politically in the way Clinton's Democrats had captured 'Middle America' from President George Bush and the Republicans – largely by borrowing many of their clothes. It was Ed Balls who arranged for the New Labour modernists to meet Larry Summers, the advocate of central bank independence.

Balls formally joined Brown as his economic adviser in the autumn of 1993. But the two got on so well that he rapidly seemed to become 'economic adviser plus most trusted confidant' and it was Balls whom Brown chose to accompany him when he went to meet Blair for the fateful Granita Dinner of (31 May) 1994. Balls even stayed for a drink and the first course, before discreetly retiring to let the two leading Labour politicians come to their formal agreement on what was going to constitute a duumvirate in government.

Brown had not had things all his own way in Parliamentary thrusts against the redoubtable Kenneth Clarke during the course of 1993. However, on the principle that attack is the best form of defence, he nagged away at the theme that taxes and public spending as a proportion of gross domestic product had risen under the Tories, and one or two opinion polls began to indicate that, even if Labour itself was still trying to shake off its own reputation as a Party of taxation, the Conservatives were not so trusted on tax either. Brown and Balls had a particular victory in fending off Kenneth Clarke's plan to raise VAT on domestic fuel from 8% to 17.5%, which was defeated in a Commons vote in the autumn of 1994.

Brown was absolutely in tune with Blair when the latter let it be known in his first Labour Conference speech as leader (October 1994) that Clause Four – public ownership of the means of production, distribution and exchange – was finally being dropped from Labour's aims, a battle a previous moderniser, Hugh Gaitskell, had failed to win in 1959. After that, the major effect of the new team of Brown, Balls and associates, with the Labour MP and businessman Geoffrey Robinson closely involved (key meetings frequently took place at Robinson's flat in Grosvenor House, Park Lane) was in preparing for a foolproof economic policy and election manifesto.

In a series of speeches and policy documents, the essentials of a 'fail-safe' electoral economic strategy were developed. From March 1995 the Shadow Chancellor was given the not inconsiderable role of being in charge of election planning – although the election was not due until spring 1997, John Major was having such trouble with his euro-sceptical backbenchers, in the face of a majority being reduced at almost every by-election, that an earlier general election was always possible.

The essentials of the strict approach to public spending were on display well before 1997, as was the defensive taxation strategy. But it was not until early 1997 that the remarkable commitments on the basic and higher rates of tax were made to a surprised public.

In March 1995 Brown began by saying, 'After twenty years of being on the defensive, we are now on the offensive'[20] and promising that he would not reverse any tax cuts made by the Conservatives before the election. Such a move would be one of the many snares in what Brown time and time again was to refer to as 'the tax trap'. But despite having promised 'to be fair to pensioners' (17 March 1993) in circumstances where 'as a result of breaking the link between pensions and earnings, many pensioners are hard up', Brown was by the time of the 1996 Labour Conference resisting pressure from Labour veteran Barbara Castle and the retired trade union leader Jack Jones to restore the link, because of the estimated £5 billion a year annual cost.

On 17 August 1993 Brown had stated: 'Labour is not against wealth. Nor will we seek to penalise it ... our aim is not increased opportunities to tax – we will not tax unless we can increase opportunities.'[21] Again, on spending the theme was 'better *use* of resources'. Criticisms from earlier times that 'Tory cuts' had damaged the public services were not, from now on, to be followed by the logical step that perhaps more should be spent on these services, because that would imply more taxation. New ways would have to be found to finance the needed improvements in public sector infrastructure, with 'partnership between private and public sectors'.[22]

In the end there were to be two areas in which Brown *would* plan tax increases in opposition, one of which was to receive a lot more advance publicity than the other. From 1993 onwards Brown was promising a 'New Deal' for the young unemployed, and a programme of 'Welfare to Work'. This was hammered home in countless speeches and radio and television appearances during the

1994–97 period. It would have to be paid for, and there were few better targets than the 'fat cats' of the privatised utilities for raising revenue.

The 'Welfare to Work' programme was to be self-financing, and Geoffrey Robinson was heavily involved from June 1996 onwards with accountants Arthur Andersen – a more impressive name to conjure with in those days than after Andersen's involvement in the Enron fraud – in drawing up the details of the tax. The first number Robinson thought of was £10 billion, but the figure eventually settled on by Gordon Brown – ever-cautious – was £5 billion.[23]

The plans for a 'Welfare to Work' programme and its financing by a tax on the excess profits of privatised utilities were aired so loudly and repeated so monotonously for so long that nobody could have complained about being taken unawares by 'old-style socialism' when Labour finally came into office and went ahead. More surprise – indeed consternation – would be caused by separate and less publicised plans to reduce the structural budget deficit (that part of the deficit which is not accounted for by the ups and downs of the business cycle) with the removal of tax credits payable on Advance Corporation Tax (ACT) – a move which eventually caused widespread controversy because of its impact on pension funds. Again, Arthur Andersen, Geoffrey Robinson and Ed Balls worked closely on these, but so far from being trumpeted like the proposed windfall tax, the plan was kept under wraps: indeed, the precise details were locked in a safe at Grosvenor House (where Robinson had his flat), along with chapter and verse of the windfall tax, which had of course received less publicity than the broad proposal.

The utilities tax had first been proposed by John Edmonds, General Secretary of the GMB trade union, at the Blackpool Labour Conference of October 1992, and seized upon by Brown. Apart from its appeal to the left – at a time when the general thrust of Brown's prudence was to upset them quite a lot – the idea of an extra tax on the 'windfall' profits of utilities had an impeccable Thatcherite precedent, in the shape of the tax introduced by Sir Geoffrey Howe in the 1981 Budget on the 'windfall' profits of banks at a time when everybody else was having a hard time during the early 1980s recession.

Although the heavy detailed work with Arthur Andersen was not done until 1996–97 in the run-up to the election, Brown had stated on 9 November 1992 (*Labour's Campaign for Recovery*) that: 'To pay for additional current expenditure we would retain stamp duty on share transactions and introduce a one-off public dividend for the utilities in the light of their excess profits, a measure modelled on the 1981 windfall measures in relation to the banks.' Interestingly, in the light of the huge delays Labour was going to encounter in government with its plans for public–private partnerships, Brown said on the same occasion: 'The investment measures we propose can be advanced quickest through agreements with the private sector.' Many of Brown's speeches during the mid-1990s suggested a sense of urgency about what needed to be done in the public sector – a sense of urgency that did not fit well with the subsequent adoption of Conservative spending plans for the first two years of Labour's 1997–2002 'first term'.

Brown's disavowal of John Smith's Shadow Budget and 'tax and spend' had been his first major act as Shadow Chancellor in the summer of 1992 – a period when more public attention was focused on the travails of sterling and the Major government in the run-up to Black Wednesday. Members of the Tribune Group are sore to this day about the way a Tribune meeting was packed with Brown's acolytes in Tamany Hall fashion, and the consummate machine politician stamped on plans for a Tribune pamphlet that would attack his newly rigorous approach to 'tax and spend'. Little did they know that he was playing a very long game – that in effect he was putting 'tax-and-spend' policies on hold for some years, but not, for all his protestations, abandoning them forever.

Sloughing off the tax-and-spend image, and disavowing any further adventures with the ERM until the basis of the embryonic Eurozone's economic policies was reformed – these were two defensive and somewhat negative policy decisions taken by Gordon Brown well before his partnership with Ed Balls began. They were also decisions that he felt able to take spontaneously – there was no question of his having to bow to the extra concerns shown by Tony Blair towards the sensibilities of Middle England and the *Daily Mail*. But Balls's arrival reinforced the strategy and contributed to the macroeconomic framework.

While many people were involved, not least members of what became known as the Millbank 'spin' machine, the essentials of the economic strategy with which Labour approached the 1997 election were worked out between Brown and Balls, with Geoffrey Robinson – who had, after all, been around in Labour circles since 1963 – playing a vital role and Blair and his entourage exercising a right of veto on matters such as the top rate of tax, but giving the Treasury team the go-ahead on the ambitious plan to grant independence to the Bank of England.

'Red Gordon' had not lost all his spots, but he had certainly developed chameleon-like qualities of concealment and adaptation. He recognised that Thatcherism had captured that streak of individualism and belief in personal liberty which was embedded in the British character but sometimes neglected by the centralist left (not by all: Roy Jenkins had been a most humane and libertarian Home Secretary in the 1960s). But, for all his 'modernising' tendencies, Brown still felt strongly about poverty in a way the Conservative governments under Thatcher had manifestly not. 'The causes of poverty are unemployment, a welfare state that isn't working, and poor skills,' he once summarised.

Ed Balls had been a member of the Labour Party since he was 16. Balls, too, cared strongly about unemployment, poverty and the distribution of income. He believed that better economic policy could improve the economy's growth rate and afford the scope for redistributionist policies to help the poor. But, as he had emphasised in his Fabian pamphlet, he believed that Labour had to earn 'credibility' and that its European adventure should not be unduly hasty. The economy had first to be in good shape.

Balls's two major contributions were to be the influence he exerted in pushing for central bank independence, including the unique shape this took, and his work on the 'fiscal rules' via which, with balanced budgets (for current spending) and an emphasis on low debt ratios (as a proportion of domestic product), Brown would earn a reputation, at least in his first term, as 'the Iron Chancellor'. From there it was hoped that, such would be 'New' Labour's reputation for being trusted with the nation's finances, Brown could be more adventurous in the latter years of the first term and especially during a second. This would not exactly constitute a return to Old Labour, but he hoped to be a good deal more like a Labour Chancellor than many of his actions and words might suggest during the run-up to the election and the early years of the first term.

It helped that the Conservatives, via the big increases in taxation introduced by Lamont and Clarke to reduce the fiscal deficit, were ripe for attack on the tax front too. In January 1994 the Treasury admitted that, taking direct and indirect tax together, the burden of taxation would shortly be higher than under the previous Labour government. 'These figures destroy the Conservatives' only political claim. Never again can they say they are the Party of low taxation,' proclaimed Brown, by now ably assisted by both Balls and the relatively new spin-doctor Charlie Whelan.

Later in the month (26 January 1994) Brown was telling the BBC's *Today Programme*, 'There is no commitment to spend money on anything. We will only spend what we can afford to spend.' Despite Brown's long-term interest in the health service and notwithstanding his previous references to the need for emergency public spending in such areas, he was now forcing Shadow Health Secretary David Blunkett to remove from a policy document any pledges to restore cuts that had been made, or would be made, by the Conservatives in spending on health. The atmosphere between Brown and Blunkett became so tense that Blunkett subsequently refused to believe that it was Blair, and not Brown himself, who was responsible for the decision not to raise the top rate of tax from 40% to 50% – a prospect that many top rate taxpayers regarded as almost inevitable and hardly revolutionary, even if they were opposed to it.

It is a measure of how debilitated the Labour Party had become after all those years in opposition that it headed for the 1997 election with such cautious, indeed pusillanimous, policies towards public spending and taxation. The country had endured (and voted for) four successive Conservative governments that had given tax cuts (or at least personal tax cuts, especially for higher income earners) greater priority than spending on the public services. Over the years the original aim of Mrs Thatcher and her colleagues, to cut public spending as a proportion of gross domestic product, had first given way to attempts to freeze it and, in due course, to measures to arrest its rate of growth. The bias of the Conservatives was always against public spending (except for defence, law and order and a few other areas) and such spending as was sanctioned on the public services and the infrastructure was grudging. It was, for instance, a matter of established fact that Mrs Thatcher herself hated railways, although even she baulked at the political risk of privatising the rail network, which took place under John Major.

While the macroeconomy prospered under Kenneth Clarke's Chancellorship (1993–97), with good growth and falling unemployment, there was a strong sense in which, from the point of view of transport, health and education, more and more voters felt that 'Britain wasn't working'. Politically, although Mrs Thatcher had ridden the tide of a revolt against union barons and high taxes in the late 1970s, the public mood now was to acknowledge that there *was* such a thing as 'society' and that something had to be done about Britain's run-down public services. The obverse of Clarke's success in reducing the Budget deficit was that the Conservative government was imposing strict limits on public spending that were not calculated to do much to satisfy the public's appetite for improved services.

All this was mulled over and heatedly debated by Blair, Brown, senior colleagues such as John Prescott, David Blunkett and Robin Cook, the spin-doctors Peter Mandelson and Alastair Campbell, the focus group expert Philip Gould, and their acolytes. Caution bred of four successive electoral defeats reinforced Blair's obsession with pleasing 'Middle England' and Gordon Brown's natural prudence. Nervousness about winning, even with the state the Conservative Party was in, gradually gave way to the feeling that if they did win, as seemed increasingly likely, they would need two terms to achieve what a Labour government ought to do.

What was not obvious for a long time was that the first term would consist largely of an attempt to show that New Labour could be as niggardly in the matter of financing the public services as the Conservatives had been. The first term would consist not so much of an immediate 'post-war reconstruction' as of another four years of trying to win electoral respectability while pursuing a few 'Labour' policies by stealth.

But the clues were all there in the run-up to the 1997 general election. Having told the *Today Programme* in January 1994, 'We will only spend what we can afford to spend', by May 1995 Brown was telling the *Financial Times* that he would be 'very tough on public spending', and close confidants such as the economist Gavyn Davies were saying that the new Brown–Balls search for credibility meant that they wanted not only 'street cred' but also 'Wall Street cred'. Davies explained: 'Policy credibility has a precise definition. It means that the public believes that the government will carry out its stated plans.'[24]

The Brown–Balls fiscal strategy was unveiled in an important speech in May 1995. 'Labour in government will be the Party of wise spenders, not big spenders. My strategy is not based on an irresponsible programme of tax, spend and borrow, but of prudent investment for growth.' Then came the essence of what was going to be repeated *ad nauseam* for years to come – the fiscal rules. 'First, Labour will be committed to meeting the golden rule of borrowing – over the economic cycle, government will only borrow to finance public investment and not to fund public consumption. Second, alongside this golden rule commitment, we will keep the ratio of government debt to GDP stable on average over the economic cycle and at a prudent and sensible level.'[25]

In this important speech Brown committed himself to carrying on with an inflation target. He then said, 'In addition, for the first time, the next Labour government will make raising the trend rates of economic growth an explicit long-term objective.' In fact, the Wilson government of 1964–70 had also tried, in a very public commitment, to raise the trend rates of economic growth and had made it an explicit long-term objective. The inflation target became the central focus of Brown's macroeconomic policy after 1997. Not much more was heard of the growth targets.

The following week (22 May 1995) Tony Blair gave the keynote Mais Lecture at City University and emphasised the impact that 'globalisation' was having on his and Brown's approach. 'The growing integration of the world economy – in which capital, and to a lesser extent labour, moves freely – means that it is not possible for Britain to sustain budget deficits or a tax regime that is wildly out of line with other major countries. One of the requirements of our tax structure is to attract enterprise into the UK from overseas.'

Such was the degree of the Blair–Brown cautionary approach that Blair on this occasion even cited the 1976 speech by James Callaghan to the Labour Party Conference, when a Labour Prime Minister had been forced (to please the markets and the US Treasury) to say that the UK could no longer expect to borrow and spend its way out of recession.

In the policy document produced for the Labour Conference in October 1995, Gordon Brown was still playing for time on detailed tax plans: 'It would be irresponsible for Labour to make commitments on the precise level of tax rates and allowances, so far away from the election,' the document stated, before listing a rather mundane list of Labour's 'tax principles', the first of which was: 'Tax should encourage work and opportunity and reward effort: we do not tax for taxation's sake, to penalise or to punish, but we will end the privileged treatment of windfall gains and monopoly profits.' Brown's speech to Conference on 2 October 1995 did not give much away but contained the nice line: 'In three years the only tax cut people have seen is a Labour tax cut – Labour defeating the Tory plan to raise fuel VAT to 17.5%.'

Over a year later, on 19 November 1996, Brown made an important speech to a City audience entitled *The Budget and Labour's Economic Approach*. It was interesting because, although it was obviously short on detail, it brought together Brown's major economic themes, even containing the words 'This is the Budget I hope to deliver in 1997.' First, he promised the Ed Balls recipe of 'stability' with 'a tough inflation target' and 'consistent and tough fiscal rules'. Second, there would be an emphasis on encouraging investment and on closing the investment and technology gap with the UK's competitors. Despite this emphasis on investment, some of Brown's colleagues were concerned at this time that Labour were, for 'image' reasons, playing down the importance of manufacturing. Certainly, before this City audience, Brown seemed to be courting the financial sector, saying: 'it is a sign of the times that manufacturing accounts for 20% of our GDP and now financial services account for 18% of UK GDP.' What such comparisons omitted was the importance of manufacturing; that one-fifth of the economy contributed two-thirds of the export earnings that paid for Britain's imports – and even then there was a trade deficit.

The third theme of Brown's promised Budget was that it would 'improve our education and skills by switching resources from welfare to education'. But as for specific details of taxation, all there was in the fourth theme was: 'a Budget for fairness that will, with the decisions on VAT on fuel and the windfall levy, show that Labour is the Party of fairness.'

The Shadow Chancellor took the opportunity to summarise New Labour's adaptation to the modern world. The Old Left's idea of a siege economy no longer made any sense. The notion of a job or trade for life was out of date: the real test of employment and industrial policies was whether they equipped people 'to master change'. Battles between the public and private sector, the state and the market were also outmoded.

At the end of quite a long speech in this vein, listeners or readers were encouraged to contact one Charles Whelan at the Gordon Brown press office. It is doubtful, however, whether they received much further detail about Labour's tax plans. These were reserved for listeners to the *Today Programme* on 20 January 1997, when the world was alerted to Labour's Tax Bombshell. Brown was due to be interviewed by James Naughtie, and in this case Whelan contacted him – at home, the night before (a Sunday) – to hint, 'You will ask about tax, won't you?'

What had happened was that, despite Labour's large lead in the opinion polls at the beginning of 1997, Labour's focus group experts maintained that 'fear of Labour was growing' and that there could yet be another Conservative 'Labour Tax Bombshell' scare (on the lines of 1987 and 1992), despite Gordon Brown's prudence with his tax-and-spend promises.

Brown and Blair had a tax 'summit' at Blair's Barnsbury (Islington) home on 5 January. In his prudent way, Brown at least wanted to keep open the option of raising the top rate of tax from 40p to 50p. Apart from raising revenue, this would also be a signal that the former 'Red Gordon' still remembered where he came from, for the fact of the matter was that, although he kept his links to Labour traditionalists throughout the 1992–1997 period when he and Blair were forming New Labour, he had conceded a great deal of ground. Blair was firmly against retaining the option to raise the top rate, and Philip Gould's research with his focus groups reinforced Blair's basic instincts. An increase in the top rate would not be popular with Middle England, according to Gould, even when set at £100,000.

Ed Balls, whose 'fiscal rules' were an essential part of the 'stability' that Brown would offer country and markets, dared to suggest that a Labour government could still responsibly raise the top rate of tax to 50%. Blair replied, 'Wash your mouth out.'

The bombshell was that there would be no bombshell. The policy was unveiled by Brown to Naughtie while Britain's nation of reluctant taxpayers was having breakfast: 'It is because of the importance which we attach to work and because people have been dealt such a harsh blow over these last few years that we will leave the basic rate of tax unchanged and we will leave the top rate of tax unchanged.' Furthermore: 'I will be making commitments for our manifesto which are commitments for a Parliament. And the basic rate and the top rate will remain unchanged.' Asked 'Throughout Parliament?', the Shadow Chancellor – who for years before and for years after this interview was capable of going through an entire interview without saying anything new or of substance – replied 'Yes.'

Further explanations were given in the speech ('Responsibility in Public Finance') that Brown delivered in London later that day

(20 January) at the Queen Elizabeth Conference Centre. Brown had in effect been leaking his own speech – a practice in which New Labour was to indulge almost as a matter of course when in government. But, master of the media that he was, he kept the other bombshell for the speech itself: Labour, a Party out of office for almost two decades, with a Shadow Chancellor who had devoted a fair proportion of his early career to promulgating the need for higher public spending to deal with the problems of the public services and the infrastructure, was going to freeze spending levels for its first two years in office.

There was an obvious link between not increasing tax rates and not raising public spending. Ironically, it was a pledge by Labour *not* to raise income tax rates in 1959 – in the face of a Conservative 'scare' that it planned a 12.5p rise in income tax – that contributed to Gaitskell's defeat in October 1959. Labour had also promised to cut indirect taxes and Gaitskell, whose honour was seldom questioned, found he lost the trust of the public on the issue. People did not believe the Labour claim that its programme could be financed by economic growth.

When asked whether New Labour's pledge nearly 40 years later not to increase income tax rates made any difference to the outcome of the 1997 election, the pollster Robert Worcester, Chairman of MORI, said: 'Not much'; 61% of electors expected Labour to put taxes up anyway.

CHAPTER SEVEN

In central banks we trust

We shall never know what would have happened in the general election of 1 May 1997 if Neil Kinnock had still been leader of the Labour Party, or John Smith, or even if Gordon Brown had stood for the leadership in 1994 and won. What was manifest was that the modernising effort of the Labour Party was a collective effort in which all these senior figures in the Party had played their part, but 'New Labour' was very much a joint imprint superimposed by Blair and Brown after John Smith's death. The phrase began to appear in Blair's Party Conference speeches and Kinnock himself joked, at the victory party held by the London Region of the Labour Party, 'After all, *je suis Labour Nouveau*' (July 1997).[1]

There was little doubt about Tony Blair's campaigning skills in the television age, or about his added appeal to Middle England. What matters in general elections is where the defectors place their votes. For the first time on record, more voters switched from Conservative to Labour than from Conservative to Liberal. For the first time on record Labour received more votes from the middle class and home-owners than did the Conservatives.

The most common reason given for the defection from the Conservatives was that it was 'time for a change'. It was a 'landslide', in the sense that Labour won a huge majority of 180 seats. Yet, such are the quirks of Britain's 'first-past-the-post' electoral system that Labour won this majority with a slightly smaller share of the popular vote (43.2% against 43.4%) than Harold Wilson had received when winning with a majority of only four seats in 1964.

The country thought the Conservatives had been in too long; but it was the country that had kept them there. Even John Major later observed that the 1992 result had 'stretched democracy's elastic too far'. The Conservatives were deeply divided, notably over Europe, and heavily associated with 'sleaze' – opportunities which Labour leaders, especially Gordon Brown, had been superb at exploiting. The Calvanistic streak in Brown's rhetoric, and his stern mode of delivery, had invariably managed to combine derision, scorn and censure on the subject of Tories, sleaze and 'fat cats'.

But the 1997 election was about something more fundamental than 'sleaze' or vague feelings that it was time for a change. Labour had campaigned against 'Thatcherism' for almost two decades, although 'New' Labour had gradually come to accept certain aspects: it had become more 'market-orientated'; it had accepted the alteration in the balance of power between employers and trade unions (with the exception of a commitment to end John Major's opt-out from the European 'social chapter'); and it was prepared to let sleeping privatisations lie.

The electorate, however, in the shape of the Conservative defectors, had finally noticed the other side of the Thatcherite coin. They loved their material prosperity but they were increasingly frustrated by what J. K. Galbraith had many years ago pinpointed as the contrast between 'private affluence and public squalor'. In the words of one Conservative commentator, some years later, 'The 1997 election showed that the electorate wanted dramatic enhancements in their quality of life.'[2]

This implied a need for higher spending on public services, which in turn implied higher taxation. But higher income tax rates had been explicitly ruled out by the compact Tony Blair and Gordon Brown had made with Middle England in order to be elected. After all those years in Opposition, Labour was still desperate to win 'credibility' with the electorate, whether or not the Conservatives had lost it after Black Wednesday and via the increases in taxation that took place in successive budgets after 1992. Above all, Blair and Brown had decided that 'credibility' meant sticking to their pre-election promises on 'tax and spend'. Perversely, this involved not addressing with sufficient will and resources the very appetite for enhancement of the quality of life – specifically, in the quality of public services and the infrastructure – which they had been elected to satisfy.

There were two well-publicised weapons in the battle for credibility. The first, pledged and now adhered to, was the commitment not to raise the basic and top rates of direct taxation for the lifetime of the Parliament. The second was the (connected) promise to adhere to the strict limits on public spending for the first two years of the Parliament – as it turned out, for *half* the Parliament – already announced by Kenneth Clarke.

But there was a third arm to the assault. This was the least publicised and the least expected. In order to establish their credibility with the financial markets – markets that were deemed to have wrecked the chances of all Labour Governments of the past – Blair and Brown were prepared to hand over the vital reins of monetary policy, operational control over interest rates, to the Bank of England.

The devolution of this important democratic power and the setting up of the Bank of England's Monetary Policy Committee were New Labour's best-kept secrets in the run-up to election day. The preservation of secrecy owed everything to the fact that this was a last-minute – or, rather, a last-weekend – decision.

When the Treasury announced that Gordon Brown was holding a press conference on the Tuesday following the election, the financial and political commentators and City analysts assumed that this would be to reveal that he had decided to raise interest rates after the scheduled monthly meeting of Chancellor and Governor. It was; but that was not the only reason. The new Chancellor also announced that he was handing over operational responsibility for interest rate changes to the Bank of England. The effect was electric – but not on everyone. One agency reporter asked him when he was going to change interest rates again. He was not. That was the whole point – except, as the details of the announcement indicated, in times of national emergency, when the new Monetary Policy Committee (MPC) might have to be overruled.

In many years of covering Treasury matters, I had never seen anything quite like it. After the press conference, Sir Terence Burns, then Permanent Secretary, came across the room to ask what I made of it. Frankly, I could hardly believe it, and told him so. My generation had been influenced by the hard times Labour (and, for that matter, Conservative Chancellors such as Churchill in 1925) had had at the expense of an independent Bank of England. Some of my best friends were central bankers, but central bankers had a deflationist streak that went with the job. James Meade, one of Britain's few Nobel prize-winners in economics, had once observed: 'We nationalised the Bank of England in 1946 to prevent another 1931'[3] – by which he meant all the deflation that went with the return to the gold standard at an overvalued exchange rate in 1925, and the impalement of the Labour government on that hook in 1929–31. That episode had ended with Ramsay MacDonald at the head of a National Government, and was deeply embedded in Labour folklore. It was not, for example, an episode that endeared MacDonald to Gordon Brown's hero, James Maxton.

This was not something Gordon Brown felt he had to do in a hurry because of a manifesto commitment. On the contrary. Whereas the manifesto stated, 'To encourage work and reward effort, we are pledged not to raise the basic or top rates of income tax throughout the next Parliament' and 'For the next two years Labour will work within the departmental ceilings for spending already announced' (i.e. a two-year 'freeze'), the only commitments with regard to the Bank of England and monetary policy were, 'We will match the current target for low and stable inflation of 2.5% or less. We will reform the Bank of England to ensure that decision-making on monetary policy is more effective, open, accountable and free from short-term political manipulation.'

The phrase 'reform the Bank of England' did not immediately conjure up a vision of independence day. On the other hand, the more one reflected on the phrase 'free from short-term political manipulation', the more it could only mean taking up the suggestion of Ed Balls (via Larry Summers) in that 1992 Fabian pamphlet that the Bank should, indeed, be made independent.

But it has to be said that this was not a point commentators or analysts had latched onto after publication of the manifesto. If anything, the general feeling was that New Labour was annoyed with the Bank of England for its role in failures of banking supervision (the Johnson Matthey affair in 1984 and BCCI in 1991) as well as its association with the 'bust' that followed the Lawson Boom, not to mention the fiasco of Black Wednesday itself.

It was a measure of how important the influence of Ed Balls was in the policy decision that, while Sir Terence Burns, the Permanent Secretary of the Treasury, was passing the time of day with me as the press conference broke up, most of the rest of the press and the news agencies' representatives were crowding around Balls for extra briefing, a number of them standing on chairs in order to see and hear what was going on. At this stage Balls was nominally only a 'political adviser' and not even a fully-fledged Treasury official. Still not being able to take it in, the author repaired to a local coffee house with Robert Chote, then of the *Financial Times*, and Gary Duncan, then of the *Scotsman*, all three of us shaking our heads and wondering just what madness had got into New Labour – and so soon after the election!

Yet from the point of view of Brown and Balls, this was not some deranged return to the past, an open invitation for the latest Labour government to be subjected to a latter-day Montagu Norman attacking socialism on behalf of vested interests in the City. If anything, the granting of power over monetary policy to the MPC was a stratagem to *avoid* such an outcome: a means by which a Labour government could, in the words of Balls, 'do the things a Labour government should do' without being brought down by some chance financial crisis.

It was in the course of the last weekend before the May 1997 election that Gordon Brown finally came round to the view that he would make the Bank of England independent, and do so as soon as possible. Reflecting at home in Scotland, he concluded: 'What a release an independent Bank of England would be – a release from a "bankers' ramp"!'

Certainly the new Chancellor enjoyed the element of *coup de théâtre* in springing this announcement on a surprised world ten days after that pre-election weekend. But he had given it long and serious thought.

Whereas Ed Balls had been urging it upon him from the time of that 1992 Fabian pamphlet, Brown had displayed characteristic prudence before eventually accepting what in effect became his alternative lodestar to the discredited exchange rate mechanism. All British governments seem to think they need some kind of lodestar: in the case of the Thatcher/Major governments, their various experiments with giving primacy in the battle against inflation to a series of monetary indicators, then shadowing the Deutschmark, then joining the ERM, had all ended in tears. The ERM could no longer be Labour's lodestar either. From the start of his association with Gordon Brown, Balls was preaching independence of the Bank instead. His advocacy became especially strong from 1995 onwards. His message was: 'You should make the Bank independent. You should lose control in order to gain greater control.'

Balls ensured that Brown discussed the subject of central bank independence with other central banks, on the Continent and in the USA. When addressing Federal Reserve Chairman Alan Greenspan at the opening of the newly furbished Treasury building in September 2002, Brown paid public tribute to Greenspan: 'I am personally grateful to you for your advice between 1994 and 1997 when you regularly met me and Ed Balls – now the Chief Economic Adviser to the Treasury – and we discussed privately with you how central bank independence would work for Britain.'[4]

These discussions helped to clarify in the minds of Brown and Balls the way a central bank could operate more to a Labour government's advantage than history-minded critics might fear. The brief of the Federal Reserve, after all, was to achieve price stability *and* maximum employment, not just price stability.

The European Central Bank was only in embryonic form at this stage, and did not start operating until January 1999, eighteen months after the inauguration of the MPC. But it was already firmly established that its brief would be 'price stability', its statutes having been made even more rigorously counter-inflationary than the Bundesbank's.

Brown had of course already accepted Balls's fiscal rules aimed at ensuring that the financial markets would be content with Labour's budgetary policies, and that there would be no return to the panics of 1976 under Wilson and Callaghan. The last of his meetings with Greenspan on the subject had been on 20 February 1997 in Washington, when he was accompanied by Ed Balls and Geoffrey Robinson. In Robinson's words, Greenspan had said it was 'unfair' to expect elected politicians to take unpopular decisions on interest rates. This remark seems to have struck all three of his British visitors, although on its own it is an odd line of argument for central bank independence. By the same logic, quite a lot of other 'unpopular' decisions could be taken out of politicians' hands, and they might end up being short of a job.

But what Brown had told Balls and Robinson on several occasions after this last Greenspan meeting was, again in Robinson's words, 'that the external pressures would inevitably push us into Bank independence.' This led him to conclude that in that case it was better to seize the initiative and win not only political kudos but also moral authority for having bitten the bullet. Balls, long the proponent of the move, thought it would be a sign of weakness not to do it immediately. One fear was that being forced eventually into the move would look like failure – despite the fact that Brown was strongly minded to do it eventually – the public impression being that independence would only be awarded after the Bank had, as it were, 'earned its spurs'. This was because at one stage Brown and his camp did let it be known that the Bank should be seen to earn the right to independence, via a good performance by a monetary committee which would be new but still only advisory.

Labour governments always worried about 'external pressures'. But as we have seen, it so happened that every Conservative Chancellor since 1979 except John Major had eventually been reduced by pressures external and internal to the conclusion that the Bank should be made independent. There was also a sense in which the Establishment, the great and the good, the institutional backdrop to British economic policy, having once placed their faith in the ERM, had been coming round to the view that the Bank needed to be made independent.

But Kenneth Clarke (Chancellor 1993–97), while keeping his views about independence away from the public, gave the go-ahead to Gordon Brown to meet Eddie George, the Governor, on a number of occasions during the eighteen months before the May 1997 election, to discuss the possibility and what it might entail.

Ed Balls confessed to Geoffrey Robinson, 'I've always wanted to sort the Bank out.'[5] The manner in which the Bank was 'sorted out' was to give great offence to Eddie George, even to the point of thoughts of resignation – something which would hardly have helped the long drawn-out campaign of Brown and Balls to win a public reputation for 'credibility'. Indeed, even after their secret meetings with George began, exploring how the Bank could be made more transparent and accountable, a report appeared in the press suggesting that George himself was not even on the shortlist of favoured candidates for Governor under a Labour government.

The Brown camp was suspicious of the Bank in general and of George in particular. So were some key witnesses to the House of Commons Treasury and Civil Service Committee, which conducted an enquiry into 'The Role of the Bank of England' in 1993. The Committee recommended 'the transfer of authority (over monetary policy) from the Treasury to the Bank' and also 'the creation of a strong and independent Monetary Policy Committee'. Powerful witnesses such as Denis Healey (Chancellor 1974–79) had said that the transfer of responsibility for monetary policy from the Treasury to the Bank was 'a gimmick' and that the Bank's record did not inspire confidence that it would 'necessarily' be 'better than ... a good Chancellor'.

The evidence of Sir George Blunden to the Treasury Committee was especially interesting. Tough and widely respected, Sir George was a quintessential Bank of England man; indeed, he was considered so invaluable that, having retired from the post of Executive Director in 1984, he was brought back as Deputy Governor from 1986 to 1990. Regarded for years as the human face of what was then both a bureaucratic and a paternalistic institution, Sir George, with his wealth of experience, surprised the Committee by opposing the derogation of monetary policy to 'the central bank not answerable to Parliament'.

Asked how he would rank certain other central banks 'in order of perceived monetary credibility', Sir George had listed the Swiss National Bank as Number One, the Bundesbank as Number Two, the Fed as Number Three and the Bank of England as Number Four. He agreed that there was a connection between the fact that his top three were 'credible' and independent, but added that Britain was different because of the fact that interest changes were 'nearly always ... made in relation to sterling and what is happening to sterling' and it was generally accepted 'even in the countries that have independent central banks, that the level of the exchange rate is a truly government matter'.

Sir George was of the view that, if independence were nonetheless to be granted to the Bank, its structure would have to alter. As he pointed out, in the top three he had mentioned: 'the central bank structure in all of them which leads to the independence that they have is a structure which is not dependent on one man.'

Sir George, who knew the Bank inside out, was well aware of the top-down nature of decision-making. He was essentially saying – in what some observers also took to be a swipe at the near-dictatorial powers of Bank of England Governors, such as Eddie George – that the well-established central banks made their monetary policy decisions by committee, and so should an independent Bank of England.

Sir George Blunden made these important points on 20 October 1993, around the time that Ed Balls joined Gordon Brown as his full-time economic adviser. And the remarkable thing is that the veteran 69 year-old who had spent his whole life at the Bank was making the same point about the need for a committee, with no collusion, as the young Ed Balls was urging on Gordon Brown.

Right from the start, in his 1992 pamphlet, Balls had emphasised that 'independence' would not mean 'independent of the political process'. The power to set interest rates should not be transferred 'from an elected official to an unrepresentative and unaccountable group of bankers who need pay no attention to the wider economic consequences of their actions'. On the contrary, if carefully reconstituted, and statutorily controlled, an 'independent' bank 'would make policy more representative and more accountable than at present'. The Bank must be directly answerable to Parliament, as the Federal Reserve was to the US Congress, and the House of Commons would be given powers to override a decision by the Bank in extreme circumstances, 'a power that is available in Australia and New Zealand but not in Germany'.[6]

Way back in 1992, Ed Balls was emphasising that: 'These Parliamentary powers would, in effect, prevent the Bank from pursuing zero inflation without considering the wider consequences. The Bank would need to reflect the Parliamentary and public consensus about the desirable long-term rate of inflation to pursue.' The Bank, with its new 'decision-making council' would have to be 'a very different institution from the Bank of England ... whose credibility has been so undermined by recent regulatory failures, particularly over the Bank of Credit and Commerce International' (BCCI). The buzzwords of the future were there in the Fabian pamphlet – monetary policy would have to be 'transparent, accountable and predictable'; so was the proposal to remove City supervision from the Bank and 'surround' the Governor with 'outsiders with proven track-records in economic or financial management'.[7]

By the following year, 1993, the essence of Balls's thoughts had already begun to evolve into Party policy. In *Labour's Economic Approach*, Gordon Brown oversaw the writing of the following passage: 'It is now time to reform radically the Bank of England and the conduct of monetary policy. The Bank must be made more accountable and its decision-making bodies be made both more open and more representative.'[8]

Tony Blair was in favour of exploring the idea of central bank independence when Brown, urged by Balls, first tried it out on him in mid-1995. As a result Balls was given leave to write a paper developing the ideas he had first voiced in the 1992 Fabian pamphlet. Brown asked Balls to update this paper on the Tuesday before the election, after he had made his decision over the weekend in Scotland to go ahead with independence.

The fruits of Brown and Blair's 1995 agreement that Balls should do further work on the subject had been seen in a speech Brown made on 17 May 1995 ('Labour's Macroeconomic Framework'). In this, Brown was both moving towards his new lodestar – Bank independence – and reacting against the way in which the Treasury's own version of a more open monetary policy had evolved. As we saw earlier, the government had made the inflation target the centrepiece of its monetary policy after the Black Wednesday fiasco and 'suspension' of our membership of the ERM. Mervyn King, the Bank's Chief Economist since 1991, had been an ardent advocate of inflation targets, while Eddie George, then the senior monetary official, had been opposed, being very much a central banker who preferred 'judgement' to 'rules'. 'His own judgement', as a Treasury official observed. Economists prefer to talk about 'discretion' rather than 'judgement' in this context.

There was a flourishing academic debate over 'rules' versus 'discretion', with rules gaining the upper hand. Brown and Balls were to favour the concept of 'constrained discretion' (a phrase they borrowed from a lecture given by King in 1997) to describe the strategy on which they eventually settled. What was abundantly clear in mid-1995 was that Brown did not like the way the discretion at that time was largely the Chancellor's – to the point of the monthly meetings between Chancellor and Governor being fixed (and even the timing changed) at short notice, 'leading to understandable suspicions that meetings are moved because of particular political events' (such as postponing a meeting that might – but did not in fact – arrive at a decision to raise interest rates, until after the May local elections that year).

It offended the prudent Shadow Chancellor in spring 1995 that Clarke had not raised interest rates at the latest meeting despite being told by the Bank that the 2.5% inflation target was likely to be breached by the end of the Parliament. A more enduring bee in Brown's bonnet was the personalisation of the monthly meetings between Clarke and George as 'the Ken and Eddie Show' (the term for which the present author fears he was originally responsible). The idea that the relationship between the Treasury and the Bank of England should be 'cast as a relationship solely between the Chancellor and the Governor ... makes the decision-making process unstable and risks undermining the credibility of policy,'[9] said Brown.

Under the Lamont/Clarke reforms the publication of a quarterly Bank of England *Inflation Report* and monthly monetary meetings had become an important feature of economic policy and had captured the public's imagination. But it was still the Chancellor who decided whether interest rates should change, the Bank's discretion being confined to its freedom to give its own unvarnished advice, freedom not to have the *Inflation Report* vetted by the Treasury, and freedom to choose the timing of any interest rate change decided upon by the Chancellor.

Brown and Balls had decided by May 1995 that: 'reversing the reforms which have occurred since 1992 would not be a sensible step. It would mean cancelling the monthly meetings, dropping the inflation target and returning full operational control to the Treasury.'[10] The alternative was to move the process forward.

Brown wanted dates of meetings published up to a year in advance, and decisions about interest rates to be announced immediately, and 'properly justified to the public'. Minutes should be published 'as soon as possible'. It was in his May 1995 speech that Brown proposed 'a new Monetary Policy Committee'. But at this stage, of course, Brown had not yet made up his mind about full independence, and the MPC would simply be an advisory committee of eight (not nine, as eventually decided in 1997). Apart from the Governor and Deputy Governor (there was then only one deputy), the six other 'directors' on the MPC, including the Bank's Chief Economist, would be appointed by the government, not the Bank, but 'in consultation with the Governor and Deputy Governor'.[11]

Balls's original idea of a 'decision-making council including people from industry and trade unions as well as the City and representatives from regional offices of the central bank'[12] had been transformed into suggestions that the Court of the Bank of England, which oversees the Bank, should be expanded and strengthened to reflect other interests. The Court would hold the MPC accountable to its mandate; the Bank's accountability to Parliament must be made statutory; the MPC must be accountable for its advice; and the Governor and Deputy should give evidence to the Treasury and Civil Service Committee on a more regular basis.

One can see here much of the structure that Brown set up after he came into office, with the vital difference that the MPC as originally envisaged would be advisory, not actually in charge of monetary policy. Throughout the regular meetings Brown and Balls had with Eddie George in 1996–97, the discussions were about an advisory committee, not an operational body. George had little alternative but to accept that his existing dominance of policy would be diluted by external members; but he was always insistent that the MPC should be staffed by technical experts, not vested interests. The term 'directors' used by Brown in 1995 was ambiguous.

Another significant way in which the ideas of Brown and Balls evolved was that in 1995 they were thinking of seven-year terms for members of the MPC, not the three years that was eventually settled on, a point that will be explored later.

While in 1995 Brown had not yet made up his mind about independence – he is a great 'agoniser' and this was certainly an issue of such major importance that it called for a lot of agonising – he certainly gave a heavy hint that he was going 'to consider whether the operational role of the Bank of England should be extended *beyond its current advisory role* [author's italics] in monetary policymaking'.[13]

But, crucially, he added: 'Government has a responsibility to the public in setting the objectives of economic policy and that means that the government rather than the Bank of England must set the targets for monetary and fiscal policy.' He was sure that any proposal for central bank independence which denied government this responsibility would not command public support. In no country was the central bank 'truly independent of democratic control and accountability'. In all cases a central bank's room for manoeuvre was subject to legislation 'and its legitimacy is dependent on the willingness of the legislature to continue to sanction it'.[14]

Brown was already attracted to the openness of debate and decision-making at the US Federal Reserve, 'the internal democracy and decision-making' at the Bundesbank, and the way the New Zealand government set the inflation target for the central bank. But the Bundesbank did not have an inflation target set by the government, and the Reserve Bank of New Zealand personalised the decision-making process. 'We are not,' warned Brown, 'in the business of depoliticising interest rate decision-making only to personalise it in one independent Governor. That is a form of independence I reject.'[15]

This, if anything, was advance warning to Eddie George, but Brown ended by hinting that, while it was certainly time to strengthen the Bank's advisory role, and internal reforms were needed at the Bank, 'the Bank must demonstrate a successful track record in its advice.'[16] It was this last point that was to lull commentators into mistakenly thinking that Brown would not grant independence almost immediately on taking office.

Gordon Brown's most indicative advance thinking about the MPC was revealed in a speech on 26 February 1997, with the somewhat unpromising title 'Building a Recovery that Lasts', delivered to an economists' forum in London. This was a speech influenced by what those close to him regarded as the seminal meeting with Alan Greenspan only six days before, and by some half dozen discussions during the preceding eighteen months with Eddie George, including a dinner at which Tony Blair, Brown and colleagues had discussed the possibility of independence with George and his colleagues. One Bank official complained: 'The dinner was rather ruined by the fact that it was dominated by John Prescott, who seemed obsessed with finding ways of disguising the public sector borrowing requirement.'

George had said to Chancellor Kenneth Clarke that he thought it sensible to have occasional 'chats' with the Opposition team – he did, after all, give presentations to groups of MPs from time to time.

Clarke had said, 'Of course you must; one of these days you might have to work with these people.' One Bank official noted wryly that 'it would have been regarded as treachery if Robin Leigh-Pemberton had talked to the Opposition.' This was a reflection of the fact that, while George was a career Bank official, having served the Labour governments of the 1960s and 1970s in his time, Leigh-Pemberton had been a Conservative appointment, chosen personally by Mrs Thatcher and regarded as close to her until he 'broke ranks' and supported the move towards a single currency. Indeed, there were those in the Bank who thought the Bank's economic pronouncements at the time of the 1990–92 'ERM' recession were more supportive of the government's line on the economy than the bare statistics warranted.

While Eddie George encouraged the Labour team in its switch from the idea of having regional and sectoral representatives on the MPC, he was happy to see them on the Court, where the CBI and TUC had been represented for years. George was impressed that Brown and Balls saw the need to draw the external members of the proposed (advisory) committee from expert, technically qualified economists. But at this stage the length of term they should serve, or even changes to the inflation target, do not appear to have been discussed.

The relationship between Gordon Brown and Eddie George (who was going to become Sir Edward in due course) eventually settled down to one of considerable mutual respect. But that was after a very rocky start. The fact of the matter was that the Brown camp began, in its preparations for office, by being anti-George and its attitude continued in that vein for some time. Ideally, they wanted George to fall on his sword; but in any case they wanted to surround him and dilute his domination of Bank policy.

Between 1995 and 1997 Brown's distaste for the 'personalisation' of monetary policy, as embodied in the 'Ken and Eddie Show', grew and grew. He complained that monetary policy was 'descending into an open, running dispute between the Chancellor and the Bank of England'.[17] This was undermining the 'credibility' that he and Balls greatly prized. The objection was that Clarke had ignored Bank advice to raise rates in January 1997. But the Chancellor had listened to the Bank on 30 October 1996, and raised rates by 0.25% to 6% – exactly as Eddie George had advised. What concerned Clarke in January 1997 was the strength of sterling and the possibility that another rise in rates might cause it to strengthen further.

After the vehemence of Brown's speech on 26 February 1997, it was difficult to believe that he wished, if elected, to have a 'Gordon and Eddie Show'. And indeed there was only one – on the day, six days after the election, 6 May 1997, when he raised rates, on George's advice – but also to make a political point – and then proceeded to announce Bank independence. But the fuss made about the previous outcomes of the 'Ken and Eddie Show' seems somewhat exaggerated. The last published minutes for the monthly meetings between Clarke and George before the election (those published on 23 April, concerning the meeting on 5 March 1997), showed that Clarke was becoming more and more concerned about the level of the exchange rate. No doubt Clarke did not wish to follow Bank advice to raise rates on the eve of the election, but he had a reasonable point in saying that he and the Governor 'remained 0.25 point apart in their views on the appropriate level of interest rates'. As the agreed minutes noted: *This reflected a small difference of judgement about the outlook for inflation one to two years ahead, and about the balance of risks.*

Indeed, there has always been a fundamental paradox about Gordon Brown's approach in these matters. While seemingly very ambitious in his desire to demonstrate that New Labour was, to coin a phrase, 'tough on inflation and tough on the causes of inflation', Brown always had longer-term Labour goals at heart. Eddie George had memorably been described by one member of the Treasury select committee as 'an inflation nutter'. This was unfair: George also acknowledged wider goals, such as high employment and economic growth; but there is no doubt that his central banker's natural instincts made him even more cautious than Brown and Balls, who were seeking 'credibility' in the financial markets but who were neither central bankers nor, at the time, especially enamoured of that breed.

In due course George was to say, in an interview just before his retirement in June 2003, that he regarded the 'inflation nutter' charge as 'a compliment' because 'with inflation under control, the past decade has seen a better economic performance than for donkey's years'.[18]

But in those early weeks of the new Labour government in May 1997, the new team thought George was far too hawkish in discussions about the inflation target. Ironically George, a quintessential central banker of judgement, had at first been resistant to the concept of inflation targets. Later he came to regard Lamont's introduction of targets in 1992–93 as a seminal move on the way to independence.

The same was true of Kenneth Clarke's later decision to publish the minutes of the 'Ken and Eddie Show'. This had been a huge step in the direction of the greater 'openness' or 'transparency' to which Brown and Balls also subscribed. Before that there had been, in the words of one senior Bank official, 'Parliamentary accountability but not public accountability'. Even though Eddie George by no means got his own way at the meetings of the 'Ken and Eddie Show', his advice was there for all to see. A Governor who had been brought up in a culture of paternalism and secrecy had become converted to transparency by the time he started having regular sessions with Brown and his team in the run-up to the election. As one of George's colleagues observed: 'Before that, only a dozen people knew whether monetary policy decisions had been made on rotten advice from the Chancellor, the Bank or England – or, for a long time, Mrs Thatcher.'

For years economic and financial journalists had had to use all their skills to obtain the most minor pieces of inside information about what the real Bank or Treasury view was: when Brown came in he inherited a system that was already much more open. For many officials, Bank independence was the logical next step and a Labour Chancellor, encouraged to have advance talks with the Bank by a sufficiently confident Conservative Chancellor, took that step with considerable panache.

In both his speech of 26 February 1997 and subsequent remarks before and after the election, Gordon Brown made much of the fact that, while keeping inflation within the 1–4% range, the Conservatives had frequently missed the 2.5% target. Indeed, Brown spoke with such passion about the horrors of missing the target that one might have imagined he was talking about a return to the days of 20%-plus inflation, instead of the forecast of 'over 3%' that greeted him when he arrived at the Treasury. As he said, 'the government has clearly failed to achieve an average inflation rate of 2.5% over the course of (the 1992–97) Parliament.'

When it came to the discussions with a surprised Bank immediately after the election, George argued strongly for '2.5% or less' and Sir Terry Burns, Permanent Secretary to the Treasury, and Sir Alan Budd, the Chief Economic Adviser, joined George in urging '2.5% or less; and preferably 2%', for the new MPC's inflation target.

Brown and Balls were unhappy with this advice, but the Treasury and Bank can be forgiven for being surprised, for in his speech of 26 February 1997 the then Shadow Chancellor had declared: 'Labour in government will set a target for low and stable inflation which will match the target for the next Parliament formally set out by the Chancellor in a Written Parliamentary Answer in June 1995: "to achieve underlying inflation (measured by the RPI excluding mortgage interest payments) of 2.5% or less", which "should ensure that inflation will remain in the range of 1–4%."' And the commitment to 'match' the '2.5% or less' target was repeated in the manifesto.

Thus, as close to the election as 26 February 1997, a Labour Shadow Chancellor who was to make a virtue out of sticking to his published plans for limits on public spending and income tax rates was committing himself to an inflation target that he chose to alter as soon as he achieved office. And he had put this commitment in the context of matching the Conservative commitment, as he had done with regard to 'tax and spend'.

The target of '2.5% or less' was the manifesto commitment that was broken within weeks – but hardly anybody noticed (Michael Dicks, Economics Analyst at Lehman Brothers, was one who did).

Ironically, it was broken in connection with the move – an independent Bank of England charged with a 2.5% inflation target – that was widely considered the outstanding success of Brown's Chancellorship.

But, in another twist to the story, that success is closely associated with the consequences of Labour's going back on the manifesto commitment, and introducing what later became known as a 'symmetrical' inflation target. As it turned out, the promise of matching the existing Treasury target of 2.5% served the purpose of 'fooling the burglars', i.e. of keeping the financial markets happy in the run-up to the election.

The whole point of the way Brown and Balls introduced the MPC was that, provided inflation was reasonably under control, policy should aim at growth and high employment, even though the MPC's sole official task was to 'achieve' a specific inflation target of 2.5%.

The MPC episode brought out Brown's strategic and long-term approach. Just as by being so rigorous about 'tax and spend' in the early years he was already planning a more 'Labour' government approach later, so the granting of independence to the Bank, for all the worries more historically-minded observers might have, was designed to give him peace of mind for longer-term objectives. As he himself has said, he saw the announcement of 'the new monetary and fiscal regime' as being 'in pursuit of the 1944 objectives of high and stable levels of employment and growth'.[19]

But the 'symmetric target' seems to have emerged from the discussions Brown and Balls had with officials between Friday 2 May 1997, when they arrived at the Treasury, and 12 June, when they published the 'remit for the Monetary Policy Committee'. They wanted to impress the markets and gain peace of mind for a Labour Chancellor, but they were shocked by suggestions of '2%' and reacted against them. The concept of the symmetric target evolved after the decision to grant independence, and it was to be some time before the new team began to refer to the target as 'symmetric' – after which they frequently crowed about it.

The new formula assumed more and more importance, both in the conduct of policy and in showing up differences between the British model of central bank independence and that of others, notably the ECB. Indeed, the inflation target and the accompanying instructions to the MPC were also to form a vital element in the big debates to come over Britain's relationship to the Eurozone. The whole point of the 'symmetric' inflation target adopted by Brown and Balls in June 1997 was that it was *not* 'or less'. The MPC would be obliged to take measures to stimulate the economy, via lower interest rates, should inflation show signs of falling *below* 2.5%. It was not to try to make further inroads into inflation at the expense of output and employment.

Writing some years later (2002) Ed Balls and Gus O'Donnell said: 'If the target was not symmetrical – e.g. it was 2.5% or less – policy makers could have an incentive to drive inflation as low as possible to ensure they met their target comfortably, even if there were detrimental consequences for output and employment.'[20]

When Brown and Balls decided on an inflation target of 2.5%, they were being ambitious by historical standards and certainly worried commentators such as the present author, not least because such a low inflation rate had only been achieved on a handful of occasions since the Second World War. But it so happened that the move to Bank of England independence coincided with the remarkable disinflationary pressures brought upon an increasingly competitive international economy by the phenomenon known as 'globalisation'.

As Treasury officials saw it, a very important consequence of the setting up of the MPC was to neutralise a traditional battleground between Prime Ministers and Chancellors, a battleground which had sometimes seen a worrying deterioration in the most vital relationship in government.

Mrs Thatcher, for instance, often tried to intervene in her Chancellors' decisions about interest rates. She might have subscribed to 'Monetarism' but she disliked putting up the mortgage rates of 'our people'. Her most notorious intervention was when she insisted, as a *quid pro quo* for entry to the ERM, on an immediate reduction in interest rates – a reduction that gave her European counterparts the impression that Britain was not serious, from the start, about the 'discipline' of the ERM.

But, as the next few years were going to show, the mere fact of removing decisions on interest rates from the arena of prime ministerial and chancellorial debate did not preclude heated discussions, not to say outright rows, on many other subjects, not least Europe. The battleground simply moved. Perhaps the most important practical consequence of the derogation of monetary policy was that it gave Gordon Brown time to concentrate on all the other myriad areas of policy, and politics, in which he was interested. It is probably an exaggeration to say, as some have claimed, that decisions on interest rates took up half the time of previous Chancellors; but they certainly absorbed a lot of time and effort. Now Gordon Brown was free to conduct, under the terms of the Granita agreement, his role as Chief Executive of a government run by the Blair/Brown duumvirate, and delve into parts of other ministries that previous Chancellors had never reached.

∽✺✺ ✺✺∽

CHAPTER EIGHT

Battle of the titans

$\mathcal{T}$he Treasury was a little more prepared for Bank of England independence than the Bank itself, but only by twenty-four hours. On Thursday 1 May 1997, election day, Sir Terence Burns, Permanent Secretary to the Treasury, told a young official, Tom Scholar: 'Having talked to Ed Balls, I think something is going on on the Bank of England and European front.' Scholar, son of Sir Michael Scholar, then Permanent Secretary at the Department of Trade and Industry, was a rising star and in due course took over the running of Gordon Brown's private office before moving on to become Britain's senior Treasury representative at the British Embassy in Washington and the International Monetary Fund. The job allocated to him while the rest of the country was going to the polls was to work far into the night on a paper about Bank of England independence. The presumed connection between Bank independence and the euro was that, although Labour had hinted that it would not join the single currency in the 'first wave' on 1 January 1999, it was a requirement for eventual membership that the Bank of England should be made independent in advance of becoming part of what was known technically as 'the European system of central banks'. Burns and Scholar deduced that this was what lay behind a remark Ed Balls had made.

Balls had been in touch with Treasury officials for some time. Contact between the Opposition and Whitehall officials in advance of a general election was encouraged by John Major. Even in 1992, Whitehall had taken the prospect of a Labour government seriously, and some Labour advisers had almost got to the stage of measuring the curtains in Downing Street. By 1997 a Labour government was regarded as a foregone conclusion, and Balls and Geoffrey Robinson had been actively meeting Treasury officials behind the scenes in order to size them up and make their own judgements. The sounding-out process also embraced former Treasury officials who had gone on to colonise other Whitehall departments. Ed Balls had almost a year of regular meetings with Burns, many of them ostensibly to prepare for a meeting between Brown and Burns, at which many courtesies were exchanged but little discussion appears to have taken place about actual policy.

It soon become clear that, notwithstanding his prominent display of public welcome for the Chancellor after the election, seen on television, as far as Brown and Balls were concerned, relations with Sir Terence Burns were not going to be easy. There was nothing new about this. When the Thatcher government came into office in 1979, Ministers associated the then Permanent Secretary, Sir Douglas Wass, with the so-called 'corporate' approach of the Callaghan/Healey government, when efforts were made to bring the unions, especially, into the counsels of policymaking. Sir Douglas had found it difficult to disguise his intellectual disdain for 'monetarism' and for a time he was effectively frozen out of policymaking. In the end Wass survived all this and the Conservatives began to appreciate his worth. But the Treasury was ill-prepared in 1979 for either monetarism or what became known as Thatcherism.

Ironically, one of the younger political appointments who found themselves part of the freezing-out process was Terry Burns, who was brought into the Treasury from the London Business School as Chief Economic Adviser in 1980. Eventually Burns joined the official Treasury hierarchy and rose to become Permanent Secretary. But as far as Brown and Balls were concerned, Burns was tarred with monetarism, as well as with the 'boom-and-bust' economics of the Lawson Chancellorship. As if that were not enough, after a slow conversion to the exchange rate mechanism he was one of the most senior officials involved with the Black Wednesday debacle (although it had been John Major and his closest Ministers, not officials, who insisted on vainly supporting the pound for most of that day, losing most of the reserves in the process).

Relations between Ministers and officials are a delicate matter. British civil servants traditionally see their job as being to give Ministers the best advice possible, including warnings of potential pitfalls, before proceeding to carry out policy decisions as well as they can. It may help if they are of the same political persuasion – Sir Leo Pliatzky, senior public expenditure official under Denis Healey in the 1970s, had been at Oxford with Healey, was a Labour supporter and a natural sympathiser with what Healey was trying to do, but this did not prevent him from giving stern advice about the need for 'cash limits' on what he regarded as areas where Labour's ambitions inclined them towards profligacy.

Civil servants who vote Labour can work happily with Conservative Ministers, and *vice versa*. In the end, much of the job at the highest levels involves the ability of all concerned to work as a team, and this in turn depends on personal chemistry as well as perceived ability and mutual respect. But the political element is seldom absent. Mrs Thatcher used to ask, 'Is he one of us?' Gordon Brown has always been sensitive to political allegiance and, as became apparent when he refused to wear tails, or even a black tie, at official functions, Brown also dislikes anything that smacks of upper-class 'flummery' or patronage.

Burns himself came from a Durham working-class background and was even, while being classed as a 'monetarist', rumoured to have voted Labour in his time. But along with his association with past economic policies of which Brown and Balls thoroughly disapproved, Burns somehow seems to have irritated the new chancellorial team from the beginning and they, likewise, him. The indefinable 'personal chemistry' aspect of this is illustrated by the fact that Brown and Balls got on perfectly well with Gus O'Donnell, who had been John Major's Press Officer at both the Treasury and Number Ten before escaping back to the Treasury in 1994. Indeed, Brown and Balls got on so well with O'Donnell that he was soon brought back from the Treasury Embassy/IMF job in Washington – which he had only taken up in 1996 – to become a trusted and highly valued member of 'the team', first as Chief Economic Adviser and head of the government economic service and later as Permanent Secretary. O'Donnell was also the Treasury representative at meetings of the Monetary Policy Committee after Sir Alan Budd retired as Chief Economic Adviser in 1997.

The other difficult relationship was that between Gordon Brown and Eddie George, Governor of the Bank of England. At one stage (January 1996) Brown and Balls had a list of possible Governors, including the respected City figure Sir David Scholey; the economist Gavyn Davies – then at Goldman Sachs, but with long-lasting Labour affiliations, including a spell in Number Ten under James Callaghan in the 1970s; Martin Taylor of Barclays; and the Bank's Chief Economist, Mervyn King. Someone very definitely not on the list was Howard Davies, then Deputy Governor, who had offended Brown by something he said about Labour in his previous role as Director General of the Confederation of British Industry. His closest associates, especially the old Scottish ones, knew that Brown could harbour grudges for decades.

As previously noted, Brown and Balls associated Eddie George with past economic failure and with an excessive devotion to fighting inflation – the 'inflation nutter' charge. They half hoped, with little tangible evidence it must be said, that George would fall on his sword and leave the way open for a new Governor, appointed by Labour. They could hardly sack him without causing just the kind of Labour financial crisis they wished to consign to history. What they did not wish to do was to reappoint him.

David Scholey had in a sense missed his chance. His name was very much in the frame in the run-up to the appointment of Eddie George, who succeeded Robin Leigh-Pemberton in 1993. But Scholey deeply admired George and, disarmingly, regarded him as the better candidate. There was no way that Scholey would have wished to succeed George had the latter been forced to resign – indeed Scholey, given the chance, would almost certainly have warned of a City crisis.

Gavyn Davies was thought by close associates to be keen to become Governor but there was the little local difficulty that his wife, Sue Nye, was Gordon Brown's secretary. There was also a feeling among at least some of those sounded out that Davies, while deeply respected as an economist, did not quite have the manner of the archetypal central banker. This might have been considered a bonus in Labour Party circles but there were wider considerations. In the end there was only one candidate, namely Eddie George, who after all still had more than a year of his term to serve and showed no inclination whatsoever to fall on his sword.

It was not that Brown expected Eddie George to resign after election day, but the hope in the Labour camp was that George would not wish to serve a second term. His first term was due to end on 30 June 1998 – a mere thirteen months after the election – and Brown and Balls had been thinking about a possible successor for at least eighteen months before the May 1997 election. Even though some members of the Opposition associated George with the Conservatives, it was abundantly clear to all who knew him that George would not resign simply because there was a change of government, although he would certainly consider resignation over policy changes of which he disapproved.

There was also speculation in the public domain that Brown and Balls were considering hiving off banking supervision to a separate agency. If supervision remained at the Bank, they were contemplating the appointment of an extra Deputy Governor, so that one would carry out the normal function of running the Bank and the other take care of supervision and regulation. As was reported in the press on 28 January 1996: 'one theory is that it [the Bank] may be offered greater independence in monetary policy in return for losing its supervisory role. This would be a big concession from a Labour government in order to please the financial markets.'[1]

This is exactly what happened, but the manner in which it happened, and the interplay between the strong personalities involved, was to be the stuff of high drama and did bring Eddie George almost to the point of resignation. But first there was an internal Treasury meeting the weekend after the election, at which the Chancellor and his officials discussed how they would go about the plans for the Bank and how they would break the news.

The bad news for the Bank was that it would lose banking supervision. In the opinion of the Treasury officials involved – and some at the Bank – this should not have been regarded as bad news at all. There is a conflict of interest within a central bank that is responsible for both monetary policy and banking supervision – in its role *qua* supervisor it might not want to alter interest rates in the way its role *qua* maker of monetary policy dictates. Also, of course, the central bank does become tarnished by association with banking failures, as the Bank had in the case of Johnson Matthey, BCCI and Barings.

But institutions and bureaucracies prefer to expand or stagnate rather than contract. There are always vested interests at stake. And Gordon Brown was planning not just one assault on the Bank but two: simultaneously with the good news about monetary policy would come the bad news that it would lose its traditional responsibility for selling gilt-edged stock – the management of government debt. All of these proposals had been contained in Ed Balls's paper of mid-1995 and were now presented to the Treasury.

One of the little-noticed aspects of the combined proposals was that the original *raison d'être* for appointing an extra Deputy Governor – to run banking supervision – disappeared with the plan to hive supervision off to a separate agency. But the new Chancellor went ahead with the appointment of an extra 'administrative' Deputy Governor, who became one of the nine members of the new Monetary Policy Committee, chaired by the Governor. The Governor, his two deputies, the Bank's Chief Economist and a senior financial official would be on the MPC, and there would be four outside experts, appointed by the Chancellor. Geoffrey Robinson, in his interesting account of his time at the Treasury, writes: 'In short, the old Bank coterie would be replaced by a group of experts who could bring specialist knowledge to this vital area.'[2] In fact it was not so much a question of 'replacement' as dilution or augmentation by outsiders. And, as Sir George Blunden's evidence to the Treasury Committee had indicated, previous advice on monetary policy might have come after discussions with a 'coterie' but the dominant voice in that coterie, under a strong incumbent such as Eddie George, was that of the Governor himself.

On the face of it, there was always a danger under the Brown/Balls prescription for the MPC that the Bank they so distrusted would have the majority of votes against the outside experts who became known as the 'externals'. In other words, the Governor was not quite as 'surrounded' by the new arrangements as Labour might have intended, notwithstanding the fact that the Chancellor would himself appoint the four externals. The (perhaps unintended) subtlety of this was that it would please suspicious minds in the financial markets that, even if the influence of the Governor was being diluted, that of the Bank itself was still preponderant. Indeed, for a time in practice it looked very much as if there was a Bank 'politburo' vote. But eventually key members, such as the Bank's markets expert Ian Plenderleith, did break ranks and all members showed signs of genuine independence.

Brown and Balls were certainly pleased with their move to nominate four of the appointments themselves. The paper presented to the Treasury soon after Brown's arrival made it clear that this was a subtle form of independence – one might even say a 'third way' – by comparison with what historically-minded critics might fear, because the Chancellor retained responsibility for setting the inflation target. The proposal was detailed to the point that the MPC would meet monthly, announce its decisions immediately and publish minutes later.

After intense discussions with Treasury officials and the Governor, Brown and Balls stipulated that the MPC should not *undershoot* its target by more than 1%, as well as not *overshoot*. Brown and Balls were evolving a system designed to reassure concerns that they were not handing monetary policy over to a committee with a deflationary bias: this was politically astute, and undoubtedly a source of relief to those historically-minded critics with folk memories of Montagu Norman – reassuring provided one was happy that the inflation target itself was not to be set unrealistically low. Geoffrey Robinson himself was concerned about the new Government 'tying itself down' but was reassured by the fact that the Chancellor retained the right to set the target, which meant that 'the target could move up as well as down'. And Robinson claims credit for insisting that the eventual document should put the MPC's approach in the context of 'taking due account of the importance of economic growth.'[3]

In the crucial, indeed historic, decision to opt for what became known as a 'symmetric' target, Balls was in tune with the results of academic research pointing to the dangers of a deflationary bias under arrangements where the target was not symmetrical. Indeed, events were to show over the next six years that even under a 'symmetric' target there still seemed to be a bias towards 'underachieving' the target. One might add *a fortiori* under non-symmetrical arrangements. But the word 'symmetrical' (or the alternative 'symmetric') was not used at the time.

The 'symmetry' arose as follows: the government would aim at 2.5% but demonstrate its good intentions by requiring the Bank to explain itself should inflation rise 1% above the target, and take measures – higher interest rates – to correct the position. Correspondingly, the conservative approach of the Governor and Treasury officials prompted Balls to devise the requirement that inflation must not be allowed to undershoot by more than 1% either.

This was interpreted by the Bank not so much as a 'range' but as a pair of 'trigger points' prompting a letter of explanation from the Governor to the Chancellor. This was a very important distinction, allowing the Bank the flexibility to explain why it was *not* bringing inflation back to target quickly after an external shock, such as a sharp rise in oil prices. The fear was that if inflation were to be brought back to target at 'normal' speed this could have an unacceptable impact on output and employment. The discussion soon centred on a two-year horizon for the target. This was essentially a Bank decision: it decided that the timescale could be stretched further if necessary.

But what was lost in all the excitement about the MPC was the way the exchange rate, for so long at the centre of monetary policy decisions, was to take second place, if that, in the government's macroeconomic policy decisions. Sir George Blunden had pointed out to the House of Commons Select Committee to the Treasury (TSC) that in his experience most interest rate changes had been dictated by exchange rate considerations – rates would be raised in order to protect sterling, or lowered if the pound was considered too high for the competitiveness of British industry.

The government and the Bank had overreacted after Black Wednesday, moving from a culture where intervention in the exchange markets to buy or sell foreign currency and influence the pound's value was the natural order of things to a position where such intervention was ruled out. Even Kenneth Clarke had lost his faith in intervention in the currency markets. Nevertheless, he had resisted advice from the Bank to raise rates on occasion largely because he was worried about making the pound even stronger and British industry's competitive position weaker. From now on the pound was virtually ignored as a target of policy: all the emphasis in monetary policy was on the inflation target. Ed Balls himself had shown concern about manufacturing industry and about the deleterious impact of an overvalued exchange rate in his original Fabian pamphlet, but such concern was now largely swept aside from the point of view of operational policy, with potentially very damaging consequences. At his press conference on Tuesday 6 May 1997, when he unveiled the news about the MPC, Gordon Brown was asked about exchange rate policy and replied that he believed the exchange rate should be 'stable and competitive'. It was not obvious that, over the following years, he was prepared in practice to do much about the pound's manifest loss of competitiveness.

For the moment, however, that first May Bank Holiday weekend was dominated by the energy that gripped the Treasury and Bank as they thrashed out the proposals for independence. The main decision – the one that was to provoke such bad blood between the Chancellor and the Governor – was taken at a traditionally large Treasury meeting, attended by Ministers and officials. One Treasury official subsequently observed: 'It was about the last large meeting Gordon Brown ever held. After that everything was decided in small groups, often consisting of the Prime Minister and Chancellor with no one present even to take minutes.'[4] There was also many a meeting between Gordon Brown and Ed Balls by themselves. One Treasury official noted, after some years: 'Gordon Brown and Ed Balls never disagree in front of others. If there is a potential problem between them, they simply adjourn the meeting.'

Whatever their prejudices against Sir Terence Burns in advance, it was the fall-out from the big meeting on the handling of the MPC decision that set relations between the Chancellor and his Permanent Secretary off to a bad start. Brown entered the meeting wanting to announce the Bank of England reforms as one big 'package' – the Bank would gain the inestimable prize of independence over monetary policy, but lose banking supervision and its responsibilities in the gilt market. Sir Terence Burns and his colleagues said the plans were fine, and the Treasury wished to do all these things. But Burns said that to do it all at once would be 'too much for Eddie George to take in'. Steve Robson, one of the top officials beneath Burns, took the view that 'you don't give the good news now and the bad news later'. Robson agreed with Brown's original proposal, but other senior officials agreed with Burns. In due course, the new Chancellor was to establish a reputation among his officials as one who believed in arguing everybody into submission and winning every encounter; but on this occasion, very early into the role, he bowed in *Yes, Minister*-style to the predominant civil service advice.

Eddie George went to see the Chancellor on the Bank Holiday Monday (5 May) and was overjoyed by the news that he had won the prize of Bank independence, even though he was also told that he was losing responsibility for the gilt-edged market. It was at this point that yet another two-man meeting involving Gordon Brown became shrouded in confusion. The new Chancellor gave the experienced Governor two letters, one setting out the proposals for the MPC, the other the proposals about banking supervision. Both were obviously 'confidential': the MPC proposals would be revealed to the public the following morning, after the official monthly meeting of Chancellor and Governor – the one and only 'Gordon and Eddie Show'. But none of the contents of the second letter was to be revealed the following day, and Eddie George took this to be no more than a 'consultation document'. It was also extremely brief.

Of course, the Bank did not really want to lose anything. Being responsible for gilts and supervision contributed to the Bank's function as a financial powerhouse, with huge influence over what went on in the City. Many traditionally-inclined officials in the Bank were deeply upset by the thought of the diminution of any of its powers. The Bank would never be the same again, for all the celebrations about independence with regard to monetary policy. But for Eddie George the prize of monetary policy was worth the loss of gilts. On the other hand, for the Bank's chief expert on gilts beneath him, Ian Plenderleith, it was an almost unmitigated disaster. 'I suppose it's not *all* bad news,' Plenderleith said that evening, 'We *have* got independence.'

According to Geoffrey Robinson, that same evening 'Gordon was very clear that the Governor knew the whole picture'. According to an official closely involved: 'Gordon Brown thought he had given Eddie George some kind of a hint. But Eddie George either didn't believe it or didn't hear it. He had such an adrenalin rush from the news about independence that his feet were not on the ground.'

The thought of Eddie George's feet not being on the ground is a difficult one to swallow for those who have known him over the years. George, whose principal pastime for years had been weekend sailing, always gave the impression of the sturdy captain in the engine room, or a safe pair of hands on the tiller. George was even on occasion heard to say that he 'loved' the Bank. It is almost impossible to conceive of his failing to pick up any audible threats to its position, even in circumstances where his immediate reaction was of triumph and joy about monetary independence. George was not a man to take his eye off the navigation charts. It was not for nothing that he was nicknamed 'steady Eddie'.

The second of the letters George received by hand from the Chancellor on the eve of independence day made the general point that the future of supervision was to be reviewed. The Bank focused on the sentence stating: 'We will of course consult you on how it happens.'

A very senior Treasury source maintained: 'we had clear conversations with the Bank, from day one.' Sir Alan Budd, the Treasury's chief economic advisor at the time, recalled ringing the Deputy Governor Mervyn King and saying: 'You've lost it. You gain interest rates but you lose gilt-edged sales. You keep the money markets. At some stage there will be a transfer of banking supervision to the FSA [Financial Services Authority]. Meanwhile, Howard Davies will be Deputy Governor for Supervision.'

For George the package as understood did not imply a *fait accompli* and twenty-four hours' notice. The 'how' included 'when'; and consultation would obviously take weeks, if not months, after due warning about 'when'. George eventually came to have a very good working relationship with Brown. But when, a mere two weeks later, he was summoned to Number Eleven Downing Street and told that the loss of the regulatory role would be announced in the Commons the following day, without consultation, he was furious. According to one Bank source he went back to his official car and began to dictate a letter of resignation over the car-phone. George denies this account, but one senior insider has said: 'It took us twenty-four hours to calm him down.' At a press conference the following day the man from the *Daily Express* asked: 'Did you think of resigning?' George conceded 'All sorts of things go through your mind, but not seriously.'

At the time the *Observer* reported the car-phone story in good faith. But the denials have been very strong. Somebody close to Eddie George subsequently said: 'As a metaphor for what happened it contained an essential truth, but Eddie is not the sort of man to behave quite so peremptorily.' Nevertheless, he did contemplate resignation when he got back to the Bank, and was in a fairly incandescent mood for the rest of the day. In the end he accepted the advice of his closest advisers that resignation should only take place on a matter of principle, and the fact of the matter was that he had no objection in principle to the removal of banking supervision. Within a day or so George in turn found himself having to calm down furious members of the Bank's Court. The principle had not upset him. But he was devastated by the way it came as a complete surprise that day, and never understood why. As far as he was concerned, the implication was that he and the new Chancellor would discuss everything. He had never told the 500 people working in banking supervision of any immediate threat. Now he was in a position where he could not even tell them whether they would have a job. As it turned out, 450 or so were duly transferred to the FSA.

The immediate reason for Gordon Brown's haste and change of mind over banking supervision was the discovery from the Lord Chancellor, two weeks after the first meeting with George, that there would be legislative time for only one Bank of England Bill in the first Parliamentary session. Gordon Brown was to show an inclination as Chancellor towards being 'sequential' – concentrating on one thing at a time. But he wanted to get the regulation proposal out in the open reasonably soon, and decided that the only way to do it was to tack it onto the Bill creating the MPC.

Unfortunately, after that first meeting two weeks earlier, Eddie George had gone back to Threadneedle Street and told the staff that, while regulatory changes were in the offing, they need not have any immediate worries: there would be full consultation. It would not have helped George's mood if he had known at the time that his Deputy Governor, Howard Davies, had been informed about the move before him. He had known for one simple reason: the team of Brown, Robinson and Balls had decided to offer Davies the super-regulator's job, and the Treasury had telephoned him the Saturday before – in Argentina, where Davies had a speaking engagement. Robinson, with his City contacts, had said that Davies was the right man for the job, and Davies was well known to the Treasury, having worked there for a time, and kept in close 'networking' touch ever since.

Davies was asked to make up his mind that same Saturday evening. This was characteristic of New Labour's brusque approach – but not unique to them. Earlier in the decade Norman Lamont, as Chancellor, had asked Rupert Pennant-Rae, then Editor of the *Economist*, to make up his mind with indecent haste when offering him the Deputy Governorship of the Bank. On this occasion Davies accepted, after some to-ing and fro-ing to the telephone from his seat at dinner next to Carlos Menem, President of Argentina. Friends of Davies knew that he would have much preferred such a dramatic long-distance phone call to raise the issue of the Governorship, but that was not on offer. And there were at least some in the Brown camp who agreed with the view of senior Treasury officials that banking and financial supervisors were 'on a hiding to nothing' and regarded the offer to Howard Davies as something of a 'punishment posting' for the way Davies had allegedly given offence to Brown while at the CBI.

Years later, after developing a warm relationship with Brown, George was to tell friends of his regret that the new Chancellor 'had not got the confidence to take me into his confidence'. This applied partly to the Davies episode but more importantly to the way the Chancellor's team went about the supervision issue. George was disappointed that anyone in the New Labour team could think that the Bank of England would breach confidences. George himself was not particularly exercised about the supervision issue *per se* – if anything, he cared more about losing the gilt-edged department, which he regarded very much as his engine room. Many was the meeting within the Bank and at Number Ten or Eleven Downing Street or the Treasury over the years where George had nodded wisely and said that whatever the political or economic arguments, the fact of the matter was that the markets would not wear this or that proposal – or, alternatively, that interest rates had to be raised to restore market confidence.

Some Treasury officials thought there was an element of witch-doctory in arguments from authority – or arguments from 'feel'. And there were those in the Treasury who were only too delighted when Gordon Brown arrived and announced that he was removing responsibility for sales of government debt from the Bank to an agency controlled by the Treasury. Things got quite personal. One very senior Treasury official entertained a dislike for Ian Plenderleith, the Bank's senior markets official beneath George, and observed – only half-jokingly – 'I favour this in order to annoy Ian Plenderleith.'

The sensibilities of Plenderleith were very much on Eddie George's mind during this entire episode. He had been a loyal and trusted colleague of George's for many years; a great expert on the markets, he was widely liked and respected in the City. George himself had recognised the international trend towards Treasury control of government debt sales in other countries. He knew Labour had had discussions with the Treasury about the debt management side of the Bank; that public accountability for all financial matters had become a big issue; and that over the previous decade the Treasury had been taking a 'hands-on' attitude towards the management of official debt. George also thought it not unreasonable that the Treasury should gain debt management, having lost monetary policy.

In the end, the Bank still retained a presence in the financial markets. As one senior official put it: 'Our money market operations continued as before, and, although we have less of a role in gilts, we have quite a portfolio of gilts for our own customers, and we continue operating (for the exchange equalisation account) in the foreign exchange market. Our concern would be to lose market experience. It has been no great problem.'

Eddie George had already had talks before the election with the Treasury about how supervision should be organised in an environment where the boundaries between financial operators and areas of supervision were becoming blurred. But Treasury officials, before Brown's arrival, while wanting to tidy up financial supervision and put it all, including banking, under one large umbrella, were still nervous of George's reaction. Treasury officials had urged a change on Kenneth Clarke, but, in the words of one, 'we could not see how Ken would take away banking supervision from Eddie.' It should not be forgotten that, while occasionally differing over interest rate policy, Clarke and George had an extraordinarily good relationship. But Clarke at the Treasury was nowhere nearly as active as his successor Gordon Brown (to put it mildly) and no great reformer. 'We all knew,' said the Treasury official, 'that if the Bank of England got independence, that would be the moment for a deal.'

Despite the Treasury's concerns about Eddie George's sensitivities over supervision, Peter Rodgers, the Bank's Secretary and head of public relations, has recalled that George's office called to fix an appointment for a job interview with the Governor on the very day in late 1996 that he had written an article – as a journalist on *The Independent* – advocating the hiving off of supervision. Rodgers drew his own conclusion from this when the issue surfaced in the summer of 1997.

Ian Plenderleith was reportedly 'spitting blood' over losing technical management of government debt. Brian Quinn, previous head of the Bank's supervisory role, might well have been very angry about loss of supervision, but he had retired at the end of February 1997. His successor, Michael Foot, was quite relaxed and in due course went to the FSA in a very senior position. Quinn had always been very close to George. For Eddie George to have to return to the Bank after his second meeting with Brown, and tell his banking supervision staff – at a memorably stormy meeting in the neighbouring Guildhall – that, notwithstanding his earlier reassurances to them, no consultation had taken place and the deed was to be done, was an almost unbearable humiliation.

Eddie George had been at the Bank since the 1960s and spent his formative years in a City of London where the great saying was 'a man's word is his bond'. To the outside world, via the 'Ken and Eddie Show', he had become a friendly and congenial figure but, in the words of one member of the Bank's Court, he 'ruled the place with a rod of iron'. At one stage the Bank had been divided internally into two camps, the George camp and the Walker camp. The George camp focused on the markets and monetary policy; that of Sir David Walker, former Treasury official, was heavily involved in City regulation, Big Bang and so on. When the Conservative government could not decide between the competing claims of George and Walker for the Deputy Governorship, Sir George Blunden was brought back from retirement as the compromise solution. Blunden championed the cause of Andrew Crockett, a Bank official who had at an early stage been an obvious rival to George, but who left the Bank for a long spell at the International Monetary Fund before returning as Overseas Director. By this time Eddie George was firmly entrenched as the obvious man to succeed Blunden, and

Walker had left to join the investment bank Morgan Stanley. Andrew Crockett left the Bank again in 1993 – the year Eddie George became Governor – to join the Bank for International Settlements. Eddie George reigned supreme.

George in 1997 bestrode the Bank of England like a colossus. To have to go back in front of the staff on his reassuring words of two weeks earlier – treated in the Bank as having been delivered with almost papal authority – was one of the worst experiences of George's career. The rest of the staff were told by circular or e-mail. As far as the staff and his closest affected colleagues were concerned, it was small consolation to be told later: 'at least we can avoid another Barings.' Apart from the obvious shock to the system, Bank employees were naturally concerned about their jobs. As it happened, there was no great surplus of would-be banking regulators on the market, and most of the redundant staff were in due course reallocated to the FSA in Canary Wharf. The Bank also retained its Financial Stability wing and close contacts with the City. But there was nevertheless great distress within the Bank during the intervening period – even talk of nervous breakdowns.

No one likes having their empire invaded, and George was quite an emperor at Threadneedle Street. But, as noted, he was not personally too troubled by the loss of banking supervision – it was never an area that had especially interested him. When the Johnson Matthey crisis broke, George himself, just back from a trip to the IMF in Washington, seemed more interested in the details of what had happened than embarrassed for the Bank or City.

But the sequence of Johnson Matthey, BCCI and Barings had been a 'triple whammy'. George had become very concerned about the bad press the Bank had received as a result of its association with banking supervision. He had perhaps not been quite so aware of how this contributed to the Brown camp's hostility to him personally. But from his point of view he had been subject to some pretty cavalier treatment. His pride must have been wounded by his initial dealings with the new Chancellor, and he genuinely felt for the blow to his staff too.

The Barings remark was genuine as far as George was concerned. As the excitement grew about the good news – the award of monetary independence – it became almost axiomatic that the Bank and the MPC would be better off without the encumbrance of banking regulation. Another banking failure would have done no good to the reputation of the new monetary authority. As things turned out, there wasn't one in those earlier years. But a weight had been taken off the Governor's mind.

The dust eventually settled. By 26 January 1999 George was telling the Commons Select Committee on the Treasury: 'We are more accountable than, I think, any other central bank in the world. I have to tell you I very, very much welcome that.' Geoffrey Robinson saw this as proof that the Governor eventually 'effectively endorsed the Chancellor's policy'. The Brown camp may insist that George should have realised what was in store for him, but it also acknowledged that it expected 'a huge row'. Sir Terence Burns was once again brought in as the culprit: whatever happened between new Chancellor and seasoned Governor at their meeting without a note taker, Burns is blamed for having subsequently made a reassuring telephone call to George that he need not worry, that supervision was not on the immediate agenda and that he would in any case be fully consulted. Plainly, he was not – at least not until after the news of the alleged *fait accompli*.

But a very senior Treasury source maintained that Burns was wrongly blamed for the phone call: 'The fact of the matter is that Eddie was right to be furious. Brown offered him independence and took away gilts. The decision to go ahead with the removal of supervision came two weeks later, when the Lord Chancellor told Brown he could only fit one Bank of England bill into the legislative timetable.'

Thus, despite its advance contacts with New Labour, the Bank was taken by surprise on both the MPC and supervision counts. Eddie George had asked his deputy Howard Davies to be the formal channel between Bank and New Labour during the year before the election, and Mervyn King, then the Bank's Chief Economist, had also been in touch with Brown and Balls on a private basis.

When a senior Bank economist was offered an outside job in spring 1997 and approached King to ask whether there was likely to be anything interesting coming up on the monetary policy front, the reply was 'not for two years'. Yet King was as well informed as anyone. As noted, King had been an active force in seizing the opportunity afforded by Black Wednesday. At internal Bank meetings and Bank/Treasury meetings, he pointed out that monetary policy had collapsed and there was a void to fill. He was much impressed by the New Zealand model of Bank independence, with inflation targets and inflation reports, and successfully pushed all these innovations upon a battered Treasury, which in turn pressed inflation-targeting on the Bank. Eddie George, who has always been remarkably pragmatic and, in the words of one long-time colleague, 'a wonderful rationaliser of great monetary disasters', had never been keen on the ERM and regarded Black Wednesday as a release. He was one of those who began referring to it as White Wednesday. In the years leading up to the granting of independence, King had been powerful in promoting two related causes: a modern monetary policy based on inflation targets and 'transparency'; and a realignment of power within the Bank between the traditionally strong 'markets' side and the economics division. The technicalities of inflation targeting meant that things were going King's way. Essentially, the Bank was gaining ascendancy over the Treasury before the final gift of independence, and technical economists were rising in influence. The decision to augment the Bank contribution to the MPC with outside economists, not with representatives of pressure groups, suited King's view of the appropriate evolution of monetary policy.

King had come to the Bank as an outside director in 1990 and Chief Economist in 1991. He was an academic, not an administrator. There were those who criticised his management skills and some of his colleagues found him intolerant of honest differences of opinion. Although he was known as a very distinguished economist in other fields (notably taxation and public policy), his forte was not considered to be monetary policy. But even his critics conceded that he was a fast learner. He was also described by such critics as 'a very political animal'. He had a powerful impact on the Bank and easily impressed the most discerning observers around the City. By the time the MPC was formed, King was destined to play a major role on it and to be the leading, eventually the only, candidate to succeed Eddie George.

There were some, however, who thought he nearly overplayed his hand and wore his ambition a little too obviously on his sleeve. This was particularly so during the awkward months between the formation of the MPC in June 1997 and the announcement in February 1998 that Eddie George would indeed be reappointed.

Meanwhile, the energetic King was so excited about the MPC news that he persuaded the Governor to have rehearsals even before the external members had been appointed. He insisted that these should take place with the full panoply of modern technology – charts, slide shows, and so on – in a properly designated conference room. Participants in the rehearsals recall a particularly telling moment when the Governor peremptorily began to take issue with a Bank official who was acting the role of an external member, and the official pointed out that under the new order of things the Governor would have to let external members have their full say. It was an outward sign of the way the papal authority of the Governor in monetary policy advice would give way to decision-making by committee, which is of course what Brown and Balls wanted all along.

Senior Bank people assumed that the reason why Brown had moved so fast in granting independence was the size of the majority, which meant that he need not worry about any backlash from his left wing. The sequence of events described earlier suggests that he made the decision before knowing the full size of the majority but when the polls were already indicating that it would be healthy. The weekend he decided to opt for Bank independence immediately, Brown thought the Labour majority would be between fifty and sixty.

Treasury officials were convinced that Gordon Brown, the putative 'control freak', could not face the idea of monthly confrontations with Eddie George in an area where he was not confident of his expertise, and that this was at least one of the influences on both the MPC decision *per se* and the timing of it. (It should be emphasised in this context that in other areas, such as his Welfare to Work programme and the bewildering array of tax credits he championed, Brown was seen as very much the master of his material; but he did not strike the official Treasury as being especially interested in macroeconomic policy.)

From the Treasury's point of view, although monetary policy was a loss, it was a loss that had been on the cards for a considerable time. Officials had worked briefly on Lawson's proposal for Bank independence during the latter phase of his Chancellorship, and the institution as a whole was weary of the endless trouble between Numbers Ten and Eleven over interest rate policy.

Indeed, on the one and only occasion that there was an old-style 'Gordon and Eddie Show' the Treasury and the Bank wanted to raise rates on Tuesday 6 May by 0.5%, but the Prime Minister and his economic adviser, Derek Scott, wanted only 0.25%. They did not wish to sour the euphoric post-election atmosphere. As it turned out, Gordon Brown bowed to Tony Blair. After all the fuss he had made about Kenneth Clarke's putative negligence in resisting Eddie George's calls for higher rates, Gordon Brown's one and only interest rate hike was hardly sensational. It was the 0.25% that had divided Kenneth Clarke and Eddie George.

Eddie George's travails with New Labour did not end with the fiasco over the bad news that followed the good news of Bank independence. Neither did the travails of Sir Terence Burns. George was a great survivor and a man who had an almost Panglossian ability to adapt to any circumstance. Colleagues used to say of the Governor that for him, economic policy at any one time was the inevitable and logical outcome of everything that happened before, not the lurch from one illusory panacea to another that had so often characterised British economic policy. Colleagues used to say of Sir Terence Burns that he travelled a long way from the monetarism of the early 1980s to his highly pragmatic and eclectic position of the late 1990s.

Both of these distinguished public servants were 'marked men' in the sense that, had British constitutional practice been like the USA's 'winner-takes-all system', Burns would almost certainly have been given his marching orders when Labour came to power and George might not have been reappointed. Burns and his Chief Economic Adviser, Sir Alan Budd, while respected economists and very popular and accessible figures, had after all been among the most prominent architects of the monetarist policies Gordon Brown had abhorred and excoriated in the 1980s. Eddie George, despite his avuncular popular image, was considered dictatorial and, even for a New Labour team that had modernised and craved respectability with the financial markets, George was regarded as just a little too zealous about counter-inflation as opposed to growth and employment. But he once explained: 'We are talking about means and ends. I am extremely keen on growth. It irritates me that people think I'm not. The objectives are growth, a higher standard of living – all the ultimate goals. The debate is about the means. If we want growth to be more than a flash in the pan, we have to have greater stability.'

Sir Douglas Wass, one of Burns's illustrious predecessors, was generally credited with Whitehall's highest accolade: that is, having a 'Rolls Royce mind'. But the job of Permanent Secretary at the Treasury is only partly policy: it is principally that of actually administering the Treasury, making it run like a Rolls Royce, as it were. Wass once observed: 'Some journalists think I spend all my time on macroeconomic policy, but in fact it takes up no more than a tenth of my time.' Burns was considered by his colleagues to be extremely able in matters of policy and an extraordinarily good handler of people. 'He is one of the most thoughtful people in handling others and getting them to do things – quite exceptional,' said an official who worked closely with him. 'Given that Gordon Brown is not good with people and doesn't like dealing with them, Terry ought to have been a great asset to the new Chancellor. But the great strength of Terry Burns in dealing with people just deserted him when dealing with Gordon Brown.'

The relationship between Burns and Brown never really recovered from the initial misunderstandings that surrounded the inept handling of the altered role of the Bank of England. And Burns was sharply critical of the 'raid on pension funds'. The final straw for Burns's relationship with his new political masters was the news, in

November 1997, that Geoffrey Robinson, whose duties as Paymaster General included the closing of tax loopholes, was himself the potential beneficiary of an offshore trust. Robinson maintained that he had told Burns all the pertinent details of his arrangement. Burns disagreed. 'After that,' said a Treasury official, 'Robinson went on at Brown about the need to get rid of Burns.' Some adverse stories began to appear in the newspapers about Burns. But the latter, who for some time had only occasionally enjoyed the traditional direct access of Permanent Secretary to the Chancellor, rode the storm. He departed in his own time in June 1998. It is perhaps not surprising that it was Tony Blair, not Gordon Brown, who proposed Burns for elevation to the House of Lords. Burns was succeeded by Sir Andrew Turnbull, who was considered to have one of the safest pair of hands in Whitehall and who went on to become Cabinet Secretary in July 2002.

At all events, when assuming right at the beginning that Brown and Balls were thinking primarily in a European context when making the Bank independent, Burns (in common, it should be said, with many others) was not on the right track. The whole point of the build-up to Bank independence, from Balls's Fabian pamphlet onwards, was to give a Labour government a viable macroeconomic policy; it was emphatically not about immediate preparations for entering the euro. If anything, it was even offering an alternative to the ERM and the euro. The euro might come later, when 'credibility' had been established. Brown's 'euro' policy, labyrinthine at times, was effectively an each-way bet.

If the relationship between Brown and Burns was to begin and end in tears, that with George was eventually going to become almost rock-solid, to the point where the Governor became a great admirer of the Chancellor's and vice versa. But this evolution would take several years. While the details of banking supervision and the new arrangements for sales of government stock were sorted out and the new MPC came into operation, the cloud over the rest of 1997, as far as George was concerned, was the atmosphere of plotting and intrigue by which he was surrounded as speculation became rife about whether he would be reappointed.

New Labour's sporadic search for a successor to Eddie George had begun at least some eighteen months before the election, and therefore well before the bad start to Brown/George relations when they came to office. As noted, among the early names mentioned before the election as possible Governors were Martin Taylor of Barclays, Gavyn Davies of Goldman Sachs, and Mervyn King, then the Bank's Chief Economist. In the 'reappointment stakes' the name of David Scholey had also been mentioned, but by this time he was probably a non-runner. Meanwhile, the name of Sir Christopher Hogg, another prominent City figure, had come on to the race card. 'A number of candidates were produced, and some were sounded out,' said one official involved, 'but there was no one of exceptional merit outside the Bank who was prepared to do it.' It was generally thought that Gavyn Davies, Howard Davies or Mervyn King would have jumped at the opportunity if asked, but Howard Davies was by now the City's supreme regulator and in the end King was not asked.

What seems to have secured Eddie George's future was the way the City rallied round him when there were press reports in October 1997 that Labour did not wish to reappoint him. In particular, there was an episode when a Labour spin-doctor said that Eddie George had 'played into our hands' with what were regarded as unhelpful remarks revealing his doubts about the European single currency. This coincided with speculation that Brown wished to put in a New Labour sympathiser, such as Gavyn Davies. A letter to *The Times* in support of Eddie George seems to have done the trick, with heavyweight signatures on it, such as those of Lord Alexander of Weedon (then Chairman of NatWest). Labour was trying to please the City, not antagonise it. It was also very important that Tony Blair was a strong supporter of Eddie George, for in the end the Governorship is a Prime Ministerial appointment. Number Ten's private soundings established that George was overwhelmingly the City's candidate, that Gavyn Davies was regarded as too close to Gordon Brown, and that Mervyn King would be a stronger candidate after he had served his period as Deputy Governor. A source at Number Ten said (at the time,

January 1998, that George's probable reappointment was reported): 'Who else is there?'[5] Eddie George's reappointment, for five years from July 1 1998 to June 30 2003, was duly announced on 18 February 1998.

∽∽ ∽∽

CHAPTER NINE

The independent bank in action

There is little question that Gordon Brown's announcement of monetary independence for the Bank of England was a great political coup. Both the fact of Bank independence and the surprise combined to impress the political world and the financial markets, nationally and internationally. For some commentators it was the most dramatic event in the Bank's long history – surely an exaggerated claim: the nationalisation of the Bank in 1946 was not without its drama either. For many commentators it was a masterstroke, arguably *the* masterstroke, of the Blair government's first term. And it was all Gordon Brown's show: while Blair approved of the move, indeed gave Brown and Balls the go-ahead for drawing up a blueprint as early as in spring 1995, Gordon Brown received the lion's share of the credit.

Neither Brown nor Treasury officials were in any doubt as to where the buck would stop if things went wrong. Sir Andrew Turnbull, who succeeded Sir Terence Burns when the latter's difficult relationship with Brown finally led to his resignation in June 1998, told the Treasury Committee that the ultimate responsibility for monetary policy still lay with the Chancellor.

Brown could hardly have hoped for a better press initially. Most political, economic and financial commentators praised the move; only one or two expressed reservations. And, in spite of the inevitable criticisms levelled at the MPC from time to time, the overall impression was that the MPC was a great success, a model, even, for Europe and the rest of the world.

As so often in British economic affairs, however, both the move itself and praise for the Chancellor responsible conformed to an historic pattern whereby successive British governments tend to lurch from one ostensible panacea to another. The British have a worldwide reputation for pragmatism, but in economic policy they often take more of a doctrinal approach than that reputation might imply.

In this case, one needs to take a rather longer view of the way in which policy 'lurched'. As we have seen, to a certain extent the formation of the MPC was the logical outcome of a monetary policy that had been evolving since September 1992, when Black Wednesday destroyed the credibility of ERM membership as Britain's buttress against inflation.

The Conservatives had introduced inflation targets: the emphasis of policy was on defeating inflation (it was not for nothing that so many Bank resources went into the publication of the *Inflation Report*, not a Monetary Report, let alone an Economic Report); and the background to decisions on monetary policy was much more openly discussed, with minutes actually published.

Monetarism itself might have been discredited, but lurking in the background all the time was the prevailing view of the 1980s that, if inflation were defeated, sustainable economic growth and general harmony – what economists like to call 'equilibrium' – would naturally follow.

In his Remit for the Monetary Policy Committee, sent to the Governor on 12 June 1997, Gordon Brown emphasised that: 'the monetary policy objective of the Bank of England will be to deliver price stability (as defined by the inflation target) and, without prejudice to this objective, to support the government's economic policy, including its objectives for growth and employment.' The formal order of priorities was clear: price stability first, growth and employment second.

Traditionalists in the Labour Party, and elsewhere for that matter, could be forgiven for being concerned at what the 'modernising' Gordon Brown was up to. True, Eddie George was no Montagu Norman; and, yes, he would be Chairman of a committee with four outsiders appointed by the Chancellor, aiming at an inflation target set by the Chancellor. But the target of 2.5% – while less obviously biased towards deflation than '2.5% or less' or plain '2%' – looked a pretty tall order. For all the obsession of the Bank, and of Treasury officials, with reducing the target to 2%, the fact of the matter was that Kenneth Clarke, concerned about the strength of the pound and the competitiveness of British industry, had been more flexible in practice than his official target implied. Indeed, as Gordon Brown had reminded him in February 1997, 'the target of 2.5% or less has not been met since December 1994.'[1]

If one goes back further, one finds that the RPI had risen by 2.5% or less on only a handful of occasions since the Second World War. Brown could have added that the last time (before 1994) that inflation had been as low as 2.5% was in 1967.

The 'flexibility' of Brown's new procedure lay in his statement to the Governor that he would require an explanation and corrective action (details and time-table of such action to be explained by the Bank) 'if inflation moves away from the target by *more than* one percentage point in either direction' (author's italics). On the face of it, this implied that if inflation were to be 3.4% or even 1.6%, that would be tolerable. The upper limit of 3.5% had not been breached in the previous four years. The lower limit implied that, for all their objection to the George/Burns/Budd view that the target should be 2%, Brown and Balls were prepared to accept an even lower figure.

But the rider to this was that such toleration could only be temporary. There was confusion about this, because the Conservatives had stipulated under the previous arrangements that the target was '2.5% or less in two years' time' whereas the MPC was charged with aiming at 2.5% at all times, although there was to be much discussion about how abrupt, or not, its approach should be if the occasion arose when it had to take corrective action. In fact, during the period 1997–2002 the Governor never did have to write what was known as an 'Open Letter'. On the other hand, there were times when the MPC was criticised, from both within and outside its ranks, for 'undershooting' the target, and there was controversy about the quality of its forecasts of inflation: both DeAnne Julius and Sushil

Wadhwani questioned, during their periods on the MPC, whether the Bank's forecasters were making sufficient allowance for the disinflationary forces prevailing in a world of intense competition in the markets for internationally traded goods.[2,3]

There was also a feeling among some of the outside members of the MPC at times that it was not necessarily a question of the Bank's forecasters failing to appreciate the full extent of deflationary forces when constructing their equations: there might be a 'hawkish bias' in the Bank itself, which actually affected the forecasting process. After one occasion when the MPC was having difficult discussions and the atmosphere was tense, one member applied the 'inflation nutter' charge to Mervyn King. This was in the relatively early days. Subsequently, as the voting records piled up, King was to gain a reputation as a hawk simply from the way he voted.

Although the early fear of those relatively few critics of the new system was that the inflation target was ambitious by historical standards, disinflationary pressures around the world made the choice of target less 'deflationary' than it seemed reasonable to infer in May 1997. Thus, inflation in the Group of Seven (G7) largest industrial nations taken as a whole had been less than 2.5% in only two of the ten years 1985–94, but was under 2.5% in every year during 1995–2002. And the much-vaunted 'success' of the new British arrangements has to be seen in the context that, during the years 1997–2002, inflation in the UK was lower than the G7 average in only one year (2001).

It is important that there was no mention of the fact that the inflation target was 'symmetric' at the time the MPC was set up. The concept was there, though, in the instruction that inflation of plus or minus one percentage point away from the target was to be considered an aberration, and should set in motion policies to direct inflation back towards the target.

Much was made later of the advantage of Britain's symmetrical inflation target, notably in contrast to that of the European Central Bank (which began operating in January 1999). This was especially so in discussions about whether or not Britain should join the euro. Indeed, reform of the ECB became something of an additional 'test' to the Chancellor's 'famous five' (covered in a subsequent chapter). For a time the perceived success of Britain's 'independent' monetary policy became a reason in itself, in Treasury circles, for hesitation about the euro. 'After years of searching around vainly, we have now found a monetary policy that works,' said one Treasury official. 'Why should we sign up to an inferior version?'

Despite the growing use of the term, the word 'symmetry' was not used in the Chancellor's original pronouncements. 'Frankly, we wish we had thought of it at the time,' Ed Balls said some years later, 'but the truth was we stumbled upon the concept when resisting Treasury and Bank attempts to lower the target, and thought of the word "symmetry" much later.'

One early use of the term was in a pamphlet by Willem Buiter (*Alice in Euroland*), published in April 1999. Buiter was far the most colourful character during the first three years of the MPC's existence. A distinguished international macroeconomist, he had returned from Yale to Cambridge and was a choice for one of the first four 'external' places with which no one could disagree. That is to say, they could not disagree with his appointment: there was plenty of scope for disagreement between Buiter and the other members of the MPC, especially with the Bank or 'politburo' members.

In fact, the Bank did not always act like a politburo when it came to voting, although it took some time for the fact that *all* members of the MPC, including the politburo, were *independently* accountable to Parliament for their voting decisions to show up as independent in their actual voting records. There were also teething troubles over the amount of resources allocated to the outsiders. 'There is no denying that this was a very fraught episode,' said one Bank source. The publicity centred on their access to research and Bank assistance, but it was also apparent to visitors in their physical accommodation.

Thus, in the early days, while the Bank members of the MPC were housed in some style, the 'externals' had to be content with rather cramped conditions. In one sense this was unimportant, but it was indicative of the general divide between insiders and outsiders that took some time to settle. In due course, however, the external members were given better physical surroundings and more assistance. And there was a marvellous moment when one senior insider said that the outsiders were more full-time than the insiders because the former could, if they so chose, work entirely on MPC matters, whereas the insiders had their other Bank duties to fulfil.

Notwithstanding Sir Terence Burns's earlier hunch, the MPC was not set up in a way that would lead obviously to membership of what was then known as the European System of Central Banks. On the contrary, when the Bank of England Bill was finally published on 28 October 1997 (although the MPC had been operating since June), the legislation was proposed as a specifically British model. The Brown camp took almost sadistic pleasure in pointing out that separate legislation altogether would be required for adapting the Bank of England to the European model.

The job of the MPC members was to meet formally once a month, usually on a Wednesday afternoon and the following Thursday morning, with a dinner in between on the Wednesday evening; they had to decide whether, on the basis of the Bank's briefing and their own analysis, interest rates needed to be changed in order to keep the economy on course to achieve the 2.5% inflation target. As noted, they were also charged 'without prejudice to this objective' to 'support the Government's economic policy, including its objectives for growth and employment'.

In *Reforming Britain's Economic and Financial Policy* (2002), the Treasury stated that these objectives were: 'not simply to ensure low and stable inflation and sound public finances but to deliver high and stable levels of growth and employment by ensuring economic and employment opportunities for all. Growth, jobs and fairness are the tests against which this Government will be judged.' In this book the Treasury said that this was the aim 'as set out in the Chancellor's 6 May 1997 letter to the Governor'. In fact, that letter referred to 'high and stable levels of growth and employment' but omitted the reference to 'opportunities for all' and the statement that 'growth, jobs and fairness are the tests against which this Government will be judged'. Although references to full employment, and indeed to Keynes, were to appear in subsequent chancellorial speeches, they were not there in the formal brief for the MPC.

The Bank's *Inflation Report*, which emerges after the Bank's regular quarterly forecasting exercises, delves into many areas of the economy, with sections on 'demand and output' and the 'labour market' as well as 'money and financial markets', 'costs and prices', 'monetary policy since the last report' and 'prospects for inflation'. And the monthly minutes of the MPC's meetings show that the MPC examines all the main macroeconomic issues, both national and international, that one would expect from economists interested in demand management.

Nevertheless the MPC was given only one instrument – interest rates – with which to affect the economy or, more specifically, the outlook for inflation; and the way that instrument was expected to work was by tightening (higher interest rates) or loosening (lower interest rates) credit conditions in the economy in order to work towards the desired outcome.

The MPC knows what the stance of the government's fiscal policy is at any one time – or is briefed in broad terms if that stance is about to alter, e.g. in a forthcoming Budget – and the Treasury representative is always on hand at meetings. The Friday before the week of the monthly meeting the MPC is briefed by about 100 Bank staff; and the week following the meeting it regroups to agree the final version of the minutes. These discussions about the minutes can be quite intensive: although not formally identified in the minutes, members' views can often be traced through the links with 'a view' and the actual vote. The minutes assumed greater importance in the eyes of members as the years went by. Some insiders even thought they detected 'revised views' during arguments about the minutes. If 'information is power' so is the ability to have a forceful say in the way that information becomes 'transparent'.

In the past, fiscal and monetary policy – i.e. changes in levels of taxation and public spending, as well as interest rates – were in the hands of the Chancellor, and at first sight Bank independence suggests that monetary and fiscal policy are less coordinated. The Treasury under Gordon Brown would argue first that coordination

of policy was not always impressive when it was under one roof;
and second that, in any case, while having what is technically
called 'operational independence' the Bank does not possess 'goal
independence' – the independence to set the inflation target.

Unquestionably, fiscal policy under Gordon Brown has been
consciously set in a medium-term context – we shall examine this
later – with the emphasis on 'fiscal rules' designed to achieve
'stability' rather than active management of demand, i.e. total
spending by government, industry and consumers in the economy.
There was a time under previous Labour governments when 'Mini-
budgets' were fashionable and fiscal policy was very active. The MPC
sees the Chancellor's medium-term projections for revenue and
spending and the annual budgetary changes, but the only changes
in fiscal policy between Budgets are the degrees to which spending or
tax revenues unexpectedly differ from forecast.

It proved possible for the MPC to meet every month for over a year
without altering interest rates, from November 2001 to December
2002, and (almost) from February 2000 to February 2001 (rates
had been held at 6% from 10 February 2000 to 8 February 2001,
when they were reduced to 5.75%). But rates were changed five
times in 1997, four times in 1998, six times in 1999 and seven
times in 2001. The four occasions in 1997 were of course in
the shorter period, June–December, because the MPC's first ever
meeting was in June that year.

The impression given during four of the first six years is of a
hyperactive MPC, trying almost monthly to manage demand in the
economy through changes in interest rates. The question has to be
asked whether this is the best way to manage demand in the economy.
There is also the important issue of whether the MPC's brief was ever
an entirely appropriate one for an economy with Britain's particular
problems. An illustration of the thinking behind the first question
was provided early on in the MPC's life, when an MPC member
privately expressed his agreement with a point that had been made
in the press, that increases in interest rates to cool domestic demand
were exacerbating the problem of the continuing rise in the pound,
and that specific taxes on consumers might ease the problem.

In other words, a more active fiscal policy would have eased the very problem highlighted repeatedly by Mervyn King in his capacity as Deputy Governor and spokesman for the MPC when he presented the quarterly inflation reports. This problem, sometimes referred to as 'The Tale of Two Cities' or 'The Tale of Two Economies', was that for much of the period 1997–2002 services were booming but manufacturing industry wasn't; houses prices, in particular, were soaring.

After the 1988–89 house price boom, the collapse of which made a major contribution to the disappearance of talk about a 'Lawson Miracle', Eddie George had said that the monetary authorities must ensure that there should never again be such a boom in house prices. Gordon Brown had talked until he was blue in the face about the importance of avoiding 'boom and bust'. Yet, in the pursuit of 'stability' – growth at around the rate of productive potential and inflation of 2.5% – the MPC often found itself divided between those who wanted to raise interest rates in order to cool the housing market, and those who wished to lower them because they were concerned about the feeble performance of manufacturing output and investment in new plant and machinery. 'Investment' had, after all, been a preoccupation of Gordon Brown's all the way to office; the need for more investment to raise the nation's productive performance and growth rate was one of the central themes of successive Brown Budgets. Capturing the Treasury, so that it should be 'long-termist'; making the Treasury into the kind of Department of Economic Affairs that had effectively been 'seen off' by the Treasury in the 1960s – these were the dreams of Gordon Brown and Ed Balls in particular. The Bank – operationally independent but still nationalised under the 1946 Act – was supposed to deliver much of the stability that provided the backdrop to improved economic performance. The rest would be provided by the new 'fiscal rules'.

Yet under the fashionable and widely acclaimed formula to which it worked, the MPC found that its job became, in effect, to stoke up consumer demand in order to make up for the fact that manufacturing output, investment and exports were severely hampered by a manifestly overvalued exchange rate, and by the collapse in overseas demand after the Wall Street bubble burst.

It was one of the many attractive features of the new system that there was far more information available about what members of the MPC thought about the state of the economy and the problems facing them.

With nine members all making speeches, and both the insiders and the externals taking the view that it was part of their job to get out and about the country explaining themselves – as well as finding out what was happening on the ground – the public speeches flowed thick and fast. One was reminded of the old joke about the frequency with which the Fleet Street journalist Edgar Wallace turned out his detective and horse racing thrillers: 'Have you read the midday Wallace?'

Then there were the frequent appearances before the Treasury Committee, where MPC members had to account for themselves and their actions. Much good information and background thinking was provided to both the Treasury Committee and to the infelicitously entitled House of Lords 'Select Committee on the Monetary Policy Committee of the Bank of England' (for ages there was a wonderful Freudian slip in the spelling of the latter committee's name outside in the corridor: it was termed the 'House of Lords Select Committee on the *Monetory* [my italics] Policy Committee of the Bank of England').

The Treasury Committee seemed to make a speciality out of embarrassing, even 'dusting up', new members of the MPC at their so-called 'confirmation hearings'. The term is inappropriate because, unlike the US Congressional Committee, the Treasury Committee cannot veto an external member appointed by the Chancellor. So it confines itself to making a stir. In the case of Sushil Wadhwani, appointed on 1 June 1999 to succeed Alan Budd, the TSC found an uncannily close resemblance between some of his written answers to their questions and the Bank's official line at the time. In the case of Chris Allsopp, appointed on 1 June 2000 from Oxford (with Steve Nickell of LSE) to replace Willem Buiter and Charles Goodhart, Allsopp was not on top form (he was in the middle of marking examination papers) and was given a very hard time by the

Treasury Committee. But both Wadhwani and Allsopp went on to become strong members of the MPC and few would question their right to have been chosen.

It was interesting that Ed Balls's original idea of a seven-year term was whittled down to three. The reason for this was the difficulty in getting the right people to commit themselves for such a long time. But given the time it takes for new members to play themselves in, some 'externals' argue – with the House of Lords Committee on the Monetary Policy Committee – that five years would be a better length of service. Buiter thought that 'one five-year term only' would eliminate the danger of politically-motivated actions shortly before the question of 'renewal' arose. The first external member to be reappointed for another three years was Steve Nickell. Goodhart was not offered the chance of renewal but might well have liked it. Wadhwani and DeAnne Julius were asked, but turned the offer down, preferring to return to the private sector. Allsopp was not asked, but was offered, and accepted, an important brief to improve the economic and monetary statistics available to the government and the MPC.

The Governor and two Deputy Governors (one for monetary policy and one for financial stability, under the 1998 Bank of England Act) are appointed for five-year terms (renewable) and serve on the MPC concurrently. The two other Bank members, one responsible for Monetary Analysis, the other for Financial Markets and Operations, are appointed by the Court of the Bank of England, and serve three-year (renewable) terms on the MPC.

One can conveniently divide the first six years of the MPC into, roughly speaking, a first period, when the 'outsiders' were Willem Buiter, Charles Goodhart, DeAnne Julius, Budd and Wadhwani, and a second period when the outsiders were Chris Allsopp, Steve Nickell, Kate Barker and Wadhwani (Wadhwani straddles the two periods because there was an interim spell when Alan Budd went over from the Treasury to the Bank from November 1997 to June 1999, before retiring to become master of Queen's College, Oxford).

The first year of the MPC – June 1997 to June 1998 – can be regarded as the fledgling or embryonic year. On 5–6 June 1997 the

MPC had only six members and a mere two of the Chancellor's four external nominees had arrived – Willem Buiter, who was undoubtedly to make the biggest splash of all those who entered the MPC pool, and Charles Goodhart, who had had long experience of the Bank from the inside. Howard Davies, then the only Deputy Governor, left to become Chairman of the new FSA after only two meetings. David Clementi, formerly of Kleinwort Benson, joined the Bank as Deputy Governor in September, immediately becoming an ex-officio member of the MPC – an outsider turned insider, as it were; and DeAnne Julius joined the MPC as the third 'external' from British Airways (having previously worked with Shell).

From June to December 1997 the MPC was, in the neat words of Mervyn King, 'Unanimous on all six occasions.'[4] They had inherited inflation forecasts of above 3% – which Gordon Brown had most certainly made a meal of – and interest rates were raised in June, July, August and November. As King put it: 'Output appeared to be above trend, the labour market was continuing to tighten, and there was a need to slow the growth of domestic demand in order to reduce pressure on supply capacity.'[5]

The unanimity of the votes during the second half of 1997 prompted the first accusations that there was a 'politburo' at work. The Bank members – Eddie George, Mervyn King (by now Executive Director, Monetary Analysis) and Ian Plenderleith (Executive Director, Financial Markets and Operations) and the Deputy Governor (Davies in June and July, Clementi from September) all seemed to vote in concert, and the outsiders – Buiter and Goodhart, joined by Julius in September and Budd in November – while not 'politburo', were very cautious. Goodhart, given his long years at the Bank in the past, seemed at least half an insider; Budd, given his early history as a monetarist and his position after the election on the need to reduce the inflation target, could reasonably be described as a 'hawk'. DeAnne Julius (and subsequently Wadhwani), while in due course making real names for themselves as independently-minded, owned to a nervousness at the beginning. It took five months or so for the real outsiders to play themselves in and pluck up the courage to make their mark.

Thus, insofar as Gordon Brown was trying to 'surround' the Governor and, while granting the Bank independence, to influence that independent policy with the weight of his own nominees, there was not much sign of 'outsider' influence in those early days. But this did not concern Brown at all. After remaining at 6% from October 31 1996 – the last occasion on which the 'Ken and Eddie Show' raised rates – and being increased to 6.25% by Brown on 6 May, rates had been edged up by the MPC in quarter point stages to 7.25% by 6 November 1997. There were signs that the Bank would have liked Brown to do more on the fiscal side (by raising indirect taxes) than he did in July 1997 with his first Budget, and that by December the Bank was reluctant to raise rates further because of the impact on the pound. The average value of the pound had risen in every quarter of 1997. But there was no indication that the Chancellor was unhappy with the course of interest rates; indeed, there was even a suspicion that he would have liked them to rise further in December when the MPC desisted.

On the whole, the MPC was almost as prudent as the prudent Chancellor would have liked during those early months but was showing concern about the high exchange rate – as was the IMF, which gave the Chancellor's economic policy and new monetary arrangements a broad seal of approval but would also have liked to see higher consumer taxes to ease the burden on monetary policy.

The inflation forecasts *were* indicating that, in the absence of corrective action, inflation was likely to breach the 2.5% target. The 'interim' MPC of six members that raised rates by a quarter percentage point at its first meeting on 5–6 June 1997 noted that the previous appreciation of the exchange rate had not yet had an effect on the relative volume of exports and imports but concluded, reasonably, that the impact had merely been delayed. It was clear from the minutes that members expected the increase in rates to lead to a further rise in the pound, but the main concern was 'inflationary risk'. By July, when their only question was whether to raise rates by a quarter or half percentage point (they opted for a quarter) they were taking refuge in the hope that the markets would begin to bring the overvalued pound down. By August the MPC was expressing 'considerable concern about sterling's level and its unbalancing effects on the economy'. The new inflation forecast was still pointing to above 2.5% but, given the concern about the pound, the MPC owned to an acute policy dilemma. It even asked itself whether 'alternative policy instruments' should be considered: 'Apart from quantitative controls, these were of three main types: (1) variable reserve requirements on the banking system; (2) changes to debt management; and (3) foreign exchange market intervention.'[6]

The MPC concluded that financial markets had now become too liberalised for quantitative controls or a call for the banks to make special deposits with the central bank (devices used in the 1960s and 1970s) to be efficacious. They did not think extra sales of government debt – to absorb liquidity – 'would contribute usefully to addressing the current policy dilemma'. The MPC actually agreed on 7 August 1997 that 'intervention was worth contemplating' but this was 'only if it was accompanied by credible actions to put the economy on a course consistent with the inflation target'. The MPC also went on record as saying 'in those circumstances', i.e. 'credible actions', intervention 'could help to bring about an adjustment in the exchange rate, which might otherwise be protracted.'[7]

This was the nearest either the MPC or the Treasury ever came in the period 1997–2002 to giving anything like an endorsement to the kind of action that would have been routine in days gone by.

As Sir George Blunden had told the Treasury and Civil Service Committee on 20 October 1993 about interest rate movements in the UK in the past, 'nearly always they have been made in relation to sterling and what is happening to sterling.' The idea of publishing minutes was only in its infancy when Sir George said that, and he spoke revealingly of the old 'untransparent' days when he pointed out that 'to satisfy the jargon of the day' the explanation for interest rate changes might not have referred to sterling, 'but actually in the discussions which led to the interest rate movements, sterling has always been a commencing point.'

Blunden had warned those contemplating central bank independence: 'I see no reason why sterling will not continue to be a problem for us in the future and the rate of sterling a significant problem.' In August 1997 the fledgling, interim MPC was manifestly concerned about the overvaluation of the pound, but its brief was to *raise* rates if there was a danger that inflation would exceed the target, and there was no sign that the new government was ready to offer 'credible actions' to counterbalance the likely impact of higher interest rates on the pound (other things being equal, higher interest rates attract more money to London, thereby rendering an overvalued pound even more overvalued). The MPC did not specify what such 'credible actions' were but, having ruled out other monetary measures, it was almost certainly thinking of increases in indirect taxation aimed at cooling consumer demand. In order to avoid publishing a forecast that inflation in two years time was likely to exceed 2.5%, the MPC raised rates another quarter percentage point in August. Although the subject of the possibility of intervention was to resurface briefly in due course, that August meeting stands out as one where the stage was now set, given the MPC's brief and the government's aversion to active fiscal policy, for the 'Tale of Two Cities'[8] – booming consumer demand and inflation of house prices, alongside a struggling and increasingly uncompetitive manufacturing sector. Exports, relative to imports, were to perform increasingly badly, and manufacturing investment was not to live up to the hopes of a Gordon Brown who was so obsessed with improving the supply side of the economy by means of all manner of interventionist micro-measures.

Any queries the MPC might have had about the likelihood of 'credible actions' from the government to alleviate the weight placed on monetary policy would have been answered by Sir Alan Budd. As the Treasury's Chief Economic Adviser, Sir Alan was also the Treasury representative at early MPC meetings – a *representative*, to act as liaison man, to guide the Bank on government policy and to report back to the Chancellor – but not a member of the Committee itself. Having been Treasury representative for those first six meetings, Budd was a popular choice when he became the most 'interim' member of an interim committee, by serving on it from November 1997 until May 1999.

Budd, despite being considered a hawk by Brown and Balls, seemed to hit it off with them rather better than Terry Burns did. On 'looking at the books' the new Chancellor, who had castigated Clarke's policies from the Opposition benches, told Budd, 'I ought to be writing you a thank-you letter.' But Brown and Balls did not like Budd's support for a lower (2%) inflation target. By the time Budd joined the MPC on 16 November 1997 it had already had its November meeting – at which he was the Treasury representative – and hoisted rates a further quarter percentage point to 7.25%. The November rise took place after the MPC had seen the inflation forecast and the data and analysis to be incorporated in the quarterly inflation report the following week. The rise was explained by the fact that domestic demand had remained 'robust' and GDP was continuing to grow at 'an unsustainable rate'. From the point of view of the MPC's main brief, inflation had 'not moderated as much as expected in the light of sterling's appreciation since the autumn of 1996'.[9]

The last rise had been in August – also a month when the inflation report was published – and some members of the Bank began to develop a theory that there could be a desirable bias in favour of altering rates only during months when the forecasts and extra knowledge from the draft inflation report were available. This theory did not stand the test of time – the next increase did not take place until seven months later, in June 1998. But Mervyn King, a putative hawk, did not vote for an increase when three others did in January 1998, on the grounds that he first wanted to see the new forecasts. This was regarded as a 'feeble excuse' by another hawk.

Budd had crossed over from the Treasury to join the MPC itself in time for the December 1997 meeting. Hawk though he was, he did not vote for an increase on that first occasion, a vivid illustration of the time it takes for even the best-qualified newcomers to play themselves in – Budd was, after all, the only new member to have witnessed the MPC's proceedings at first hand. 'I am sure that, if he had had the courage of his convictions, Budd would have voted for a rise at his first meeting,' observed one MPC member. As it was, the vote at that December 1997 meeting was a unanimous 'no change', a key factor being the view that the previous rise in the pound would 'come through' via a slowdown in exports (net of imports) and a softening impact on retail prices.

The January 1998 meeting at which King decided to wait for the inflation forecast was the 'coming of age' for that interim committee, in that it was the first occasion on which it disagreed and had a split vote – five to three in favour of 'no change', the ninth member, John Vickers, having not yet taken his seat. Alan Budd joked: 'There were no divisions until I arrived.'

The January vote was also interesting because there were concerns that the Asian crisis of summer and autumn 1997 was having repercussions on the world economy: this had some influence on the 'politburo' and on DeAnne Julius. But the other outsiders were concerned about 'high-profile wage settlements' and wanted to send 'a clear and early signal to the labour market of the MPC's determination to achieve the inflation target.'[10] Willem Buiter was in the lead, but rather than be described as 'hawkish' he preferred the term 'activist'. He wanted to establish the MPC's credibility and pave the way for rate reductions later. Goodhart, who with Budd voted for a rate rise, also acquired the reputation of being an activist, especially after one meeting when he said to the others that to show they were doing their job the MPC should consider changing rates every month, even if it was only by 0.10%. If anything, the impression at this stage was that the Chancellor privately favoured the activists or hawks, if only to get the bad news out of the way. But there is no indication that, notwithstanding the difficult early start to their relationship, George ever felt any pressure from the Chancellor either way over the direction of interest rates.

This did not prevent Gordon Brown's spin-doctor, Charlie Whelan, from annoying the Bank in early October 1998, when he wandered around the press room of the IMF in Washington telling financial journalists, 'Gordon and Eddie have had a word: It's in the bag' – a reference to an imminent rate cut. The Bank insisted they had not had a word, and Bank officials were not amused by the episode. A few days later the MPC did cut rates, but only after a full meeting of the MPC.

Quite apart from regular European and international meetings at which the two would see a lot of each other, Brown and George had monthly lunches from June 1997; the Governor would also see Gus O'Donnell for monthly lunches (or breakfasts) after the latter was brought back to the top Whitehall economics job in spring 1998. O'Donnell also became the Treasury representative at the MPC meetings.

Unlike Alan Greenspan at the US Federal Reserve, George voted last, not first. All concerned regarded him as an excellent chairman, once he had got used to the fact that academics such as Buiter and Goodhart (especially the former) could liven up the proceedings no end and behave relatively informally when it suited them.

Some MPC members used to speculate about what would happen if George were outvoted. Whereas Alan Greenspan would tend to lead the Federal Reserve discussions, George did act more like a chairman, which was what Brown and Balls wanted. One member swore that there were occasions when 'Eddie says he's thinking of voting this way then later – when outnumbered – says he's been swayed by the argument!' The member implied that this indicated a desire always to be on the right side, but George himself openly claimed that he sometimes *was* unsure and was genuinely swayed by the discussion.

Another MPC member on one occasion thought it was not quite cricket when DeAnne Julius said she had very nearly decided to vote against yet another increase in a whole series but had been persuaded not to, and George openly thanked her. George said publicly on one occasion to a Parliamentary committee that he would not consider it a resigning issue if he were outvoted, and indeed never was outvoted. 'Since he votes last, he need never be outvoted,' one member observed. Some external members used to have fun wondering whether George was simply not prepared to be on the losing side, and preferred that course in the end to 'having his way'. A Treasury official stated bluntly: 'It's very important that Eddie should not be in charge.' And there is no doubt that so far from being a dictator, George became a very popular chairman.

In the early days both internal and external MPC members did seem occasionally to change their minds. One of the members appointed after several years maintained that neither he nor anyone else to his knowledge ever approached the meeting not knowing which way to vote, and that neither he nor anyone else (again to his knowledge) ever changed his/her mind. But others say they made up their minds only during the meeting.

George's natural caution rendered him less likely to be as active or 'pro-active' as people like Buiter; and, worried about the Asian crisis, the strength of sterling and a perceptible slowdown, he explained his early 1998 (non-hawkish) voting behaviour to the Treasury Committee by warning that there was a danger of an outright recession if interest rates were raised further.

George's caution about the repercussions of the Asian crisis coincided with a brief period when, notwithstanding the constraints that had been put upon him by the Chancellor's committee, he was able to dominate it in exceptional circumstances. At the meeting on 4 and 5 February 1998 his morale was already boosted by indications that he would certainly be reappointed (although the formal announcement was made a fortnight later on 18 February). Given his concerns about the dangers of a slowdown, he ended his summing-up by asking the Committee to vote on the proposition 'that the Bank's repo rate be left unchanged this month' (on some earlier occasions the proposition had been that it should be increased by a quarter point). The MPC was split four–four, with his Bank colleagues Clementi and Plenderleith, plus the 'dove' DeAnne Julius, voting with him for no change, and King plus the other three 'externals' (Budd, Buiter and Goodhart) favouring 'an immediate increase in rates'. This was a time when Buiter was gaining a very hawkish reputation. The minutes blandly state that then 'The Governor exercised his casting vote in favour of the proposition and the repo rate was thus left unchanged.' What this skates over – although the information is all there in the text – is the quite remarkable fact that, while the ninth MPC chair was vacant at that stage, George allocated the missing vote to himself, and in fact voted twice. This is not quite what the phrase 'casting vote' necessarily suggests to the uninitiated, but the legislation does allow the Governor to have two votes in an *impasse* – it specifically says that the chairman has a 'second casting vote'. Even with a full Committee of nine, the Governor could exercise a second casting vote if the Committee were split three–three–three.

Sir Terence Burns, still Permanent Secretary at the Treasury, was the Treasury's representative at the MPC from November 1997 to February 1998, before Gus O'Donnell was brought back from Washington to be head of the Government Economic Service, the senior official for overseas finance *and* the Treasury representative at the MPC. Burns, O'Donnell and Budd (by now of course a voting member) were all highly amused by Eddie George's use of two votes – a right (and duty) he exercised again 5 March 1998, when he again asked the Committee to vote on a 'no change' proposition, and they were split exactly as before – none, on this occasion, having changed views between meetings, which was not always to be the case. Again, George used his second, 'casting' vote in favour of his own proposition. This prompted one member who had voted for a rise to observe: 'Having voted for no change, he should have used his casting vote for a rise, and put the interests of the country above his personal view.'

The position of the MPC in those days was well epitomised at the time in a remark by someone very close to it: 'I was not surprised by the February vote,' he said, 'because the Bank wants to prove that it is not hawkish, and the outsiders want rates to go up in order to bring them down.'

Willem Buiter, possibly influenced by the academic 'rational expectations' school of economics, saw himself as being forward-looking and trying to influence the financial markets. 'He is trying to jump over the short run,' said a colleague in a rather mixed athletic metaphor. Alan Budd seemed to admire this approach. Buiter was not, in the end, to prove especially hawkish. What he wanted was to drive rates up faster than the central bankers would be inclined to, in order that they could reach a plateau from which they would descend, when the MPC's determination to fight inflation had been well established. The close observer prophesied in

February: 'All the hawks save Charles [Goodhart] will change direction soon' (but in fact Goodhart changed first).

These were exciting times for the 'insiders' as well as the 'externals'. The minutes were much more revealing than under the 'Ken and Eddie Show' and, *a fortiori*, the new 'transparency' brought a seismic shift in the way monetary policy was discussed and the information and analysis on which it was based became available. 'I had a huge sense of exhilaration when I realised that I could enjoy this 'transparency',' said one of the most traditional and cautious (Bank) members of the MPC. 'I can't think why we didn't open up policy like this years ago,' said one of the senior Treasury officials involved.

One of the Bank members said they all began their MPC period by trying to reverse the habit of a lifetime and 'not pay too much attention to the markets'. But he added: 'After the Long Term Capital Management debacle of summer 1998, and what happened to the yield curve (for bonds), we ended up deciding markets had something to say.' Nevertheless, this particular MPC member emphasised: 'Half the time markets are not concerned with what ought to happen, but with what they think the monetary authorities are going to do – with what *will* happen.' An interesting justification of the new transparency was provided by someone previously considered a most 'dyed-in-the-wool' traditionalist (on the MPC): 'The importance of the move from intermediate targets [like the money supply] to final targets [inflation] is that they lie a long way ahead. You *have* to explain the process of getting there.'

George's perfectly legitimate casting vote on those two occasions in spring 1998 when he was concerned about recession saw the Governor at his most influential. In his new role as chairman of a committee and not the all-powerful Bank voice he previously was, he could not normally determine Bank policy on interest rates; he could merely influence what the Bank decided now actually counted. But he was one of nine, and not so dominant in public or private as Alan Greenspan at the Federal Reserve. As noted, Greenspan steered the Federal Reserve Open Market Committee, voted first and was seldom challenged. George, while often at the end of the first day giving an indication of the way he thought the balance of argument lay, always let Mervyn King speak first on the Thursday morning and left his own final view to last. 'I sometimes don't know which way I am going to vote when I enter the room,' George once said disarmingly. After letting King go first on the Thursday morning, George would then invite members to speak in a random order, as they explained which way they were inclined to vote and why.

It is an immense tribute to George that, notwithstanding the initial hostility towards him on the part of the Brown camp, and despite the fact that the Committee system was designed in part to 'surround the Governor', he seemed to go from strength to strength in public esteem. True, he received stick from the press and from industrialists in the North-east in particular when he emphasised that achieving the inflation target took priority, under his brief, over the problems of manufacturing regions suffering from too high an exchange rate.

But George's authority and reputation during the MPC years 1997–2003 seemed to grow and grow. While the other members of the MPC all made frequent speeches and established themselves in their own right – they were, after all, personally accountable for their contributions to monetary policy – George reigned supreme. When appearing with MPC colleagues in front of the Treasury Committee (TSC), George tried to bring others into the debate. But the TSC tended to concentrate on the Governor – so much so that when George on one occasion did manage to bring in a colleague towards the end, that particular member recalled: 'I had become so bored that I began counting items on the flock wallpaper. When asked I had no idea what they were talking about and was reduced to saying, "I agree with the Governor".'

At the April 1998 meeting of the MPC the dilemma that would become more and more apparent in later years was already there: a two-speed economy, with services booming and manufacturing, hit by the high pound, threatening to go into recession, but only one instrument, interest rates, to deal with it. One of the external members said at the time: 'We are in no man's land. I don't really know what's happening to exports or wages. This is a humbling experience.' Another said, 'before we arrived, we had the idea that it would be a brave member who stepped out of line from the Bank's "politburo" consensus.' In fact Mervyn King, gaining his reputation as a hawk, had voted for a rise in rates in February, March and April and stepped out of line from his 'politburo' colleagues. That was the beginning of the end of the 'politburo' theory. In due course Ian Plenderleith, regarded as a quintessentially Bank man and a close acolyte of George's, would establish his independence too – on one occasion being in a minority of one because he did not like the arguments of the others. When trying to weigh up the impact of the Asian crisis that April, one 'outsider' commented, 'It would have helped if the Bank hadn't abolished its overseas department'. The overseas department was in due course reconstituted in different form.

As well as contrasting 'activists' and 'cautious bankers', another way of looking at the differences to emerge at the MPC in the spring of 1998 was not so much between insiders and outsiders but between 'the professors and the central bankers'. The professors, notably Goodhart and Buiter, wanted to raise rates to a peak to show they had control over inflation. The central bankers, including George, did not wish to lose 'credibility' by changing them too often.

King, although 'Bank', was also in the professorial category. While being described as a 'hawk', King objected to the categorisation. As far as he was concerned, he and the rest of the MPC were trying to achieve an inflation target of 2.5%. No one was hawkishly saying 'let unemployment rip', neither were the so-called 'doves' tolerating inflation above 2.5%. Otherwise they would be in breach of their contract.

Thus, the professors at this stage were in a hurry and influenced by all the economic literature about nurturing 'expectations'. By contrast, the natural reaction of central bankers such as Eddie George was to wait for the next month's figures – 'more data'. But as soon as one member was 'categorised' he could easily change his mind. Thus Goodhart, a professor, suddenly voted against a rise in April – probably influenced by the latest rise in the exchange rate.

Some members have admitted that, over the years, they suspected one or two others of voting a 'popular' way to make a point, in the certain knowledge that the majority of the committee was moving another way and they would not affect their decision. In May 1998 one Bank official observed: 'It is easy to ride a trend. The difficulty is spotting turning points in the economy. What the present position shows is that half of them think the economy is close to a turning point (where the danger becomes recession and further interest rate rises risk overkill) and half don't. That's what you'd expect statistically.'

One insider, close to the MPC but not on it, said at the time, 'They are finding they don't know how monetary policy works' (in April 1999 John Vickers, the new Bank Economics Director and ex-officio MPC member, produced by popular demand a document on the 'transmission mechanism' of monetary policy – not just for the benefit of non-MPC members, it appeared).

Echoing Harold Macmillan, who when Chancellor in the mid-1950s had described steering the economy as trying to catch a train with 'last year's Bradshaw' (then the official railway timetable), one MPC member observed in those early days, 'We find ourselves in a swamp of uncertainty: we don't know where we're going, where we are or where we've been.'

Given that Gordon Brown was setting fiscal policy for the medium term, and largely eschewing changes in tax rates or levels of public spending as weapons of demand management (i.e. of influencing the overall level of spending in the economy), the MPC effectively found itself trying to 'fine-tune' the economy on a monthly basis. One member said that Gordon Brown, who had hired him, might be obsessed with 'stability in the long run' but 'they forget that the long run is a series of short runs'.

The level of the exchange rate, i.e. the rising pound, was a continual matter of concern for many members of the MPC, but their brief was that the exchange rate only mattered insofar as it affected inflation. Nevertheless, they knew it was having a bad effect on the competitiveness and profitability of exports. They were also aware that the higher the pound went, while bad for exports and long-term investment, the more the process helped them to achieve the inflation target in the short run. Built into the MPC's *de facto* procedure was the paradox that if, not least because of the rising pound, the inflation figure looked like falling short of the 2.5% target, then the MPC would be obliged to stoke up consumer demand (and house prices) in order to achieve the target. The pursuit of 'stable inflation' meant the deliberate creation, or at least aggravation, of instability in certain sectors.

On a couple of occasions during the period mid-1997 to mid-2000, Charles Goodhart and Sushil Wadhwani, supported by DeAnne Julius, raised the question of intervention in the exchange markets with the intention of deliberately lowering the value of the pound. The reaction from the majority of members – not just the putative 'politburo' but also from the highly influential Willem Buiter – was that intervention was a waste of time and unlikely to achieve the desired result. The tendency was to blame the strength of the pound on the weakness of the euro, about which the majority of the MPC, supported by the Bank staff, said they could do little. In any case, intervention was largely the province of the Treasury, which was responsible for exchange rate management. The original letter from the Chancellor to the Governor on 6 May 1997 had stated: 'The Government will be responsible for determining the exchange rate regime.' But it did add that: 'The Bank will have its own separate pool of foreign exchange reserves which it may use at its discretion to intervene in support of its monetary policy objective.'

The entire Whitehall/Bank of England machine had been so wounded by Black Wednesday that – even under the Chancellorship of Kenneth Clarke, who was undoubtedly concerned about the strong pound – it had gone from one extreme to another. A whole generation of officials, such as Eddie George in the Bank and Sir Nigel Wicks and David Peretz in the Treasury (senior officials on the overseas side, with responsibility at various times for exchange rate policy), had moved from the position that intervention in the markets should be an almost routine affair to the view that intervention was both undesirable and ineffectual.

Charles Goodhart, the most distinguished monetary economist on the MPC, argued that at the very least, even if others did not agree with his view that they should intervene, there was a case (if you believed that the pound was overvalued and would eventually fall) for selling sterling and buying dollars and euros in order to improve or protect the Bank of England's balance sheet. Incidentally, the majority of the MPC members who were opposed to intervention would also say that the Bank's balance sheet restricted their scope, and any serious intervention would have to come from the Treasury. At various times the Chancellor would be asked at press conferences about his policy towards sterling and he would always answer, whatever the level at the time, that he believed sterling should be 'stable and competitive'.

Intervention seems to have taken place on no more than two occasions during the 1997–2002 period, and then as part of a G7 effort to calm the markets. For instance, the Chancellor sanctioned a small British contribution to a G7 effort to steady the euro in the week before the annual meetings of the World Bank and IMF in Prague in September 2000.

On the whole, at least until the storm clouds descended on the world economy in the autumn of 2002 and the imbalances in the UK became more obvious – poor manufacturing performance, a huge and growing trade deficit, but a consumer boom encouraged by debt and rising house prices – the MPC had a remarkably good run in popular esteem. It became fashionable to describe the formation and workings of the MPC as the greatest success of Brown's Chancellorship, and there was widespread international admiration for the UK 'model'. As the restrictive nature of the statutes of the European Central Bank (ECB) became more and more manifest, the MPC's 'symmetric' approach became an object of admiration in the Eurozone too, and in spring 2003 the ECB itself went some way to making its approach more symmetrical. It announced that it was aiming at an inflation rate of 'close to 2%'. But this was interpreted as meaning 'close to but under' 2%, rather than 'close to and possibly over' 2%.

Although Gordon Brown had intensely disliked the 'showbiz' aspect of the meetings between Kenneth Clarke and Eddie George, the MPC itself became a rather glamorous body, not just in the City but also in the public eye generally. From the more serious point of view of *policy*, economists and City analysts noted that after the formation of the MPC the differential between British and German bond yields narrowed (although it has to be said that there was an upward 'blip' in the second half of 1997). Reviewing the MPC 'two years on', Mervyn King noted that both earnings and prices had grown less than would have been expected from past relationships and that this seemed to be due to 'a fall in inflation expectations'.[11] But he was careful to emphasise that there were other factors at work: 'Part of the performance of the last two or three years can be attributed to a combination of the "credibility windfall" resulting from the new monetary policy framework and the benign impact on inflation of the higher exchange rate and lower commodity and import prices.'[12] The Treasury had to admit in 2002 that, while 'professional expectations' (i.e. of the financial markets) of inflation one or two years ahead had fallen to around the 2.5% target, the expectations of the general public were still of inflation in the 3.5–4% range.[13]

In November 2002 King was able to point out that: 'over the past decade inflation has averaged 2.5% and has been no lower than 1.5% and no higher than 3.3%.'[14] This period embraced the ten years of 'inflation targeting', including five and a half years of the MPC. Over the same period, real gross domestic product had grown at 2.76% a year, compared with a long-term average (1956–2002) of 2.42% (but of course output had been depressed in the base year 1992–93 by the recession that preceded Black Wednesday). Output had also been 'much more stable than before'. He also argued that 'shocks to the UK from the world economy and from the sterling real exchange rate have been as large, if not larger, over the past five years than in earlier periods.' In theory, acknowledged King, the causation could have run from a more stable economic environment to lower inflation. Wadhwani and DeAnne Julius had many times drawn attention to the impact of more intense competition in 'globalised' product markets, a trend which was independent of both inflation targeting and the formation of the MPC. But from King's point of view the new thing was that now 'businesses and families expect that monetary policy will react to offset shocks that are likely to drive inflation away from target.'[15] At the very least, monetary policy was not *adding* to the volatility of the economy in the way that it did in earlier decades.

Or was it? While the 'overall' picture might look benign, there was a case for saying that the way economic policy in general and the MPC in particular worked during the 1997–2002 period was to aggravate the problems of manufacturing industry and the traded goods sector, with the potential threat of great instability in the future. The same could be said of the way the MPC found itself stoking up demand for personal consumption and housing, in accordance with its brief.

George summarised the situation in evidence to the Treasury Committee and in many a speech: 'The responsibility of the MPC is absolutely clear and that is to deliver inflation around the target.' The MPC did 'take account of the exchange rate in setting monetary policy,' Sir Edward said, but all the MPC could do was 'recognise that the impact of monetary policy, and particularly the impact of the strong exchange rate, have differential impacts on differing sectors of the economy and that in turn can have differential impacts on regions in which those sectors are concentrated'.[16]

The Treasury Committee found that: 'The strength of sterling has had a disproportionately severe effect on the manufacturing sector of the UK economy, with many companies finding it difficult to remain competitive particularly in European markets.'[17] The minutes and speeches of the MPC almost from its inception are strewn with references to the impact the strength of sterling was having on the trade balance, and in one notable speech Sir Edward George acknowledged, in May 2002: 'Of course, we'd all have been much happier with better balanced growth. Stimulating domestic demand to offset the external weakness – the only option available to us – was very much a second-best option. It is not without its own risks, including the build-up of household debt and the current exuberance in the housing market.'[18]

Sir Edward maintained: 'It was better than doing nothing at all. This would have meant a much sharper slowdown, and probably recession in the economy as a whole.'[19] And, of course, quite apart from the fact that the MPC was frequently criticised for over-estimating the dangers of inflation and undershooting its target, under its terms of reference it was not allowed 'to do nothing'. It was charged with aiming at 2.5% inflation at all times, with the proviso that, if there was a big shock to the economy, it could use its discretion about the speed with which it tried to return towards the target.

A good 'bird's eye view' of the case for the success of the MPC was included in the Treasury's *Reforming Britain's Economic and Financial Performance* (2002). The argument goes that the MPC raised interest rates four times in 1997 in order to head off inflationary pressure; then in 1998 and early 1999 the MPC cut rates aggressively, thereby avoiding the danger of a sharp slowdown (in the wake of first the Asian crisis of 1997 and second, the shock to the world economy from the Russian default of August 1998 and the financial market crisis associated with the collapse of the Long-term Capital Management (LTCM) hedge fund in September 1998). After that the MPC raised rates in September 1999 in wise anticipation of future inflationary risks, despite the fact that actual inflation was below target. It later cut rates in February 2001 as a precautionary measure because of the slowdown in the USA. And it showed how it could act in a crisis by pre-emptively cutting rates between scheduled meetings after 11 September 2001.

Certainly, under the aegis of the MPC the British economy enjoyed good overall growth, low unemployment by the standards of recent decades, and did not, as was widely forecast by City analysts and the press, go into recession as a result of those various shocks from the world economy – at least not up to 2002.

But it seemed extraordinary that, after all the concerns noted above about the dangers of a slowdown, or even recession, that were being expressed in spring 1998, the MPC voted by eight to one to raise rates in June 1998, the very week that the CBI quarterly industrial trends survey had sounded the alarm bells about the dangers of a manufacturing recession. This action had to be reversed with a vengeance. There were no fewer than seven reductions in interest rates between October 1998 and June 1999. What was interesting was the speed with which Willem Buiter moved from being a hawk to a dove when he realised the threat posed by the deterioration in the world economy. He had a quite simple explanation – Macmillan's 'Events, dear boy, Events ...'. Buiter had a magnetic personality and the speed and intensity of his turnaround was a wonder to his colleagues.

It was a landmark when Buiter stepped down from the MPC in May 2000. Having made a major contribution to establishing the MPC's counter-inflationary credentials early on, he had also played an important role in recognising the gravity of the Asian crisis of 1997 and the financial crisis associated with the Russian default and the LTCM debacle in summer 1998. 'The markets froze in real time,' he observed of the panic of September 1998. When that crisis receded, he was then in the vanguard of the move to avert the possibility of 'overshooting' the target, as the MPC raised rates progressively from 5% to 6% between 8 September 1999 and 10 February 2000.

Buiter had not hesitated to take on Mervyn King in the bitter battle over the resources allocated to the MPC; neither, when he sensed deflationary dangers, was he averse to challenging King's more hawkish views. On one occasion Buiter proposed a change in interest rates of only one-eighth. On the other hand, he thought it was absurd to meet the renewed inflationary threat of late 1999 and early 2000 with a series of quarter-point changes, and would have preferred bigger moves. Although his fondness for straight talking and his distaste for bureaucracy ruffled feathers, members of the 'politburo' confessed that they missed him when he left. But he was of the firm view that members should serve for one term only, albeit a five- or six-year one. This was also the view of other MPC members, such as Alan Budd, who thought Parliament would insist on five years and then discovered what little power Parliament had in these matters. As Buiter put it, the current three-year term was 'on the short side to accumulate and amortise your MPC human capital', and there was a threat to members' independence of judgement 'from even the appearance that they might want to ingratiate themselves with the powers that be' in the hope of reappointment.[20] A neat twist to this theory was provided in June 2002 when, with the decision about the next Governor looming, Mervyn King was accused by a member of the Treasury Committee of having softened his stance on inflation in order to ingratiate himself with the government. In fact, when the minutes were published it turned out that King was the only member of the MPC to vote for an increase in rates in June – and he did the same in July.

For Buiter the biggest surprise of his time on the MPC had been the strength of the pound. In explanation he said, 'I think we are in a familiar but fearsome swamp of confidence factors, safe havens, herd behaviour and market psychology. It is both unwelcome and very surprising.'[21]

Buiter said the pound's strength was 'not rationally explained by our [the MPC's] behaviour, nor by reasonable market anticipation.' During the first three years of the MPC's existence the pound had risen by about 30%, and in February 2000 its value of DM 3.25 (in what Sir Edward George liked to call 'old money') was way above the level of DM 2.95 that had proved unsustainable within the ERM and led to Black Wednesday. There were once again signs of the kind of house price boom in the south of England that had been a feature of the late 1980s, and the economy was looking increasingly unbalanced, with imports outstripping exports and manufacturing output and investment performing dismally.

The other MPC member to depart at the end of May 2000 was Charles Goodhart, who shared Buiter's view that the pound was seriously overvalued but, unlike Buiter, thought intervention in the markets was worth trying. The conventional view of the MPC, expressed on many occasions by George and King, was that the pound's strength was due to the weakness of the euro, and that was that. The MPC discussed the possibility of intervention three times during its first three years, but never got very far. While Buiter's departure was voluntary, Goodhart's was not, and it was a blot on the Chancellor's hitherto good record that such an internationally distinguished economist was not offered a second term. On the other hand, some continuity of view was provided by the fact that Goodhart's London School of Economics friend and colleague Sushil Wadhwani's three-year term did not expire until the end of May 2002. Apart from anything else, one of the roles of the academic 'externals' was to be able to stand up to the 'politburo' both intellectually and in terms of market experience, and Wadhwani qualified on both counts. Wadhwani was especially impressive in pointing to the links between the stock market and the real economy, and showed a much greater understanding than the 'politburo' of the threat to the world economy on the stock market collapse which greeted the new Millennium.[22]

Steve Nickell, also a member of the LSE 'mafia', and Chris Allsopp from Oxford, succeeded Buiter and Goodhart on 1 June 2000. With DeAnne Julius about to depart (August 2000) Nickell's appointment was timely. Julius had been questioning the 'hawkishness' of the MPC – not that she was 'soft on inflation', but she did think the forecasts were not taking enough account of world and labour market trends; she made an impressive contribution to the debate and was widely admired by commentators and analysts.

Nickell, as an eminent labour economist, was an uncontroversial appointment. Allsopp, with previous experience at the Bank itself and at the OECD, had a distinguished record in macroeconomics, including a major contribution to the debate about North Sea oil and its impact on the exchange rate in the early 1980s.

Having raised rates in quarter-point steps between September 1999 and February 2000, because the fear of the majority was of rising domestic demand and the need not to overshoot the inflation target, the MPC kept rates at 6% for a whole year before lowering them to 5.75% on 8 February 2001. They were then reduced progressively in quarter-point stages to 4.50% on 8 November 2001, amid fears about the ramifications of the US-led world economic slowdown (the September reduction was announced 'between meetings' as part of the general central bank reaction to the extra fears for the world economy that arose after the 11 September attack on New York).

Concern about the US slowdown spreading to Europe had been voiced by the doves towards the end of 2000 and in January 2001. The early reaction of the 'politburo' was that Europe would remain isolated: on 11 January Allsopp had joined Julius and Wadhwani in advocating a cut, and the relatively new arrival as Bank chief economist, Charlie Bean of the LSE (officially Executive Director, Monetary Analysis) had also voted for a cut. At this stage Bean would definitely have been seen as an 'outsider' still being transformed into an insider. The doves lost that vote. Although influenced by the threat of the US slowdown hitting the UK, they put their argument in terms of the remit: inflation had been below target since April 1999 and recent developments were likely to push it further below. Given that the MPC's remit was inflation, not demand management, there was a case for action. The majority, however, wanted clear evidence that the labour market and the pace of growth of consumer spending were easing. Yet the next month (February 2001) the MPC voted unanimously for a quarter-point reduction. While they were deliberating they received a 'flash' estimate from the government statistical services that inflation between January 2000 and January 2001 had fallen to 1.8%; the minutes noted, 'Recent news implied that UK price and cost pressures remained benign.'

However, the underlying concerns were there for the 'politburo'. With household debt having risen relative to income and net trade having made a negative contribution to GDP growth for five years, there were imbalances in the economy. But the threat was expressed in terms of the impact an eventual fall in the pound would have on inflation.[23]

These imbalances really became the story of the MPC. While one inevitably talked about 'hawks' and 'doves' and comparisons were made between the 'symmetric' target for the MPC and the deflationary bias of the ECB target (0–2% range in the medium term, before 'close to 2%' from spring 2003), the real defect of the MPC remit was that it proved in practice to be a mechanism for exacerbating, if not actually creating, imbalances. 'Doves' could worry about the threat from the rest of the world to the overall growth rate of the economy; 'hawks' could worry about the strength of domestic demand. But the job of all was to 'achieve' an inflation target; they could fret about 'imbalances' but not do much to correct them – except via intervention in the exchange markets, which they eschewed.

If Sir Edward George was the chairman of the MPC and the foremost public face of the Bank, Mervyn King was the shop steward, the public face of the MPC at press conferences and in his frequent speeches and lectures. There were times when some of the 'externals' thought King gave a one-sided view of the inflationary dangers or of productivity trends on such occasions; but they also thought he did a reasonable job, and they themselves had the opportunity to redress the balance in their own speeches and appearances before the Treasury Committee. For instance, Wadhwani and Julius certainly got their more optimistic views about productivity and world inflationary trends across to the outside world. At the time of writing they seem to have been more right about the impact of global disinflationary trends than about productivity gains in the UK. On the other hand, as imports continued to rise at a much faster pace than exports, and the ratio of household debt to income rose and rose, the concerns of the 'hawks' about domestic imbalances appeared to be amply justified. In a typical warning in April 2000, King pointed out: 'the internal imbalances in each country – differences between growth of domestic demand and the supply of output – are the mirror image of external imbalances – current account surpluses and deficits.'[24]

As King observed almost 18 months later, after the 2001 series of cuts which brought rates to 4% by 8 November 2001, one would have to go back to 1955 to find a time when interest rates were last as low as 4%. He made it plain that the world background was a major factor – world industrial production had grown 6.5% in the year to August 2000 and fallen 3% in the following 12 months. British manufacturing output had fallen for three successive quarters, although the economy as a whole was still growing at close to its long-run trend.[25]

But the huge underlying imbalance in the economy was shown by the fact that 'over the past five years, final domestic demand has grown at an average annual rate of nearly 4%, much faster than the 2.75% growth rate of output.' The imbalance between import and export growth meant that, in the jargon, 'net trade will make a negative contribution to economic growth for the sixth year in a row.' This was unprecedented in modern history, 'by which I mean since 1800.'[26]

Frightened by these imbalances, and not feeling impelled to move rates either way by minor variations in inflation or the inflation forecast, the MPC kept rates at 4% for the whole of 2002. But as the year wore on, it became more and more apparent that the 'imbalances' were not going away: indeed, consumer borrowing was rising apace, house prices were soaring and, for all Gordon Brown's desire for stability, there was more and more danger that what was being witnessed was yet another example of 'boom and bust'. A Bank for International Settlements analysis showed that, of 15% growth in real private consumption between 1996 and 2001, just over one-third was financed by higher disposable income, most of the rest being financed by higher property prices ('equity withdrawal') and some by the rise – before the 2002 fall – in equity prices. Professor Wynne Godley noted that net lending by banks and other financial institutions to individuals rose from 3% of personal disposable income in 1992 to 15% in the third quarter of 2002. It then leapt 1.5% in October to 16.5%. As Godley said: 'It was not the rise in debt which generated the rise in demand so much as the rise in net lending – that is, the rise in the rise in debt.'[27]

This could not go on indefinitely. Godley pointed out that an eventual reduction in the lending ratio from similar heights in the early 1970s and late 1980s had ended in tears on both occasions; and King wryly noted, 'something which is unsustainable can't go on for ever.'[28] In particular, King pointed out that the improvement in the terms of trade (the ratio of export to import prices) resulting from the rise in the real exchange rate had boosted real incomes while, hit by the high exchange rate, the profitability of manufacturing industry was now 'very low'.[29]

As 2002 was drawing to a close, Gordon Brown's reputation for prudence came under attack: his growth forecasts were revised downwards in the face of the impact the worldwide slowdown was having on UK exports and investment. But these new factors were being imposed on an economy whose export and investment sectors were already suffering – in both output and profitability – from the prolonged overvaluation of the pound. Manufacturing output, remarkably, was no higher in 2002 than in 1995.

The innovation of the MPC had been widely regarded as an outstanding success, contributing to the stability and reputation for prudence that Gordon Brown and his colleagues desperately sought. The UK central bank model had drawn heavily on the work of Ed Balls, who had outlined the bare bones of it way back in 1992 in his Fabian pamphlet and alighted on the magic of symmetry only after Labour had come into office. But when urging an independent central bank upon the then Shadow Chancellor Gordon Brown, Balls himself had emphasised that 'the UK cannot achieve sustainable growth or full employment without a manufacturing and export-led recovery.'[30] Sterling, he wrote, had depreciated to 'a more realistic level' after Black Wednesday. This provided industry with a boost to competitiveness and profitability which could and should be translated into manufacturing investment, output and jobs.

Britain, Balls had argued, tended towards 'short-termism' by putting 'consumption and earnings before savings and productivity growth.' Alas, under the widely admired MPC the noble attempt at providing stability and long-termism had evolved into a position where the exchange rate rose too high, damaging manufacturing, and the function of the MPC appeared to be to stoke up consumer demand in a way which made the economic 'imbalances' even worse.

Few were more aware of the trouble lying in store than the Deputy Governor, Mervyn King, whose appointment as Governor (to date from 1 July 2003) was announced on 27 November 2002 – the day of a pre-budget report unveiling gloomier economic forecasts and higher borrowing. The very timing of the announcement of King's succession was brought forward by the Treasury in a blatant attempt to divert attention from the deterioration in the fiscal position.

Certainly the MPC has managed demand in the British economy to achieve a higher growth rate in recent years than recorded by the Eurozone. But has the MPC been the success it has been cracked up to be? Or has it been yet another example of the way successive British Chancellors – such as Nigel Lawson – search for magic 'rules' and end up abandoning the (putatively) traditional British belief in pragmatism?

'Balance the budget over the cycle and leave monetary policy to the constrained discretion of technical experts' is not an unfair summary of the brief with which Gordon Brown sought stability; and stability was meant to be the means to the end of improved economic performance, as well as other Labour goals to which Brown aspired.

The tradition grew up that every time a member of the MPC was due to leave because his term was up, he (or she) was allowed an extra five minutes' reflection in front of the others. One who left in 2002 said: 'All say it is a good time to go – things can only get worse.' Ironically, Mervyn King, perhaps the most openly concerned member of all, was now due to stay and lead. At least until the problems became more apparent in the course of 2002–03, Treasury officials were privately arguing that the 'success' of the MPC meant that Britain now had an alternative to adopting 'European' solutions such as the ERM or the euro. But there appeared to be something very odd about a much-lauded MPC system under which individual members felt increasingly divided within themselves: it seemed that one half of the typical MPC membership wished to raise interest rates during 2002 to calm the boom in consumer spending and house prices; but the other half wanted lower interest rates to assist manufacturing and make the pound less attractive to overseas investors. In the end, the pound did descend in the first half of 2003 towards more realistic levels. But a lot of damage had been done to the nation's manufacturing industry en route.

The MPC had coped with its quandary by keeping interest rates unchanged at 4% from November 2001 for the whole of 2002. Meanwhile, a Treasury official walking through the resplendent old world chambers of the Bank looked about him and sniffed: 'All this in order to decide whether to change interest rates.'

The MPC reduced rates to 3.75%, the lowest rate since the mid-1950s, on 6 February 2003 in response to new Bank forecasts which showed a deterioration in the domestic and international outlook. Shortly afterwards it was announced that Mervyn King's successor as Deputy Governor would be Rachel Lomax, a former Treasury high-flyer, who was Permanent Secretary at the Department of Transport. A welcome innovation was the appointment of Richard Lambert, former Editor of the *Financial Times*, to the MPC to succeed Allsopp. While it was strange that Allsopp had not been offered reappointment, Lambert's wide experience of the real world made him a good candidate for the first non-economist to be appointed as an external member.

On the eve of George's retirement, Gordon Brown delivered a heartfelt tribute to the Governor in his Mansion House speech of 18 June. The atmosphere that evening, during George's last appearance at the dinner as Governor, was a complete transformation from the difficult way in which Brown had first approached his relations with the Governor. Whatever lay in store for the MPC and Brown's reputation in the future, George was undoubtedly going out 'on a high'.

George's triumphal departure left a hot topic for speculation among MPC members themselves and the veritable industry of 'MPC watchers'. Although Mervyn King was pre-eminently qualified to succeed Sir Edward George, would the new Governor end up dominating proceedings in a way the MPC system had been designed – so far successfully – to avoid? Or would he himself also evolve into the perfect Chairman?

CHAPTER TEN

Gordon Brown's Treasury

*O*f Brown's Chancellorship is remembered for nothing else in years to come, it will almost certainly be for the granting of operational independence to the Bank of England. The event made an impact, not only in Britain but also in financial circles around the world.

Yet if Gordon Brown's eventual place in history is only for this, his soul will not be marching on as briskly as he would have liked. The independence of the Bank, a reputation for devotion to financial stability, the Labour Party as the Party of low inflation – all these were achievements of which a Labour Chancellor should be proud. But they were only a means to an end. They were on no account the be-all and end-all of his economic policy. For all the perceived success of the Monetary Policy Committee, Brown must often have felt the need to restrain himself when hearing or reading – as he did on many occasions – that the MPC was the finest achievement of the first leg (1997–2001) of his Chancellorship – indeed, of the first Blair government. Such accolades were all very well, and the accompanying footnote in history was that this was the first Labour government ever to have survived without being either derailed or seriously diverted by the advent of a financial crisis.

But from Brown's point of view, financial stability was not an end in itself. His strategy was to eliminate the obstacles to his pursuit of Labour policies – not 'old' Labour policies, which paid little heed to 'the market', but what one might term 'Middle Labour' policies, which were as close to traditional Labour ideas about 'social justice' as 'the market', the constraints epitomised by the vogue concept of 'globalisation' and domestic electoral considerations allowed.

Monetary policy, the power to vary interest rates, with an impact on the value of savings and the cost of borrowing, which in turn affects the level of both consumer spending and business investment, is an important tool of macroeconomic management. If anything, under Brown it was allowed to become too important a tool, so that fiscal policy – the power to alter levels of taxation and government spending – virtually fell into desuetude as a means of steering the economy in the short term.

But if fiscal policy as a tool of economic management – the management of demand for goods and services in the economy – was unfashionable, fiscal policy as a political objective became all-important. For government is not really about monetary policy. Government is about 'getting and spending' – about what Gordon Brown, both defensively and dismissively, used to refer to as 'tax and spend'.

As we have seen in earlier chapters, the Labour Party was so bruised by a succession of electoral defeats – 1979, 1983, 1987 and 1992 – that by the time it campaigned for office in 1996–97 (it never quite knew when an election might be called during this period: the Major government by this time was so dishevelled that it might have fallen apart at almost any stage) Labour had undergone a metamorphosis and become 'New Labour'.

The characteristic of New Labour that will almost certainly be recognised by the majority of the electorate is 'spin'. The desire to put the best face on things is hardly new to politics, but by common consent Labour after 1997 took the obsession with 'appearances' to new extremes. And the area to which this obsession particularly applied was the central arena for any government of the *soi disant* left: the arena of 'getting and spending' or 'tax and spend'.

Although a visitor from outer space would not necessarily deduce it from the standard rhetoric, even Conservative governments 'tax and spend'. Even the most rabid right-wingers believe in raising taxes for the purposes of defence and for the roads on which troops must be transported. The debate between left and right about 'tax and spend' is essentially one of the *degree* to which governments should tax and spend. But this did not stop Gordon Brown and his colleagues from saying, for political and vote-catching purposes, that they were against the very concept of 'tax and spend'.

This approach was a reaction, indeed an overreaction, not only to all those successive electoral defeats but also to the prevailing climate of the times. It was not just electoral votes that counted: it was also the votes of the owners or managers of 'capital' – i.e. not only the funds of the very rich, but the insurance and pension funds administered on behalf of the majority of the population – that mattered. And the prevailing view, throughout the 1980s and 1990s, was that high taxation and high government spending were somehow bad in themselves and that, in the absence of control on capital movements, governments – especially left-wing governments – were at the mercy of the vagaries of the flows of international capital.

Such factors served to reinforce the fear of being dubbed 'the Party of high taxation' which had haunted Labour during the succession of electoral defeats that preceded the rise of Blair and Brown to the position of Labour's ruling duumvirate. Close observation of President Clinton's perceived success with policies that aimed to lower the budget deficit (and, with it, long-term interest rates) reinforced the cautious New Labour views. Clinton had successfully wooed voters on the 'middle ground' while trying to do what he could for the Democrats' traditional constituency with an assortment of 'welfare to work' and 'tax credit' policies aimed at ending 'welfare dependency' and 'making work pay'.

Gordon Brown and Ed Balls studied the US system before the election and had the usual Treasury official stationed in the Washington Embassy from mid-1997, one of whose principal tasks was to study US experience, learn the lessons and pass them on. Indeed, it was soon obvious to Treasury officials that 'welfare to work' was a major obsession of the incoming Chancellor. But it also became apparent that, while the new team had worked hard on certain specific areas, such as the independence of the Bank and a 'windfall' tax on utilities to finance the initial 'Welfare to Work' programme – referred to rather grandly by Gordon Brown, in an all too conscious echo of Roosevelt, as 'the New Deal' – their preparations in many other areas were decidedly thin, for all the years they had spent in Opposition.

The Treasury itself had done what it could to prepare for the new government, including, as noted, having contact with Labour over the previous twelve months – an innovation of John Major's, previous practice having been for such contacts to be made only during the election campaign itself. There had not been a change of government since 1979, and older Treasury officials in 1997 were mindful of how ill-prepared they had been for the incoming Thatcher government in 1979. 'Frankly, the Treasury served Geoffrey Howe very poorly for two years [1979–81],' said one senior official, 'not because we were unreconstructed "pinkos" but because we couldn't get our minds round the new agenda.' In 1979 the incoming Conservatives said they wanted 'cuts' in public spending. The Treasury provided a package but, according to the memory of one senior official, 'Howe said: "I wanted cuts, not for you to fiddle around the edges".'

'The Treasury had no idea of the scale of what the Tories wanted to do, and we were determined not to make the same mistake again with Labour,' said the same official. 'We'd read and distilled everything that Brown and Ed Balls had said, and frankly it was not that difficult. But what we failed to grasp was the change in working methods that we were in for.'

This was something that came as a shock in particular to Sir Terence Burns, the Permanent Secretary, who chaired the Treasury Management Board and was in the process of making changes which did not fit in too well with Gordon Brown's approach. The normal Treasury procedure was for officials to prepare papers, for these to be discussed at big meetings and for everything to be carefully minuted. 'They had no idea that this was the normal process of government,' said one horrified official.

Brown and Balls brought the working methods of Opposition straight into the Treasury. Observers found them very informal, preferring to work in small groups, concentrating on the current issue, with a narrow focus on the problems of the moment. 'A lot of the Treasury could not adjust to this,' said one of those who seems to have adapted successfully. 'My colleagues said, "This is not the way Ministers work. It's different, therefore it's wrong. They'll learn our ways".'

But the newcomers – the political bosses – could not adjust to what they did not know, and the Treasury became divided into those who accepted them and those who did not. One or two senior officials found themselves acting as a bridge between the official Treasury and the new Ministers and political advisers. Ed Balls was technically a 'political adviser', a category which in days gone by could have implied a relatively subordinate role. Some political advisers in the past had appeared to be little more than 'bag-carriers', learning from their Ministers rather than advising them. But Balls soon became known as 'the Deputy Chancellor' and all serious issues had to be cleared with him.

When Brown and his team arrived, Burns and his colleagues were engaged in what was known as a 'Fundamental Review', which, in the words of one closely involved, required 'downsizing, flattening management structures and changing working methods'. In early discussions with the new Chancellor, Burns was concerned with organisation and 'management objectives', whereas the new, informal political masters were only interested in policy. 'Management and organisation were not what they wanted to talk about,' observed one member of the Management Board. Thus, 'there were real problems of communication' and this did not help relations between the new Chancellor and his Permanent Secretary. Neither did the plan to remove the hub of Treasury operations to a building upriver – and indeed on the other side of the Thames, near Vauxhall – while the Treasury building was being modernised. 'Brown soon put a stop to that,' said one official. He was not going to be shifted so far away from Number 10.

One official was shocked to find that the new arrivals 'didn't know the sort of thing we assumed Ministers absorbed with their mother's milk. They would ask how to get things done when it was second nature to us.' Officials were used to being asked 'to cook up ideas' but found that the new team had some firm ideas but large gaps. 'If you think in terms of an oilfield, they had drilled deep in one or two areas but hardly at all in others,' said one mystified official.

Thus, the work on the windfall tax on privatised utilities was well prepared and the Brown team had done quite a lot of work on 'public–private partnerships' and the 'private finance initiative'; but what was quite remarkable was that, after all those years in Opposition, Labour was ruling out a normal public spending round for the next two years. Instead Brown told officials he wanted 'a fundamental review' of public spending, in order to determine longer-term priorities.

One would have thought, from the widespread complaints of the electorate and the findings of the opinion polls, that public dissatisfaction with the state of the public services and the general infrastructure was obvious from the start. Did it really take a two-year freeze on overall departmental spending, and a fundamental review, in order to establish what should be done about the schools, the hospitals, the roads and the railways? And was not the very idea of a freeze on departmental spending guaranteed to make things worse and foment public dissatisfaction – dissatisfaction which had at least contributed to the election result that brought Labour in?

From the start Gordon Brown had a strategy, but it was a sequential one. Treasury officials themselves thought old habits died hard and that, whatever they had said in the Manifesto, New Labour would soon be wanting to spend, or 'tax and spend'. As set out in the first week, Gordon Brown's strategy was to do little for the first two years, other than on his pet 'Welfare to Work' scheme and tax changes to encourage investment; after that, spending would be increased in 'priority areas' (yet to be identified!) and cut back in other areas. From the start Brown was aiming at a reputation for fiscal responsibility in the early years: this was in order to establish that base and earn the credentials with 'Middle England' and the financial markets, for higher spending in years three to five and the second term 'without being blown off course'. In a sense, the election campaign for 2001 began in the first week of the new 1997 government.

In the four years from May 1997 to 2001 one sees a Labour government that was determined to demonstrate that it had learnt some historical lessons. While at one level the macroeconomic picture did not seem at all bad, beneath the surface there were all manner of problems in the public sector, reflecting decades of under-investment on the capital side and a chronically penny-pinching approach on current spending. This applied to education, health and transport – three pretty big areas of discontent – although for some reason the discontent with the transport system took a long time to register with New Labour's 'focus groups' and therefore did not disturb the Prime Minister or Chancellor – surely a serious error of judgement.

Some time before the election, Tony Blair had stated that this government would require two terms to do what was required, but most of the first term was devoted to establishing what Brown and Balls would repeatedly refer to as 'stability' and 'credibility'. On the one hand, borrowing and debt interest came down, there was a return to a current surplus on the Budget, and the nation and the financial markets witnessed a complete reversal of the traditional pattern by which Labour governments were returned to power, spent freely in the first year, then had to devote the rest of the time to 'cuts' and trying to repair the damage to their reputation. On the other hand, by instituting a freeze on public spending for the first two years and being slow to raise spending even in 'priority areas' thereafter, Brown's 1997–2001 Chancellorship saw public discontent with the state of the public services grow and grow. The MPC may have steered the economy successfully on a high consumption and (almost) full employment course but, in that famous phrase of one of Gordon Brown's heroes, Professor J. K. Galbraith, which merits repetition, there was a marked impression of 'private affluence amid public squalor'. For a long time, however, few of the Chancellor's many admirers seemed able to make the connection between his fiscal success and the growth of discontent with the state of the public services.

What was more, despite the Chancellor's commendable focus on the alleviation of poverty and making it more worthwhile for those on 'welfare dependency' to take up paid jobs, there was precious little sign of any narrowing of the gap between rich and poor – a gap that had always been a traditional focus of Labour governments. On the contrary, this continued to widen.[1]

As we saw earlier, Labour in Opposition had devoted a lot of energy to removing much of the 'baggage train' of policies with which it was traditionally encumbered, and essentially accepted many of the 'supply side' reforms of the Thatcher period. The disaster of John Smith's 'Shadow Budget' was the last throw of Labour's formal commitment to policies of 'redistribution'.

Yet from day one it was clear to his Treasury officials that Gordon Brown *was* wedded to covert policies of redistribution. Both within the UK and internationally, through his links with the International Monetary Fund (he became Chairman of the IMF's key political committee of Finance Ministers in 1999), Brown showed a concern with the alleviation of poverty and with increasing aid to developing countries that was highly unusual for Chancellors of the Exchequer. He was quite open about his ambitions for more aid and debt relief for the Third World but more cautious and circumspect about what he was up to on the home front. 'Redistribution' was a concept that dare not speak its name, especially in front of the Editors of the *Daily Mail* and the Murdoch press. It was much better to present such policies to Middle England as incentives to relieve the burden on the state of 'welfare scroungers' and the work-shy, and muddy the waters with a bewildering array of 'tax credits', of the detail of which Brown was the master. The populist approach was pushed to the limits of the patience of traditional Labour supporters (and not only them) when Brown's ally, Harriet Harman, introduced cuts in the benefits for lone parents. A former Conservative Cabinet Minister observed to me at the time: 'On social security and welfare to work they are doing what we dared not do'.

Such was Brown's interest in all aspects of what he called 'Welfare to Work' that one Treasury official, on returning from secondment to another department, commented, 'I have come back to what seems to have become the Department of Social Policy.' Although converted politically to involving the private sector in the management of public sector contracts – via the so-called Private Finance Initiative (PFI), introduced by the Conservatives, and Public–Private Partnerships (PPP) – Gordon Brown left much of the detailed work on this to others, with Geoffrey Robinson, as Paymaster General, playing a very prominent role in the early days. A senior Treasury official said: 'Gordon Brown's real interest is tax credits. He mastered the issue and understood how the benefits system works.' In this he became a member of an admired minority, because most of his colleagues found the subject of tax credits less than enthralling. Indeed, the Chancellor's obsession with tax credits became something of a joke in political and journalistic circles.

Brown also took a continuing interest in health and education and in issues such as productivity and investment, about which he had often spoken during the long years in Opposition. His study of twentieth-century history had convinced him that good policies and 'ideas' were often derailed by interest groups and the pressures of the moment. This conclusion permeated his entire strategy – not least with regard to Europe, which will be considered later.

Gordon Brown had spent decades criticising the 'short-termism' of governments. He was determined to take a long-term view of everything, from public sector investment to the euro. The problem was that the emphasis on prudence and 'long-termism' meant that much of the investment effort went into establishing 'credibility' with the public finances, so that 'stability' was certainly achieved at the financial level, but at the risk of instability in the real world of what affected the everyday experience of the general public. As one senior official observed: 'Running public services is difficult, but not that difficult. If you want people to concentrate on getting roads built, or hospitals, then the concept of stability applies here too.'

The Treasury itself regarded the Conservative public spending plans as eminently revisable. The retiring Chancellor, Kenneth Clarke, himself said that he would not have stuck to them, and Treasury officials certainly wouldn't have expected him to. At one stage Clarke had put his foot down when John Major contemplated committing his government to reducing the ratio of public spending to GDP below 40%. Despite Gordon Brown's pre-election acceptance of the planned two-year freeze, the Treasury thought the advent of a Labour government – even a New Labour government – would involve dusting down all manner of public spending projects from the shelves. From their point of view as guardians of the nation's finances, officials were agreeably surprised by this remarkable display of prudence. As citizens and users of public services, they were not so sure. 'Did Labour need to be quite so prudent? Probably not, if you look at the election results,' said one senior official.

Brown had studied how the Wilson government's attempt at a more long-term approach, through the setting up of the Department of Economic Affairs, had ended in tears – but not the Treasury's tears. Traditionally the Treasury, as the 'Exchequer', was responsible for controlling the nation's finances – raising taxes and keeping a strict eye on spending.

Nigel Lawson, who had been a Treasury-watcher, both as journalist and politician, for years before becoming Chancellor, was once asked what had most surprised him when he got there. His reply was, 'The degree to which its time and resources are taken up by controlling public spending.'[2] The Treasury had also been responsible for short-term management of demand in the economy. Sometimes under the Chancellorship of Denis Healey in 1974–79 it seemed that there was a 'mini-Budget' every few months. Then the tide of fashion turned against 'fiscal activism' and monetary policy became the main weapon of demand management. Monetary policy – essentially deciding whether and by how much to change interest rates – absorbed a mere 1.7% of the Treasury's resources before the Bank of England was made independent, but sometimes seemed to take up half the Chancellor's time, and was an endless source of bickering between Prime Ministers and Chancellors.

Gordon Brown was not especially interested in, or happy with, monetary policy. But when David Blunkett, then Secretary for Education, complained to the Treasury about a rise in interest rates a few months after Labour came in (a rise instituted by the MPC), a Treasury official muttered: 'This is precisely why we handed this over to the Bank of England.'

In the 1960s the Treasury, with its hold on the levers of short-term economic management, had always triumphed over the DEA's longer-term views. Gordon Brown made the Treasury into a kind of modern DEA with a heavy emphasis on microeconomic policies, or the supply side, improving, via tax concessions, the incentive to work, the incentive to invest and the incentive to do research and development. Although there had been signs of an interest in the supply side of the economy under previous Chancellors, such as Lawson, the predominant thrust of the Treasury machine in the past had been concentrated on control of overall levels of spending – 'The Treasury says "NO"' – rather than on how money was spent and on the precise implications for social policy. One official joked after six years of Brown's Chancellorship: 'We were never too good at controlling. It is much more fun intervening in how other departments spend their money.'

Previous Labour governments had felt captured *by* the Treasury. Brown *captured* the Treasury. Then, having hived off operational control of monetary policy – while, as noted, retaining emergency powers and vital control over the inflation target and of key appointments to the MPC – Brown built a Treasury which incorporated a DEA-style approach to improving, it was hoped, the 'supply side' of the economy and long-term prospects for economic growth. Previous Chancellors, such as Nigel Lawson, had not been averse to airing their views on the policies of other departments while attempting to control their overall levels of spending. But until the advent of Gordon Brown's Chancellorship the Treasury was essentially a *macro*-department, concerned with macro-issues such as the overall levels of taxation and spending and the balance between them – the fiscal balance. The Treasury did its best to steer the economy with a mix of fiscal and monetary policies.

As one senior official put it: 'Gordon Brown redefined the job of Chancellor: previously it was largely fiscal policy, with a micro element, now it is all micro, with a fiscal element.' Moreover, thanks to the devolution of monetary policy to the Bank, Treasury officials became firmly of the view that 'if the Chancellor did anything radical on the fiscal side, it would be offset by the Bank of England.'

By this was meant that, as the MPC was responsible in practice for short-term demand management, if it thought Brown had tried to over-stimulate the economy with dangerous tax cuts in the Budget, it would simply raise interest rates to counteract any inflationary effect. The same would apply to budgetary measures based on optimistic revisions to the Treasury's assumptions of the underlying potential of the economy for growth, e.g. if the MPC thought the Treasury was making excessively sanguine forecasts of tax revenue. In the old days the same person – the Chancellor – was responsible for both tax changes and interest rates, and would often announce a cut in interest rates on Budget Day. With the advent of the MPC, the Treasury routinely apprised the MPC of its fiscal strategy on the eve of the Budget, in the hope of convincing it that the strategy was 'fiscally responsible' and did not require any offsetting action on the interest rate front. This was done formally via a presentation by the Treasury representative on the MPC and informally at one of the regular monthly lunches at which Gordon Brown and Sir Edward George met.

During the years 1997–2002 this arrangement seemed to work smoothly. While there were occasions when the Treasury's assumptions about productivity and forecasts of future economic growth were rigorously questioned by the Treasury Committee – also the 'affordability' of the spending plans when the Chancellor finally announced more ambitious ones – there was no obvious sign of serious disagreement between the Treasury and the Bank about the overall economic implications of the annual Budgets. What there most certainly was, however, was repeated expression of concern on the part of the MPC about the imbalances *within* the economy.[3] And, once the Chancellor did unveil the scale of his spending plans for health and other areas during the second term, the MPC made it quite clear that these *could* be a factor in making it concerned about the impact on the inflation target in due course. By spring 2003 the MPC was taking issue with the Treasury's growth forecasts, regarding them as too optimistic.

Whereas Governors of the Bank of England in decades gone by had regarded it as their duty to complain about levels of public spending under Labour governments as a matter of course, Sir Edward George and his MPC colleagues were concerned entirely with the impact on the economy in general and the inflation target in particular. Indeed, in his farewell speech at the Mansion House on 18 June 2003, George declared: 'We have been helped more recently – and it's not often you'll hear a central banker say this – by a timely increase in public spending.' For Treasury officials the fascination with Labour back in office was the extent to which Gordon Brown tacitly acknowledged that the Conservatives had won the 'tax and spend' argument. While carrying out, as good civil servants, the Conservative policies of the 1980s and 1990s, Treasury officials had been well aware of the chorus of complaints about the state of the public services. Although they spent some time seriously preparing for a Kinnock government in 1992, Treasury officials thought John Smith had walked into a 'tax trap' unnecessarily because he had developed his policies during a boom, and, ironically for Labour, by spring 1992 the last thing the economy had needed was caution about 'tax and spend' – i.e. the 'fiscal responsibility' that contributed to Labour's demise at the polls might well have been unnecessary after all.

Treasury officials then watched Labour's policy review from a distance, and how Gordon Brown, the man who had a reasonable chance of being the next Chancellor, got himself off 'the redistribution and tax and spend' hooks. As Treasury officials saw it, the Conservatives had simply 'won the argument' on tax. Between 1979 and 1988 the top rate of income tax was approximately halved from 83% to 40%.

This trend towards lower marginal rates of direct taxation was followed in many parts of the world and basically accepted by New Labour. Yet, as a Treasury official observed, 'People don't want to pay but they want the services.' This had become increasingly obvious during the 1990s, and discontent with the state of the public services had contributed in no small measure to the way the electorate turned against the Conservatives.

It was soon obvious to Treasury officials after the change of government that the team of Brown and Balls had brought some of the concerns of Opposition into office with them. They might have been brimming over with confidence about their plans for the Bank of England and the windfall tax, and resolute in the face of City criticism of the 'raid' on pension funds (all in the one and only Brown mini-Budget of July 1997), but they were racked by a profound fear – that the public thought they would waste money. They had bowed to the Thatcher Revolution when it came to direct taxation; and would do what they could by way of indirect and 'stealth' taxes to make some compensation for what they felt they could not achieve politically via income tax rates. But whatever the electorate wanted in terms of better public services, Brown and Balls still feared that Labour was distrusted on the spending front. Their strategy was to prove that they could control and direct spending before they bit the bullet of taxation.

This helps to explain the extraordinary phenomenon in which New Labour presided over a slower rate of growth in public spending during their first term (1997–2001) than had occurred during John Major's premiership. At 1.7% a year, the rate of growth was below the normal growth rate of the economy as a whole of around 2.5%. Equally, it was well below what one might have expected given the generally perceived need for the UK to 'catch up' on Continental Europe. And public sector capital investment, the need for which Gordon Brown had consistently advocated during all those years in Opposition, was lower during the years 1997–2001 than in any previous comparable four-year period since the 1970s.

Thus, to the amazement of many Treasury officials, Brown stuck to the two-year 'freeze' on public spending that he had unveiled so dramatically three months before the 1997 election. But Brown always intended to return to the subject of taxation eventually, when he had (he hoped) won the public's trust with the nation's finances. Trust on 'spending' meant not spending – or, rather, not spending more, and spending wisely and to some purpose in those areas where extra spending was allowed.

It was paradoxical that Labour should come in after all those years and adopt the spending plans of the Conservatives for two whole years – plans to which the Conservatives themselves had no intention of adhering. The standstill on spending guaranteed that it would take a very long time to achieve the improvements in public services for which most people so patently longed. As David Butler and Dennis Kavanagh wrote after the election of 2001: 'The public spending standstill for the first two years meant that it took a long time to achieve any visible improvements in the core public services ... polls showed a steady increase in the numbers disillusioned with the government's performance on health and education and their resentment of spin.'[4]

Even in 2003, the implications of the pre-1997 pledges on tax rates and spending may not have been fully appreciated. Demands on public services grow year by year. The condition of the public services was considered deeply unsatisfactory in 1997, yet here was a government committed to doing very little about them for two years, and which took several years after that to get its act together. True, the odd extra billion or so was announced from time to time in the face of emergencies in the health service, but such injections were modest by comparison with the problems piling up – a drop in the ocean compared with the extra £100 billion of spending plans over five years which were unveiled early in the second term.[5] It takes months to make vital repairs to the transport network; it takes several years to train teachers, and over five years to train doctors. Investment in new equipment and buildings also requires long-term planning.

One way of looking at the time wasted – or, putting the best face on it, 'invested' in gaining 'credibility' – is that the first term, during which very little tangible progress was made with transport and the public services (which in many ways were widely thought to have deteriorated further), lasted four whole years – the equivalent of 1939–1943 if one thinks of the Second World War, or 1945–1949 if one thinks of the post-war Attlee government. That is to say, the Second World War was more than two-thirds over in the same time it took New Labour to establish its credibility with the public finances, and the first Attlee government was four-fifths of the way through. Yet the situation facing the new government had all the elements of a peacetime emergency that urgently needed addressing.

This is not to say that the Chancellor himself was not active: he was – feverishly so, interspersing his annual Budgets with well-publicised intervention in many areas of Whitehall, and in daily contact with the Prime Minister over almost every conceivable issue in which the Treasury felt it had an interest. All the time, however, his strategic objectives during the first term were: first, to prove a Labour government could control spending; second, to reduce the budget deficit – the rate of borrowing and the level of debt – to a sound base; third, to avoid all talk of 'Old Labour'-style 'redistribution' of income (while discreetly gearing personal tax changes towards helping the poor and the low-paid, and 'making work pay'); fourth, to introduce 'targets' to show what such spending as was allowed was *for*; and fifth – his ultimate aim when all this was done – to be able to come out in the open during the second term and say, 'Let's face it: if you want better healthcare you have to pay for it' – in other words, an ultimate return to the politics of 'tax and spend', but with nothing like a return to the kind of tax levels experienced during previous Labour governments. After all, had not this New Labour government demonstrated how fiscally responsible it was?

The odd thing was the way that the Conservatives had managed to keep the tax issue going for so long. For the whole of the 1997–2001 term Gordon Brown was terrified of mentioning the word 'tax' except to say he was against 'the politics of tax and spend'. In the Budget of March 2000 he even, when finally abolishing mortgage tax relief and the tax allowance for married couples, offered the 'sweetener' of a further penny off the basic rate of income tax.

By lowering the basic rate from 23% to 22% Brown caused huge dismay and disappointment in the Labour ranks – not just among the die-hard 'Old Labour' core, but also among those who had happily swallowed 'modernisation' but who, given their concerns about the state of the public sector, knew that this 'Tory-style' tax cut was rubbing salt in their wounds. Although Brown felt that this move was politically necessary to compensate Middle England for the final loss of its mortgage tax relief and the married allowance, it was also apparent from the gleeful way in which he announced this cut (it had been trailed in the 1999 Pre-Budget Report) that there was an element of being 'too clever by half'. To this day, one can hear bitter comments from Labour backbenchers about the episode.

From Gordon Brown's point of view, however, the masterly long-term planner was trying to hide the degree to which he was attempting to contrive what economists call a 'redistribution of income' to the poor. As one Treasury official confessed of the first term: 'I had thought all that stuff about "prudence with a purpose" was prudence with the purpose of prudence; but in the first term it was for redistribution.' This official early on decided that one of the Chancellor's principal preoccupations was to achieve a balance between 'negative income tax (for redistribution) and the puritan ethic: make them work!' After the July 1997 mini-Budget introduced the 'windfall tax' to get the Welfare to Work programme going (mainly aimed at the under-25s at this stage), the March 1998 Budget was designed to help families with children and introduce 'incentives' for the poor and low-paid generally. This involved help with childcare and the new 'Working Families Tax Credit'. The emphasis was on assisting lower-income households in general and those with children in particular. He built on this in the March 1999 Budget with appreciable increases in child benefit and promises of a new child tax credit by 2001, again biased in favour of low-income families. But some means-tested benefits were reduced, and it was not obvious at this stage that he was doing much for the poor in households where there were *no* income-earners.

Treasury officials were surprised that the work they were doing on tax credits, which always showed up almost *ad nauseam* in the annual Budgets, did not receive quite the attention they thought it would. David Willets, the Conservative spokesman who had worked as a junior Minister in the Treasury, observed on one occasion: 'the Treasury is a department of obsessions. For a time it was the money supply statistics. Later it was the ERM. Now it is tax credits.' Officials noted that Gordon Brown, while having fingers in every available pie, held them longest in the pie marked 'redistribution and tax credits'.

Most of the time Brown was swimming against very strong tides. Even Denis Healey, towards the end of his Chancellorship, had become concerned about a 'narrowing of differentials' in income. This was the Denis Healey who has gone down in popular mythology as having threatened to 'squeeze the rich until the pips squeak', but was in fact trying to make another point. He never said the words attributed to him. As Healey subsequently observed: 'I quoted it once in a speech and attributed it to Lloyd George or Balfour. All I said, which was absolutely true, was there would be howls of anguish from those who are rich enough to pay the highest rate of income tax – but you never hear a word of sympathy from them for those who are too poor to pay tax at all.'[6]

During the 1980s and 1990s the gap between rich and poor widened, not only as a result of 'market forces' but also because such a widening was implied as a desirable aim of 'Thatcherism'. If the Conservative right objected to policies of 'tax and spend' in the 1970s, the question was: to which did they object more? The tax or the spend? There was no question that it was the tax, and they made this the defining issue. The overall tax burden did not come down under the Conservatives, but the taxation of the rich and upper income groups fell dramatically. This was because of the remarkable reduction in marginal tax rates – from 83% to 60% in the first Conservative (1979) Budget (and from 98% for investment income) and again to 40% in the 1988 Budget. The best stealth tax of all was VAT, which the Conservatives raised from 8% to 15% in 1979 and which was later increased to 17.5%. But what happened during the 1980s and 1990s was not only the dramatic impact on the distribution of income of the reduction in marginal tax rates, but the development of a 'winner-takes-all' culture in which ever higher salaries and financial 'packages' in the City and Industry became well established. The beneficiaries may have been vilified as 'fat cats' by Gordon Brown in Opposition, but there was little energy left in the Old Labour battery to power a direct attack on 'fat cats' by 1997–2001.

Thus it was that as Chancellor, Gordon Brown concentrated much of his energy in the first term on trying to put two of his passionate beliefs into practice: helping the poor, and promoting the work ethic from the economic powerhouse of British government – the Treasury. On Budget Day in March 1988 the House of Commons had had to be suspended for fifteen minutes to restore order because of the outcry over the reduction in the top rate from 60% to 40% by Nigel Lawson. Now the tax 'argument' had resulted so overwhelmingly in a Conservative victory that it would be considered controversial and daring when Brown proposed raising National Insurance by 1% in 2002 (for his Budget of 2003). Indeed, as noted, Brown felt it necessary in the Budget of 2000 to lower the basic rate by one penny. This was itself a remarkable gesture towards the victory of the right.

'Redistribution' under his Chancellorship consisted of tax concessions or extra payments to the poor and minimising concessions to the upper-income groups. It was called 'redistribution' within the Treasury and sometimes referred to outside as 'redistribution by stealth', but it was more a policy of alleviation of poverty combined with promotion of incentives to work. The upper echelons of income earners continued to enjoy low marginal tax rates *and* a world in which very high salaries were much publicised but little questioned. The effect was that economists specialising in the statistics of 'redistribution' found little change in the overall measurement of inequality of income (known as the Gini coefficient) between 1997 and 2001. Nigel Lawson even went so far as to tease New Labour[7] for continuing the good work of Thatcherism.

But Brown was far more concerned about the 'dependency culture' and helping the poor. 'Dependency' had in fact been increased under the Thatcher governments through such devices as encouraging unemployed people to claim 'disability benefit' so that they could be removed from the unemployment register. Brown was seriously worried about the effect on 'entire communities'. The philosophy of the Treasury under his Chancellorship – 'the Department of Social Policy' – was epitomised in a speech Brown made within the first month of his arrival in office, when he addressed the CBI on the subject of 'The British Genius'. 'The government will restore the work ethic at the centre of our welfare state and modern employment policies,' he said. 'The work ethic has been undermined in large tracts of our cities and regions by the destruction of opportunity.' As a result of 'an unreformed tax and benefit system,' he said, 'unskilled people can work forty hours a week and can actually be worse off than if they had done no work at all.' That Protestant work ethic cropped up again in the next sentence: 'The government must ensure that hard work is encouraged and rewarded at all levels.'

In the James Meade Memorial Lecture of 8 May 2000, Brown once again emphasised 'the ethic of personal responsibility as we stress obligations as well as opportunities.' He said that full employment could be achieved neither by market forces nor by pulling the macroeconomic levers 'without tackling underlying structural weaknesses, not least the need for rights and responsibilities in the labour market.' He ended by trying to warm the hearts of some Old Labour listeners by saying: 'We should never lose sight of the ambition to make this country a far fairer and far more equal society.' This latter statement was interesting because examples of references to equality tended to be few and far between at this stage of New Labour's term in office. Indeed, these words were not in the official text of his lecture, but added spontaneously by the Chancellor.

It is easy to criticise Gordon Brown and New Labour generally for having apparently accepted so much of the 'Thatcherite Settlement'; and there seems little doubt that one of the constant problems facing the Conservatives since 1997 has been the way that New Labour seems to have stolen so many of their clothes. Paul Foot, in a scathing assessment of Gordon Brown's period in Opposition and early years in government (*London Review of Books*, 27 February 1999) concluded that 'Brown and Blair worked together to bring about the emasculation of the Labour government as a force for change'; and, certainly, New Labour was created by both of them.

Yet it is possible, in his obsession with 'redistribution by stealth', to see Gordon Brown trying to do the best he can for the poor and the underprivileged in circumstances he regarded as being severely constrained by public opinion. As the welfare economist and social security expert John Hills has written: 'There is very clear evidence that the general public is – as policy has been since 1997 – highly selective about spending priorities.'[8] Thus social security, with the exception of pensions, low-paid working families with children and the disabled, is not high on the list of priorities of those famous focus groups – nor of the more comprehensive annual British Social Attitudes survey. Health and education have consistently been the public's biggest concern, with health overwhelmingly in the lead; e.g. in 2000, 55% of respondents told BSA health was the priority, compared with 26% citing education and 2% social security. A remarkable 71% of respondents to the BSA survey in 2001 thought unemployment benefit constituted the biggest or second biggest item in the social security budget, whereas it was actually 6%.

But while no fewer than 87% of respondents thought 'the gap between those with high incomes and those with low incomes is too large' (in 1995), Gordon Brown, in his capacity as a Chancellor with a very powerful influence over social security, concentrated on help for the poor, rather than narrowing the gap from both ends of the income redistribution.

There was a huge increase in the inequality of incomes during the second half of the 1980s under Mrs Thatcher, and a slight fall in the first half of the 1990s under John Major. But the gap widened during the closing years of Major's government and continued in that direction during the early years of the 1997–2001 Labour government, before stabilising in 2000–01 (national statistics).

The proportion of people with income below half the average amount was 6% in 1977 (under the Labour government of James Callaghan) but over 20% by the early 1990s.[9] This is 'relative poverty' rather than 'absolute poverty' but Labour had made much of the increase in relative poverty under the Conservatives, and set out to do something about it in 1997. According to OECD comparisons, the UK moved from a position in the 1970s where it had one of the most equal distributions of income to having one of the most unequal by the mid-1990s.[10]

The phasing-out of some disability benefits and of special additional benefits for lone parents in 1997–98 – the fulfilment of a plan drawn up by the Conservatives – was not Gordon Brown's finest hour. But independent experts acknowledge that on the whole such losses were more than compensated for eventually by rises in other benefits. For several years Brown kept rises in the basic state pension to the Conservative formula: compensation for inflation, but no attempt to keep up with average earnings. The 75p a week increase in Budget 2000 was in fact in line with (low) inflation, but was generally perceived to be so shamefully low that it produced a revolt in the Labour Party rank and file. As a result, Brown announced increases above inflation in his Budgets of 2000 and 2001 but did not restore the old, pre-Thatcher, formal link with earnings for which Labour veterans such as Jack Jones and Barbara Castle had campaigned.

Brown's emphasis has been on helping poor families with children – the Working Families' Tax Credit – because New Labour had committed itself to end 'child poverty'. But reducing child poverty also alleviates the position of others in the family, and the new Working Tax Credit will top up the incomes of couples without children. It did not go down well with the strong body of opinion that believes that children are more likely to benefit if payments are made directly to the mother when the Chancellor made the Working Families' Tax Credit payable to the father; but this move was reversed when it was announced that from April 2003 the Child Tax Credit would normally go directly to the mother.

John Hills has pointed out that during the first six years of Gordon Brown's Chancellorship: 'there have been large – even spectacular – increases in particular elements of the cash benefit and tax credit system, even after allowing for inflation: 27% in the rate of the universal Child Benefit for the first child; 84% in the maximum amount of in-work support for a family with two children under the age of eleven; 17% in the total income support for a non-working, lone mother with one young child; and 29% in the total income support for a couple with two young children.'[11] In gross terms, support for children through the tax and benefit system grew by over a half, from £13 billion in 1998 to £21 billion in 2003 (in real terms, at 2002 prices).

The average support through the tax and benefit system per child rose from £20 to £31 a week between 1998 and 2003, but from £30 to £50 a week for the poorest 25% (with one child) and from £50 to £80 a week for those with two children. Such payments may not sound much when contrasted with the much-publicised increases in 'fat cat' salaries over the period; but from the point of view of social security experts they were 'dramatic'.[12]

Despite the tough rhetoric employed by Brown and others for the purposes of satisfying the prejudices of the right-wing press, increases in benefits were not confined to the 'working poor'. But as Hills comments: 'The increased cash transfers to non-working families probably have been politically possible only because they have come behind a strategy that stresses the aim of increasing work opportunities and incentives.'[13] Relatively more money has gone to working families, partly in keeping with the rhetoric of incentives; but the policy of reducing child poverty does imply, whatever the fears of the right wing about 'scroungers', that the non-working poor receive handouts from the government as well.

One unforeseen consequence of the way Gordon Brown has pursued his policy of 'redistribution by stealth' is that, having learnt about 'workfare' from the USA, he might now be in a position to demonstrate to his American teachers that 'it is possible for a government – even one alive to the constraints of the opinions of a public that is sceptical about handouts to the unemployed – to bring in reforms that have a noticeable direct impact on the incomes of all poor families, working and non-working.'[14]

Nevertheless, Brown's main obsession in this sphere has been with putting his own slogan – 'Welfare to Work' – into practice. And, apart from the intensive involvement of government officials and agencies in bringing potential workhorses to water, the financial incentives have included not only the minimum wage but also the more generous tax credits for the lower paid and changes in the structure of national insurance contributions to favour the lower paid.

And redistribution? Up to a point, especially if, as David Piachaud and Holly Sutherland have pointed out, account is taken of the £5 billion a year which Brown took from pension funds in his July 1997 Budget (by abolishing the tax credits previously paid to pension funds and companies). This undoubtedly hit middle- and upper-income earners more than the poor, and it was always a common cause of complaint in the City and elsewhere from people who otherwise thought Brown had been an admirable 'Iron Chancellor'. Admiration for iron qualities can diminish if your own pension is the object of their attention. The tax changes were dressed up as part of a package of corporate tax changes to boost investment, but the subsequent performance of manufacturing investment was far from impressive. And a tax justified at the time by the 'pension fund holiday' being taken by companies did not look so well-advised during the pension fund crisis in the early 2000s.

One minor route to 'redistribution' was the way Brown early on removed the additional tax allowance for married couples and ensured that the new child tax credit would not benefit upper-income earners. On the whole, however, what the 'redistribution' tables show is that tax and benefit changes during Brown's first term as Chancellor benefited all income groups to some extent, but were biased heavily in favour of the lower income groups. According to Piachaud and Sutherland, all the measures announced under Gordon Brown's aegis between 1997 and 2001 affecting tax and benefits, produced a gain of 17% for the net incomes of the poorest tenth of the population, falling to 1% for the richest tenth – who appear to have taken this in their stride, with the exception of the 'raid on pension funds'.[15]

Thus, for Gordon Brown and the Treasury a central aim has been to connect the alleviation of poverty with incentives to work in the pursuit of full employment – an important point being that, even in the good times, after many years of what was widely thought to be impressive economic growth, there was still widespread unemployment – open or 'disguised' – in certain areas of the country, especially inner cities and on 'sink estates'. Labour had made a commitment in its Manifesto to introduce a minimum wage, and duly did so. There has always been a gulf between economists and the general public on this issue because whereas the layman tends to think a decent minimum wage is a 'good thing', economists worry that too high a minimum wage can 'price people out of jobs'. The 'market' solution favoured by the Conservatives had been low wages topped up by some element of help from the government, but not as much as Brown favoured. The Treasury was not keen on making the minimum wage 'too high' and in fact argued for a lower rate. The Treasury's influence on Brown in this matter made him unpopular with trade unionists, who tend to have long memories. Thus, before the minimum wage was introduced on 1 April 1999 at £3.60 an hour, the Chancellor insisted that the rate should be only £3.00 an hour for under 22s. The Low Pay Commission had recommended £3.20 for under-21s. A senior trade union leader told Brown: 'Don't think you can get away with this. People won't forget.' Again, when the minimum wage was uprated in 2001 to £3.70, Brown fought against the 10p rise but was overruled by the Prime Minister, who said, 'No. We must accept the recommendation of the Low Pay Commission'. But the Chancellor insisted that he should make the announcement and the Treasury duly briefed sections of the press on a 'Gordon victory'.

The Treasury/Brown view was that the best thing to do was encourage the unemployed or the work-shy to price themselves into jobs under a system where the minimum wage was not too high; they would make work worthwhile *and* alleviate poverty by 'topping up' the wage with either tax incentives or subsidies, both of which came under the heading of a 'tax credit'. In this context, Gordon Brown would talk proudly of tax rates ranging from 40% to 'minus 200%'.

The minimum wage was one of the few left-wing causes to be espoused by Tony Blair, whose election to the Leadership had worried the Conservatives in 1994 because, as Edmund Dell commented, his 'convictions seemed to run so closely with their own'.[16]

While the concept of a minimum wage seemed decent and sensible to the general public, the Treasury and many economists used to argue that it would distort 'the market' and cause unemployment to rise. But it began to make sense to the Treasury when outside economists such as Gerald Holtham – then head of the Institute for Public Policy Research (IPPR) – pointed out that ruthless employers could happily drive wages down relentlessly and 'top up' from a bottomless pit of government subsidies. So the minimum wage became a way of reducing welfare spending. Subsequently, the Chancellor made a virtue of it.

The author recalls conversations with women known as 'single mothers' or 'single parents' in which they expressed great enthusiasm for the vital £40 or £50 they were receiving from the government and said Gordon Brown was a 'hero'. Such payments made all the difference to their ability to work and arrange child care. On the other hand it was disturbing that, according to some authoritative estimates, up to a third of people eligible for such help in one form or another were not actually claiming it. But at the very least the vast effort that Brown and the Treasury put into their efforts at 'redistribution' while coping with the constraints of 'tax and spend' placed a brake on the pace at which inequality was increasing. There was bound to be a dispute about what would have happened anyway to people who went from 'welfare' to 'work' during a generally expansionary period of economic growth. There were always going to be plenty of examples of young people who came off the unemployment roll, took part in a 'Welfare to Work' scheme and then dropped out. But the view of the Treasury officials most closely involved was that, alongside the 'deregulation'[17] inherited from the Thatcher/Major era, the Brownian programme helped the workings of the labour market and contributed, against a background of 'global' disinflationary forces, to the absence of upward pressure on average earnings that might have been expected from experience of previous economic cycles. Such upward pressure on wage inflation in past economic cycles had been the traditional signal for the Treasury and Bank of England to step on the brakes, slow the economy down and induce a rise in unemployment.

In economists' jargon, the so-called 'natural rate of unemployment' – an inaccurate as well as inelegant term to describe the rate of unemployment at which inflation rises – might have been lowered by the panoply of 'Welfare to Work' measures. The possibility of an acceleration in the earnings figures was an almost constant concern of the 'hawks' at the Bank of England. There were a number of scares, but on the whole the MPC was not too constrained in the years of rapid economic growth, 1997–2002, by wage inflation. The chronically high exchange rate also played its part in controlling inflation.

At all events, the combination of steady economic expansion in the years 1997–2002 and the 'micro' measures designed to 'make work pay' contributed to an impressive fall in unemployment. The prudent Gordon Brown had been 'dismayed' when John Smith re-committed the Labour Party to the goal of full employment in 1993. Now he was even prepared to use the phrase himself – and even make a virtue of it.

CHAPTER ELEVEN

Getting and spending

Although his obsession with, and mastery of, the 'Welfare to Work' and 'redistributive' programme came up time and again in discussions about how Gordon Brown's Chancellorship looked from the inside, it was only part of the government's 'tax-and-spend' programme; and it was, of course, designed to reduce the cost of 'welfare' and debt interest in the long run. As one official observed, 'The tax thing had run its course by the late 1980s. It was an achievement for the Conservatives to keep it going as a defining issue in the 1990s.' In this they had been helped by the way Labour led with its chin in 1992, allowing the Conservatives to make great play with another 'tax bombshell' scare. 'Cats miaow, dogs bark, Labour taxes,' said Chris Patten.

By 1997 the defining issue had indeed become 'tax and spend'. The Conservatives were deeply unpopular and the condition of the public services left a lot to be desired. But there was still a belief that, while they were widely disliked, the Conservatives could, in the words of one Treasury official, 'keep a grip' on public spending, while Labour 'would just spend'.

To Gordon Brown's new official Treasury advisers: 'In neutralising the issue, the whole business of defining what spending is for was at least as important as capping the amount.' Hence the stage was set for one of the major themes of the Blair/Brown duumvirate and Gordon Brown's Treasury: the introduction of *targets* to demonstrate, it was hoped, that public expenditure was achieving solid results. In its desperate attempt to show how it had shaken off its spendthrift ways, the Labour Party had gone into the election with very little in the way of concrete proposals, contenting itself with a 'card' of promises it thought should not be too difficult to keep, such as reducing class sizes and hospital waiting lists. Even these limited ambitions would prove difficult to realise; but after 1997 the 'target culture' was going to permeate Whitehall.

There are several paradoxes about the way 'tax and spend' was handled in 1997–2001. Historians have rightly described the years of 1945–51 as 'the Age of Austerity': a Labour government struggling to rebuild a war-ravaged economy. For much of the Attlee period, the austerity inevitably applied to consumer spending; during Gordon Brown's first Chancellorship, however, consumer spending raced ahead, while the austerity was confined to the sector that needed expansion most: the public sector. It is clear, at least in retrospect, that Brown did not have to be quite as cautious and prudent as he was. Most ironically (in the true sense of the term), when he did take the brakes off after the two-year freeze, to an alarming extent the machine did not respond – or at least not for a painfully long time, while public dissatisfaction with the railways, the hospitals and the schools grew and grew. Even the bias under the 'fiscal rules' in favour of capital investment, as opposed to current spending, took an unconscionably long time to produce results.

The last Budget presented by Kenneth Clarke had been in November 1996. It was also the last of the 'unified budgets', putting 'tax and spend' proposals together, a system introduced by Norman Lamont after many years when outside experts had argued that it made more sense to 'unify' plans for taxation and spending, instead of introducing them at separate times of the year. After his mini-Budget in July 1997, Brown restored the Budget to its traditional (pre-1992) spring timetable, preceded by what used to be called an 'Autumn Statement' but which was now a 'Pre-Budget Report'.

Clarke had pointed out that his November 1996 Budget 'reduces public spending plans further, while providing more money for priority services' (but not much more – certainly not by the standards of what Brown felt he needed to do during his second term). Gordon Brown trumpeted his own prudence in drawing up spending plans for three years ahead. In theory the Conservatives had done this, but one Treasury official said: 'Under Nigel Lawson plans for years two and three were a joke. Under Kenneth Clarke they had a degree of realism.'

Officials thought that in 1996 Clarke had 'scraped the bottom of the barrel in order to make his spending plans fiscally respectable', and that it would not be easy to stick to his theoretical plan for no overall increase over the following two years. But it gradually became clear in the course of 1997 – and abundantly so later – that the new Chancellor was inheriting a very favourable fiscal position.

There was a large element of social security spending in the 'planning total' that Clarke had frozen. In theory, social security payments affected by the economic cycle – such as unemployment benefit – were not in the planning total; in fact, Treasury officials later acknowledged that much of the so-called 'non-cyclical' expenditure was in fact cyclical. So with the economy continuing to expand fast under the 'Clarke Boom' that followed the nadir of the year of Black Wednesday (1992), unemployment was falling fast and the burden of social security payments on the Exchequer was considerably eased. 'It was a very benign set of circumstances,' said one official. 'The Treasury was in a very powerful position from the start.' On the spending side things were subdued. On the revenue side the economy was doing well and the revenues were cascading in. Clarke had ensured that fuel and tobacco duties were not merely 'indexed' to rise with inflation but to rise by significantly more than the inflation rate – the so-called 'fuel escalator'. What was more, after being scarred by the way surplus turned to deficit following the Lawson Boom of the late 1980s, the Treasury had built in very cautious assumptions to its forecasts, even before Gordon Brown and Ed Balls added their own strong dose of prudence. One official confessed that even if Labour had come in 'spending as in 1974–75', the Treasury was at least prepared for it. 'Though we were being criticised for cutting services,' this official added, 'it did create a bit of discipline.'

And that was before Brown arrived. Right through the years of Gordon Brown's first term as Chancellor, 1997–2001, the fiscal outturn was, in narrow Treasury terms, 'better than projected, because of our cautious assumptions. It was embarrassing, but good for the Treasury.' The July 1997 'Welfare to Work' Budget was, for the official Treasury, 'incredibly prudent and a sign of what the Brown regime would be like.' The welfare to work part had been carefully costed and planned in advance. 'They also found £1 billion for hospitals and some money for schools (also £1 billion). That was it.'[1]

In the view of close Treasury observers, Kenneth Clarke had had a very casual approach to the media. He just relied on his own considerable political skills and 'made it up as he went along'. The Brown team were very different and had already done a lot of thinking about the media. As noted, Gordon Brown himself had long been a past master at handling the media and had made good political use of leaks in Opposition. For several years his team of Ed Balls, as economic adviser, and Charlie Whelan, as 'spin-doctor', had had plenty of opportunity to hone their skills. With the other political adviser, Ed Milliband, and Brown's secretary, Sue Nye (inherited from Neil Kinnock), the Brown team made a formidable impression on Treasury officials, whether they liked what they saw or not. The apparent leaking of parts of the July 1997 Budget in advance was the first of a myriad of skilful uses of the press, although things were going to rebound on Brown when, in frustration at public and Labour Party criticism of the state of the public services, his team indulged in creative 'double or treble' counting of their announcements about future spending plans. This produced an angry reaction and severe criticism from the Treasury Committee.

In a way, the obsession with 'spin' proved a useful diversion from what little was being achieved on the public spending front during the first term. The watchwords were indeed Prudence, Prudence and Prudence – even when Ministers wanted to relax some of their constraints.

For the first year or so much of the Treasury action on the public spending front – outside the Welfare to Work programme – had been on the private finance initiative (PFI) and 'public–private partnerships' (PPP). Treasury officials were convinced that this was not motivated solely by a desire to get round Gordon Brown's own self-imposed, prudent restrictions on 'tax and spend'.

'It was important ideologically for New Labour to show they were not ditching all that stuff,' said one Treasury official closely involved. 'It was a way of demonstrating that they could do business with the City.' This official said that Brown and his team had had 'some successes with PFI and PPP – especially with prisons' – but 'all that business with the Tube was slightly odd.'

Another official who worked closely with Brown maintained: 'They had seen enough of the public sector at work to see that schools and hospitals went over budget, over time, and were not fit for their purpose. They had learned from Mrs Thatcher that privatisation and contracting out produced a better outcome.' But even this official, who was personally inclined to sympathise with the concept of involving the private sector in public contracts, ended up saying, in 2002 after all the controversy about the London Tube, 'The deal is now so warped that I do wonder how much good it will do.'

Treasury officials closely involved had noticed back in 1997 not only that Gordon Brown's acceptance of the PPP approach was a deliberate attempt to distance the Labour Party from the past, but also that he was impressed by the obvious point: bringing, as he did, an atmosphere of additional frugality to a Treasury that is traditionally obsessed with candle-ends, Brown deliberately placed a big emphasis on PPPs as a way of 'spending without it showing too much' during that initial two-year freeze. Ironically, delay, procrastination and political infighting meant that even this pared-down form of immediate spending was emasculated, thereby adding to the public's frustration with the state of the infrastructure.

In a way, both the decision to freeze public spending for two years *and* the almost doctrinal obsession with the PPP and PFI can be attributed to the fears that haunted New Labour after all those past defeats and successful Conservative attempts to brand it as the Party of 'tax and spend' (in the words of one Treasury official: 'The spending freeze was the price Labour paid to be elected.')

The PFI had been introduced by Norman Lamont in the Autumn Statement of 1992 as a way of increasing capital spending on the infrastructure without adding to government spending or borrowing. Private sector contractors would pay for infrastructure projects – the London Tube, new hospitals and schools – 'up front' and the Treasury would repay the capital cost over a long period of years, so the full cost would take time to show up in the government's accounts. When Kenneth Clarke became Chancellor in spring 1993, he objected to the Whitehall view that the PFI was merely a way of 'getting spending off the balance sheet' and enthused about using it to bring private sector expertise and 'value for money' into the public sector. As the Treasury Committee noted in March 2000, 'There has been some doubt about the relative advantages claimed for PFI.' When Gordon Brown unveiled the July 1998 Comprehensive Spending Review he announced additional public sector investment, and a subsequent Treasury document in March 2000, *Public Private Partnerships: The Government's Approach*, stated that the PFI and other public private partnerships would 'add to and complement' the additional public sector investment and 'relieve the pressure on public finances, allowing government to concentrate resources on other public services'.

One senior Treasury official observed how strongly Gordon Brown wanted 'to distance himself from Old Labour' by encouraging public–private partnerships. But although Brown became identified very strongly in public with his support for the PFI with respect to the London Tube, this official maintained that 'he was never that interested in, or on top of the PFI stuff'. He left it to others, not least Ed Balls and Geoffrey Robinson in the early days. 'He wanted to demonstrate that New Labour could do business with Business, but it was not his prime concern.'

Robinson and Balls recognised that the public sector had neither the confidence nor the expertise to handle the PFI, and brought in Adrian Montague from the City to head the Treasury Task Force. 'This was a gridiron of helpers to public sector organisations doing PFIs, and helped the general momentum,' said one official. Another surprise for Treasury officials was the way that, from the start, public sector partnerships and PFIs were also being pushed by John Prescott at the Department of Transport. Officials were amazed to hear Prescott – hitherto considered very Old Labour – declare, 'There's got to be a culture change at London Transport.'

Balls and Robinson were obsessed by the way costs had escalated during the construction of the Jubilee Line. Indeed, the 'Jubilee Line Overrun' became a mantra to be invoked whenever anyone questioned the supposed wonders of the PFI. There had in fact been huge physical problems associated with the construction of the Jubilee Line, and 'overruns' are not necessarily unusual in the world of big public sector contracts.

The Jubilee Line was a very special case. There was an unavoidable delay of nine months for reasons of safety because there had been a disaster during the construction of a tunnel at Heathrow, where similar tunnelling techniques had been employed. There was then an officially inspired rush to complete the extension of the Jubilee Line in time for the opening of the Greenwich Dome by the year 2000. This unseemly haste weakened the bargaining power of the public sector *vis-à-vis* the contractors and employees, and virtually guaranteed a sharp escalation in costs.

The private sector was not exactly faultless in these matters either. Indeed, Brown, who had declared some years earlier that 'the job of government today is to harness the energies of both the public and private sectors', promulgated what was known as a 'productivity reform agenda', holding high-powered seminars with prominent outsiders, where some familiar themes from the old DEA days of the 1960s soon resurfaced. How far, Brown and the Treasury asked themselves, could the British private sector leaders match their counterparts from overseas? How good – or bad – were British managers? Before long they were concluding that the 'best of British' were of world class but there weren't enough of them – just like the kind of conclusion the National Economic Development Office (NEDO) and the DEA came up with in the days of Gordon Brown's namesake George Brown in the 1960s.

But as far as the Treasury was concerned, some of the conclusions drawn by Gordon Brown were very different from the Old Labour 1960s. It was familiar stuff that 'skills' had to be improved and 'training' encouraged. But the conclusion was that, just as social policy should be about encouraging people from welfare to work, industrial policy should be about incentives for higher productivity and greater competition, rather than the Old Labour-style industrial policies of the 1960s and 1970s with their price controls, Selective Employment Tax (SET) and seemingly endless 'propping up' of nationalised and, occasionally, private sector industry.

'Once you have accepted an independent Bank,' said one Treasury official, 'tax is all about incentives, ranging from encouraging direct investment in shares to investment in run-down communities; spending is all about how you run the NHS or provide for endless generations of tiny people.' He was partly joking of course, but he was trying to illustrate the 'culture change' within the Treasury. 'There is no question,' said this official, 'that a huge amount of the time of British politicians in the 1960s was absorbed by fundamentally mistaken microeconomic management, encouraging hidden unemployment and over-manning.'

For Treasury officials, the difference between Old Labour Chancellors of the past and Gordon Brown was epitomised by Budgets in which, as his interest in competition and private enterprise grew, *reductions* in capital gains tax were introduced to encourage enterprise and competitiveness. This was a far cry from the 1960s when, advised by those 'terrible twins', the left-wing economists Nicholas Kaldor and Tommy Balogh, a Labour government had regarded capital gains tax as a device to punish 'filthy capitalists'. When summarising what he thought had been the essence of Brown's approach to the Treasury over the years 1997–2002, one senior Treasury official said: 'It's microeconomic management. It's how to make the part of the economy for which you are directly responsible (the 40% known as 'the public sector') actually *work*; and how to improve the environment of the private and voluntary sectors.'

It was these aims that provided the themes of much of what Gordon Brown tried to do in his Budgets and spending reviews. 'It wasn't a dramatic story,' said one official. 'It was slow moving.' But it reached the stage by 2003 when the Chancellor's interest in industrial and competition policy was so great and pervasive that one of his closest allies joked, 'Given what the Treasury is up to, it is not at all clear why we need a Department of Trade and Industry at all.' Nevertheless, for all the focus on 'productivity' the economy's trend rates of productivity growth did not increase.

And for all the worship of the private sector and its involvement with the PFI and public–private partnerships, it was not at all clear that the practice lived up to the theory or the rhetoric. A series of reports from the Treasury Committee, the Institute of Public Policy Research, Catalyst and the National Audit Office severely questioned both the operation of the public–private partnerships and the very concept itself. The government's attempt to distance itself from Old Labour did not prevent it from having to shell out tens of billions of taxpayers' money to bail out the railways, in the botched privatisation in which the Treasury had been deeply involved during John Major's Premiership. Then, on top of the financial demise of Railtrack, there was an embarrassing escalation in the cost – from £2 billion to upwards of £7 billion – of upgrading the privatised West Coast Line.

It was noted, however, that if other departmental ministers were the ones who delivered the bad or embarrassing news on these fronts, and Gordon Brown, like T. S. Eliot's cat Macavity, never seemed to be in the vicinity at the time, it was Treasury money that was ultimately involved.

The stalemate between the Treasury and Ken Livingstone, the Mayor of London, over the proper way to finance the modernisation of the London Tube was partly attributed by Treasury officials to the impression Gordon Brown gave that anything Ken Livingstone wanted must be wrong. The Treasury also tried to rationalise the situation by saying that in the end if things went awry it was the paymaster of last resort. It simply did not want to relinquish control.

In his dealings with the canny Ken Livingstone, Gordon Brown hardly covered himself in glory. In league with Blair, he tried to prevent Livingstone from becoming Mayor of London in the first place. Then he was obdurate in his dealings with him. Furthermore, at the time of writing, Bob Kiley, the American hired by Livingstone to sort out the Tube, had yet to gain an audience with the Chancellor after several years in his post. Yet Livingstone and Kiley won the propaganda war with the Treasury, gaining the support of the *Financial Times* and the *London Evening Standard* in their quest for bond finance. A close observer of the transport scene summarised the Tube affair as 'a grubby compromise between Prescott's distrust of the unions and Brown's dislike of Ken Livingstone'. As with the railways, problems with the Tube system tested the patience of the public to the limit. It was all very well running a widely admired macroeconomic policy, but it was not much fun if the trains could not run on time.

To a considerable extent, the bad publicity received by the government over the private sector partnerships was out of all proportion to its importance in the overall scheme of things. The IPPR think-tank whose inception Gordon Brown had supported in the 1980s was more critical of the government's lack of openness with regard to the PFI than concerned about the actual impact on the nation's finances. Paul Maltby of the IPPR pointed out that all the roads, hospitals and other infrastructure schemes financed by the PFI after 1997 had added only 2% or so to the level of net government debt. Raising the level from around 33.5% to 35–36% of GDP still kept debt well within the Chancellor's chosen margin of 40%. The criticism was that Brown should not have been indulging in 'off-balance sheet' practices – which laid him open to criticism. It seemed all the more unnecessary since he was in fact being prudent with both official and PFI borrowing.[2]

By 2003 PFI spending was a mere 12% or so of total public spending, although it amounted to some 90% of new infrastructure spending on hospitals and schools. 'You do not use the PFI to mend roofs and leaking drains,' said one official. And, of course, much the greater part of public spending is devoted to the wages and salaries of doctors, teachers and public sector workers generally. Paul Maltby said there was no obvious need for the obsession with off-balance sheet financing, which in any case in more recent years was being accounted for in the Budget report.

For all the publicity and the public endorsements he gave to PFI and partnership with the public sector, Gordon Brown himself was said by his close associates to regard it as 'a sideshow' by comparison with his longer-term strategy of achieving 'stability', building up trust and then embarking on a programme of sustained increases in public spending. What he really wanted was to be in a position where a Labour Chancellor could comfortably borrow £20 billion a year for public spending without being accused of profligacy and irresponsibility.

Treasury officials have always liked 'strong Chancellors' and Chancellors who know what they are doing. The Treasury has proved over the years that it can respond enthusiastically to the requirements of a new government, once it knows that government is serious and clear about its intentions. In the case of Gordon Brown, the younger Treasury officials in particular seem to have been enthused by the responsibility thrust upon them by Gordon Brown's many 'micro' initiatives and to have relished the challenge, if not always the long hours or the pace set by their extraordinarily hardworking political boss. One cannot but be struck by the way that even some of those officials who were most enthusiastic about the private sector partnerships at the beginning began to wonder whether, outside certain obviously successful areas such as prisons, the PFI had been worth the candle. 'The biggest example of failure is obviously the Tube,' said one official. With masterly understatement he added, 'One cannot help wondering whether a more traditional procurement strategy might have been better.' There were also doubts about the accuracy of the methods devised by outside consultants for predicting the costs and benefits of PFI projects, let alone about the wisdom of the public sector becoming so reliant on such consultants.

If one goes back to the 'conversion' that Gordon Brown underwent between his 'Red Gordon' days in Edinburgh in the 1970s and his pragmatic adoption in the 1980s and 1990s of what his friend and colleague Tony Blair was fond of calling 'what works', an awkward question arises: did Brown, and Prescott with him, jump too far from an ideological belief in the powers of the state to a naïve belief in the wonders of the private sector and what it could bring to 'public–private partnerships'? Given the manifest example of the chaos on the privatised railways, it seemed foolhardy to adopt a similar approach to the Tube. Before one of several 'restructuring' efforts with the railways, Tony Blair privately said: 'You can call it anything you like as long as you don't call it re-nationalisation.' Labour seemed so 'hung up' on the past that Gordon Brown's Treasury entered a dangerous labyrinth when they decided to abandon traditional procurement methods for the Tube because the Jubilee Line had overrun by £1.8 billion and was eighteen months late. As a result of the PPP fiasco the modernisation of the rest of the tube system was delayed a lot longer than that. A Chancellor who believed in 'what works' became hung-up on what often patently didn't work.

Meanwhile, Ken Livingstone no doubt thought there was a certain poetic justice in the way the man New Labour had tried to prevent becoming Mayor achieved worldwide fame for the perceived success of his Congestion Charge. The Treasury even began to recommend it to other British cities. It would be ironic if the Congestion Charge became the biggest microeconomic footnote in the history of the period. Certainly Livingstone thought it paradoxical that 'Red Ken' would make his biggest mark 'by charging people'.

The odd thing was that Gordon Brown's new 'fiscal rules' of summer 1998 – without a glowing reference to which few Chancellorial speeches thenceforth were complete – seemed specifically designed to negate the need for the kind of 'backdoor' route to higher infrastructure spending for which Norman Lamont's Treasury originally designed the PFI. The Golden Rule stated that: 'on average over the economic cycle, the government will borrow only to invest and not to fund current spending.' This was accompanied by the 'sustainable investment rule' – the 'second fiscal rule' – which stated: 'Public sector net debt (PSND) as a proportion of GDP will be held over the economic cycle at a stable and prudent level.' The words 'stable and prudent' were defined as 'below 40% of GDP over the economic cycle'. In a sense this was all very negative. Perhaps in years to come governments will develop a *'net asset'* criterion, rather than an obsession with 'net debt'.[3]

For years there had been complaints from all sides that all those constraints imposed by public sector borrowing targets made no distinction between current and capital spending. Sometimes the pleas for changing the rules to encourage capital spending seemed to be based on the rather simplistic notion that capital spending was by definition good and current spending bad. Much current spending by the public sector – on doctors' and teachers' pay, for instance – is absolutely vital to society. But it had been true that, dating at least from the time the Callaghan government was in the hands of the IMF in 1976, successive governments had found capital spending the easiest thing to cut back in a crisis.

Governmental rules about borrowing tend to be arbitrary. Previous Labour governments had borrowed what the market would bear, and there usually came a point when it would bear no more. Gordon Brown was proud of his fiscal rules which, as noted, had been developed in Opposition, and dated from the time in 1992 when Ed Balls gave his first advice about the need to provide a sustainable basis from which a Labour government could operate. All cavils about definition apart, the view that the public sector should be able to borrow for investment purposes seemed eminently sensible; but in theory the 40% limit on net debt placed limitations even on the scope for borrowing for investment purposes. Balancing the current budget over the cycle allowed for the workings of 'automatic stabilisers' – the tendency for borrowing to be relatively low when the economy is expanding faster than normal (or 'above trend') because revenues are buoyant and unemployment falls and social security outgoings are correspondingly less. Conversely, when the economy is in recession or expanding only slowly, tax revenues are lower than they might be and disbursements of social security rise, thereby forcing the government to borrow more.

But allowing the automatic stabilisers to work is one thing; being able to conduct an active fiscal policy – deliberately raising spending or cutting tax rates in order to recover from a serious recession – is quite another. Gordon Brown had already accepted the prevailing orthodoxy and ruled out an active fiscal policy. As it happened, despite one or two scares – and periods of genuine recession in the manufacturing sector – the economy as a whole had a good growth record in the period 1997–2002, and the fiscal rules were not a constraint. But if for one reason or another private savings rise to unusually high levels, then it makes perfect sense to run a large budget deficit to offset the depressing effect on consumer spending. There is nothing god-given about a balanced budget. But the British fiscal rules were certainly more accommodating than the rules adopted by the founding members of the Eurozone on 1 January 1999, when the commitment was to 'budgetary positions close to balance or in surplus' and the scope for 'normal cyclical fluctuations' was firmly circumscribed by the need to keep deficits within 3% of GDP. So great was the pressure on Eurozone countries such as Germany and France in 2002 that the European Commission made proposals to adapt the rules of the so-called 'stability and growth pact': it wished to make things easier for public sector capital investment; for countries whose gross debt position was considered particularly satisfactory (i.e. well within the official 60% limit of GDP); and for economies in recession. In practice, France and Germany found they had no alternative but to break the rules during the slowdown of 2003. The President of the European Commission, Romano Prodi, went so far as to describe the stability pact as 'stupid', because 'all rigidity is stupid'.

At various times over previous centuries the UK national debt had reached 290% of GDP (in 1815 during the Napoleonic Wars) and 200% (during the 1914–18 war), having been as low as 30% in 1914. Between 1918 and 1939 its lowest point was 150% of GDP. Then it shot back to 270% during the 1939–45 war. But in the 1970s, 1980s and 1990s there was both a political and 'market' reaction against high debt levels and it was against this background, and all Labour's electoral travails, that Gordon Brown opted for what, historically, seemed very tight fiscal rules, even if there was an opt-out clause for investment.

It should not be forgotten that the period when low public sector borrowing and low deficits became fashionable, the 1970s and 1980s, coincided with the general impression that Britain's infrastructure was 'running down' and public services were not functioning properly – a situation that had provoked great electoral dissatisfaction by 1997.

If the easing of rules for borrowing for investment had been that impressive, then the need for the PFI or public–private partnerships as a backdoor means of encouraging public investment would have disappeared. Thus, the Treasury Committee stated on 20 March 2000 that: 'in the new framework, the case for PFI as the main means of obtaining extra investment is very much weaker. The main justification should now be the prospect of obtaining better value for money.'[4] An astute critic, John Grieve Smith, maintained that 'the rule requiring the public debt to GDP ratio to be held at a stable level is quite inappropriate in varying and unpredictable circumstances,' and complained, 'it has also contributed to the disastrous continuation of the Public Finance Initiative.'[5]

The proud way in which the Treasury continually referred to the wonders of its new fiscal rules, *vis-à-vis* both its own past practice and that of its Continental neighbours, was threatening by 2003 to prove a hostage to fortune. There was a danger that dared not speak its name built into the new fiscal rules. It was that the Treasury might be lulled into a false sense of security and eventually be hoist by its own petard. As one perceptive observer remarked, 'prudence is not necessarily rewarded.'

For the smooth operation of the fiscal rules in the first New Labour Parliament (1997–2001) was in part due to the fact that in the end, when it began to release the clamp on spending, the Whitehall machine proved even more cautious than even the prudent Gordon Brown intended. In a curious way, Whitehall departments seemed for a time to have lost the art of spending. This, combined with the remarkable teething troubles Labour had with the operation of the PFI, contributed to the bizarre outturn in which capital spending ended up lower in 1997–2001 than in any previous comparable four-year period in recent decades. Of course, the deliberate 'freeze' during the first two years was primarily to blame, but it was ironical that when the Chancellor actually thought it was time to beef up government spending plans, the machine did not respond in the way he hoped.

The distinction between current and capital spending was introduced in the 1998 Fundamental Spending Review, and Gordon Brown and Ed Balls were openly proud of the scope this afforded them for plans to double public sector net investment from 0.6% of GDP to 1.2% between 1997 and 2001–02. The Treasury briefing was that this meant that government was 'beginning to address the years of neglect in public sector infrastructure' and that the plans were consistent with a falling debt to GDP ratio. In 1998 the Treasury was saying that, other things being equal, it was desirable to reduce the debt ratio below 40% of GDP. By spring 2000 it was forecasting that the ratio would fall to under 33% of GDP by 2004–05.

Given the scale of the problems with the country's run-down infrastructure, a gradual increase in public sector investment to 1.2% of GDP did not sound notably ambitious. But even this modest ambition, which most certainly fitted in with Gordon Brown's prudent approach to the nation's finances, proved to be on the optimistic side.

Treasury officials recalled with wry amusement in 2003 how pundits in the press and the City were concerned in 1998–2000 that the government had embarked on 'a dangerous spending splurge'. One official, looking back, said, 'the quality of the comment was ridiculous.' The announced plans were well within Gordon Brown's prudent framework and great difficulties were encountered with trying to achieve even these plans.

Knowing that the two-year freeze would be over by mid-1999, the Treasury was planning from the autumn of 1998 onwards for a significant upturn in investment from April 1999. 'Once the tap started being turned on, the frustration for Gordon Brown was the failure of Whitehall to spend,' said one senior official. 'They had not been spending for so long that they did not just spend badly, they did not spend at all. And investment projects have long lead times.'

Of the two fiscal rules, the Treasury regarded the one relating to current spending – that the budget should balance over the cycle – as more constraining than the net debt rule in practice. As the revenues rolled in, and spending remained constrained, net debt as a percentage of GDP fell steadily, and then took a merry leap downwards when the Treasury managed to auction mobile digital channels for a massive £22 billion at the height of the new technology boom in 2000. During New Labour's first Parliamentary term, 1997–2001, public sector net debt as a percentage of GDP fell from 43.7% in 1996–97 to 31.3% in 2000–2001. Conservative members of the Treasury Committee and assorted media interviewers routinely tried to lure Gordon Brown into admitting that, thanks to the general buoyancy of the revenues and his 'stealth taxes', the tax burden had actually risen under Labour, whatever political mileage Blair and Brown had secured from not raising the personal tax *rates*. But Brown made not answering that question into something of an art form – after all, New Labour did not believe in 'tax and spend', did it? In fact, net taxes and social security contributions rose from 35% of GDP in the last year of Kenneth Clarke's Chancellorship (1996–97) to 37.7% by 2000–2001 – the highest level since Nigel Lawson's seminal tax-cutting Budget of 1988 brought the ratio below 37%. (In an irony not too delicious for Labour, the tax 'burden' had actually risen under Mrs Thatcher from 33.2% in the last year of the Callaghan government, 1978–79, to 39% in 1982–83, and was still above 37% before Lawson's pre- and post-election Budgets of 1987 and 1988. But the near-doubling of VAT in 1979 had worked stealthy wonders of its own for the government's revenues.)

While the New Labour government's budgetary position was improving all the time, investment in all those areas of the public sector considered to have fallen behind was not. Public sector net capital expenditure in the four years of Kenneth Clarke's Chancellorship (which included in the earlier part the effect of budgetary decisions taken by Norman Lamont) was successively £12.3 billion in 1993–94, £12.2 billion in 1994–95, £11.7 billion in 1995–96 and £5.8 billion in 1996–97 (at 2000–2001 prices). Thus, as far as capital spending was concerned, the voluntary two-year 'freeze' was imposed at a very low level. During the four years of Gordon Brown's first Chancellorship, public sector net capital expenditure was £5.2 billion in 1997–98, £6.1 billion in

1998–99, £4.8 billion in 1999–2000, and £5.7 billion in 2000–2001 (at 2000–2001 prices).

The Budget of 1999 had heralded a doubling in capital spending – from 0.5% of GDP in 1997–98 (later revised to 0.6%) to 1.2% of GDP by 2002–2003. The financial year 1999–2000 was to see the first major advance. In fact, as the above figures show, capital spending fell sharply between 1998–99 and 1999–2000 as Whitehall failed to get its act together. Yet the 1999 Budget had forecast a rise of about 60% in the public sector's net capital spending between 1998–99 and 1999–2000.

The prolonged squeeze on capital expenditure by the public sector began way back in 1976–77, the year the Callaghan government was forced to borrow from the IMF and savings had to be found. It was cut back in successive years from £29.2 billion in 1975–76 to £5.4 billion by 1981–82, the year of Sir Geoffrey Howe's notably deflationary Budget. It only rose above £10 billion once during the 1980s (£10.9 billion in 1983–84) and was as low as £2.6 billion in 1988–89. It was in the £10–15 billion range annually during the Major years (1990–97) except, as we have just seen, for 1996–97, when it fell to £5.8 billion.

The capital spending figures for the first term of Gordon Brown's Chancellorship constitute the solid statistical confirmation of the general impression that things were already bad enough in the public sector but not much was being done to remedy the situation.

This was a New Labour Party that had castigated the Conservatives for their attitude towards the public sector and the infrastructure. Gordon Brown himself, as noted, had tirelessly campaigned from the Opposition benches on the importance of investment and the infrastructure. He and his economic adviser Ed Balls were especially proud of the way they had introduced fiscal rules in favour of investment, and made a big feature of their plans to double public sector investment by 2002. But in those first four years, public sector net investment as a percentage of GDP – the sequence was 0.6% in 1997–98, 0.7% in 1998–99, 0.5% in 1999–2000 and 0.6% in 2000–01 – was lower by far than in any previous four-year period since the cutbacks began with the

Callaghan government of 1976–79. Moreover, by comparison, during the first half of the 1970s public sector net investment averaged over 5% of GDP.

By 2001–02 net public sector investment did finally reach the 'doubling' target of 1.2% of GDP, and was projected to rise to 1.4% by 2002–03, when it was planned to total £14.4 billion (at 2002–03 prices). And what about the PFI, which had generated so much heat? Capital spending by the private sector in deals negotiated by the government was forecast to add £3.7 billion on top, thus amounting to about a fifth of the combined public sector and PFI investment on behalf of the public sector. But with all the delays and teething troubles with the PFI – most notably concerning the London Tube – PFI spending in 1999–2000, the year when Gordon Brown was trying to get things moving, was a mere £1.4 billion, rising to around £2.9 billion and £2.8 billion in 2000–01 and 2001–02.

The PFI had evolved from being an alternative to public investment under Norman Lamont in 1992, via becoming a means of bringing putative private sector efficiency and value to the public sector under Kenneth Clarke, into a 'complement' to public investment under Gordon Brown. Since it was contributing less than a fifth of total publicly-sponsored investment (i.e. public and PFI) by the early 2000s, it seemed to generate a disproportionate amount of publicity – and certainly of criticism. A typical summary of the popular criticism was the following: 'Instead of building new schools and hospitals from the money raised by taxation on today's adults, New Labour has followed the Conservatives and instructed the private sector to borrow on far worse terms than the state could obtain.'[6]

If the PFI itself was generating an inordinate amount of publicity, within the PFI arrangements the London Tube seemed to attract much of the crossfire. In fact, the PFI was being used for capital investment in 'schools, colleges, hospitals, local authorities, defence IT and property management' (HM Treasury Budget 2002).[7] As far as the Treasury was concerned, approval of a scheme depended on: 'a thorough assessment of the lifetime costs of both providing and maintaining the underlying asset and the running costs of delivering the required service.'[8] In what the more savage left-wing critics might regard as a masterpiece of understatement, the Treasury noted: 'the PFI provides considerable opportunities for the private sector.'[9] The justification from the government's point of view was that: 'the contractual relationship with the public sector ensures the ongoing delivery of cost-effective and quality services.'[10]

Integral to the PFI approach is that private firms are involved in service and maintenance of projects, as well as the initial construction. As noted, there have been a number of critical reports and the debate still rages. What was quite clear in the 1997–2001 period was that Gordon Brown had done so well in obeying his self-imposed 'sustainable debt' rule that under the label 'public spending' he could have achieved all the investment incurred under the PFI, and net debt would still have stayed well within the 40% limit. As the Treasury Committee said (March 2000), the question then arises: does the supposed 'extra value for money', via private sector expertise, scope for innovation and transfer of risk, outweigh the higher cost of private sector, as opposed to public sector, borrowing? (a government such as the UK's can usually borrow on more favourable terms than the private sector).

Other considerations arose under the PFI and the accompanying spread of 'privatisation' to the public services, such as the possible development of a 'two-tier workforce', with new employees at 'outsourced' services being given second-class status. One veteran public servant observed: 'This leaves seven million workers in a cloud of uncertainty as to whether the structures within which they serve are only there because, for the present, government cannot think of how to move them "off balance sheet" in ways which the government thinks will meet what people want more efficiently.'

Labour when in Opposition had mocked Mrs Thatcher's obsession with 'market forces' and 'value for money'. There was a strong feeling that too much emphasis on 'the market' was at the expense of basic human values, summed up in Mrs Thatcher's contemptuous dismissal, 'There is no such thing as society.' But in the words of one public official: 'By the time Labour came back to power, they discovered that the public wanted the lot: high consumption and good quality public services. With new technologies in medical care, people living longer, and demanding as of right the kind of treatment for, say, skin cancer that wasn't available twenty years ago, the demands on the health service seemed infinite.'

Gordon Brown was driven towards the Thatcherite acceptance of 'value for money' whether he liked it or not. And, given that he and his colleagues felt so defensive about the public's feelings towards them, they were perhaps inevitably drawn into what at times seemed a nightmarish world where so much emphasis was placed on 'delivery', with its accompanying instruments of 'targets' and 'public service agreements'.

The acceptance of the Conservative PFI approach – not to say of the privatisation of the railways, memorably described by a dissident Conservative as 'the poll-tax on wheels' – produced one set of problems, the principal one being that governments cannot let go of the responsibility when things go wrong. In the words of the veteran public servant referred to earlier: 'Real accountability is not "transferred" in the case of trains, the tube, hospitals, doctors, teachers and so on. All that happens is that we have newer and more costly relationships with private sector contractors.' This same official emphasised that he was all in favour of private sector contractors being contracted to do specific work, 'but it is the illusion of privatising services which are public which is the heart of the problem.'

There was no question of the government's avoiding responsibility in the case of the increase in public spending unveiled in a series of major programmes; and the problem was that, in the end, Gordon Brown was not responsible for *enough* public spending in the years 1997–2001. That was one reason why so much emphasis was placed on the Pre-Budget Report of 2001; this was sometimes known as the 'Wanless Budget', after the study on the future of the National Health Service by Derek Wanless, former Chief Executive of NatWest, whose name was cited frequently in the course of the Chancellor's Pre-Budget and Budget speeches in November 2001 and March 2002.

We have seen how the capital investment programme unveiled in the summer of 1998 was simply not realised. It is remarkable to reflect that, when introducing his *Comprehensive Spending Review: New Public Spending Plans 1999–2002* in mid-July 1998 Gordon Brown was given a hero's welcome by his backbenchers and greeted by the headline, 'Brown's shock spending spree – spend, spend, spend' in the *London Evening Standard*. The respected City accountants PricewaterhouseCooper talked of Brown's 'calculated gamble'. With the economy booming and social security and debt interest payments falling, the Chancellor had been able to include plans for health spending to grow by 4.7% a year (in real terms) and spending on education by 5.1% a year while promising that total public spending would grow by only 2.75% a year.

In truth, the calculated gamble had been the *combination* of the two-year freeze and the relaxation; for all the fears of the Opposition, of many outside commentators and of Sir Terence Burns himself (then still Permanent Secretary), even the new plans were modest taken over the expected run of the Parliament. Thus, Gordon Brown felt able to boast to the Treasury Committee on Wednesday 15 July 1998 that 'if you look at public expenditure over the last Parliament, it rose by 2.2% [a year]. If you look at public expenditure over this Parliament as a whole it will rise by less, 1.75% [a year].'

This was a truly prudent approach, and the seemingly large increases for health and education had to be seen in the context of the two-year freeze (with minor modifications) which was still in place when the Chancellor spoke.

But these increases in spending should also be seen in the light of Gordon Brown's particular interests. He had thrown his considerable political weight behind the PFI and 'public–private partnerships', ostensibly in the belief that the old ways did not work. Brown appeared passionate in his support for the PFI but it is an open question whether the PFI 'worked' in the way he hoped it would; anyway, his officials believed that the Chancellor was 'neither interested in nor on top of' the PFI issue. What really interested Brown in addition to tax credits and 'redistribution by stealth' were health and education.

Redistribution, health, education: these were traditional concerns of the Labour Party, and especially of those members of the Party who still believed in equality of opportunity. Gordon Brown had always been interested in these issues. A man who believed there was too much inequality in the 1970s, when he was making a big splash in Scottish politics (student and otherwise), had all the more reason to be concerned in the late 1990s and early 2000s.

Both Brown and Ed Balls had made it clear that one of the objects of building their 'platform of stability' was to reduce inequality; but they did not shout too much about this. Health and education were always on their agenda for extra funds once the thaw began; the Chancellor was already proclaiming in July 1998 that: 'our prudence has been for a purpose. It is because we have set tough efficiency targets, and reordered departmental budgets, that our top priorities, health and education, will receive more money than the other nineteen government departments combined.' He had taken a firm line with non-priority areas, so that 'as a result more than half today's allocations – over 50% – will be invested in health and education' (explaining that 'more than half' meant 'over 50%' was a quaint touch in a statement about education!).

But knowing that they were still not trusted to spend wisely, Brown emphasised 'it is money in return for modernisation' and 'in every area investment is conditional on reform'. Neither Brown himself nor Tony Blair displayed a particular interest in the issue that was to haunt them later, transport. But the 1998 Review did include a pledge that: 'from a 25% decline in transport investment in the last Parliament there will be 25% increase in the next three years.' As noted, however, the Whitehall machine did not, in Number 10 Downing Street's favourite word, 'deliver' anything like this ambitious investment target. The transport did not arrive on time.

An official closely involved said of the criticism of the 1998 spending plans: 'we had been running bloody great surpluses and it was sensible to spend. Debt was incredibly low.' And so it was. Public borrowing had been cut by £20 billion – 'a fiscal tightening that will be locked into next year,' Brown promised.

It was way back in 1998 that the seemingly ubiquitous 'targets' were introduced. An official said, 'There was a fear that big increases would frighten the horses, so that the public needed to get something in return.'

'Each department,' said Brown, 'has reached a public service agreement with the Treasury, effectively a contract with the Treasury for the renewal of public services. It is a contract that in each service area requires reform in return for investment.'

The menacing tones of the 'control-freak' aspect of Brown's behaviour in the eyes of his critics could be deduced from between the lines of his statement that 'the Education Secretary has agreed not just to set numeracy and literacy targets for eleven year-olds but to set government targets for nursery education, for cutting truancy ...' (and so on). The 'has agreed' conjured up a picture of the Chancellor browbeating his Ministerial colleagues into submission – something regarded as common practice under Brown's additional chancellorial role of 'chief executive' to Tony Blair's 'presidency'.

A senior official commented of Brown's first term: 'Every battle has to be won. If not the Chancellor is terribly angry. He lives life on the edge of a volcano. He drives himself extraordinarily hard and has incredibly high expectations of himself and the people around him. If things do not go right, the volcano erupts. A lot of any such day can be spent in high frustration because things are not right. Everyone around suffers collateral damage while the Chancellor is slumped over his desk.'

This was well before the days when the Prime Minister was seen to assert himself over Foundation Hospitals and university 'top-up fees' in 2003 – both issues on which Gordon Brown thought 'equality of opportunity' was threatened, and both, incidentally, in the spheres of education and health about which Brown always felt strongly. Of that first term when the Chancellor usually, but not always, won a confrontation with the Prime Minister, one of his officials commented: 'Government would be so much better if Tony Blair were confident of his authority over Gordon Brown. From observed behaviour this government is allowed to say "no" to Gordon Brown twice a year. Things would be so much better if it was allowed to say so four times a year.'

When the Prime Minister did start saying 'no' to his Chancellor in spring 2003 – over top-up fees, for example, which Brown vehemently opposed – a number of commentators began to speculate for the first time about the Chancellor's political mortality. In a sense, however passionately Brown felt about the issue – which he did – this was an example of Tony Blair's (second term) decision to follow that official's advice and say 'no' more often. But it was an issue over which Brown was true to his egalitarian instincts – in the sense of his belief in equality of opportunity – because there seemed little doubt that loading students with a far bigger bill for their university education would almost certainly deter many of the potential candidates.

In any case, the supposed threat to Brown's position was a seven-day wonder. When the Prime Minister's own position was momentarily put at risk by the resignations of Robin Cook and Clare Short during the Iraq War in spring 2003, the machine politicians, Gordon Brown and John Prescott, rallied the (back bench) troops in support of Blair. This had the effect of removing any threat to the position of both the Prime Minister and his Chancellor. And, although Alan Milburn resigned for 'personal reasons' in June 2003, one additional factor was that Brown had sat on his plans for extra finance for foundation hospitals.

Brown's intervention in the top-up fees dispute was only to be expected from one who cared so strongly about education. The spending reviews of 1998, 2000 and 2002 all gave prominence to education and health. In a sense, the Treasury was in a weak bargaining position after Gordon Brown's voluntary freeze. It wanted to spend money, yet the Chancellor felt he had to prove that the money would not be wasted so that, even though there was little doubt that the money would be forthcoming (and, in some cases, spent rather slowly), everything had to be presented as part of a 'deal'. Money for reform, rewards for fulfilling commitments and hitting targets – that was the order of the day. 'Frankly, targets were invented on the hoof,' said one official. 'Ed Balls dreamt up public service agreements in an evening, to justify the extra spending,' said another.

The government's embarrassments in failing to achieve many targets were well publicised and became the stuff of many a daily news item. There was also the problem of distortion. 'If you hit 55% of your targets you are missing the other 45%,' observed one veteran public servant. An official involved said that 'when it came to *Spending Review 2000* we had decided it was ridiculous to say "you will do *x* by *y*" because we knew perfectly well departments couldn't. So we tried to have fewer but higher quality targets.'

The 1998 *Comprehensive Spending Review* had been subtitled *Modern Public Services for Britain – Investing in Reform*. By 2000, the crucial year before the general election expected (rightly) in 2001, *Spending Review 2000 – New Public Spending Plans 2001–2004* was subtitled *Prudent for a Purpose: Building Opportunity and Security for All*.

Opinion polls and focus groups had manifested considerable dissatisfaction with the government's performance with the public services. As noted, the promises of 1998 had not been fulfilled: economic growth is an incremental process, but there had been a famine and then a hotchpotch of extra spending, with many ill-considered and unachieved 'targets'. In the March 2000 Budget (with a Budget Report also subtitled *Prudent for a Purpose*) the ground had been prepared for extra spending, with the news that the current Budget was now in surplus to the tune of £17 billion (nearly 2% of GDP) in 1999–2000 and projected to remain in surplus thereafter, while falling to 1.25% in 2000–01 and 2001–02 and to 'over 0.75% thereafter'. Debt was being repaid, but there would be 'modest deficits' in 2002–03, 'mostly reflecting the rapid growth of public investment'.

On 18 July 2000 the prudent Chancellor was able to announce that [with the help of the massive proceeds from auctioning the airwaves for third generation (3G) mobile phones] the £28 billion deficit inherited in 1997 had been eliminated. There was no sense of irony in his promise to 'make good the damage done by the legacy of decades of under-investment across the public sector' – no recognition that New Labour had added another third of a decade of neglect of such investment.

But the fact of the matter was that by the time the first Blair government faced the electorate in May 2001 very little of the 'purpose' of the 2000 Budget and Spending Review had become apparent on the ground. One of the outstanding images of the campaign is of the Prime Minister himself being publicly harangued by a woman dissatisfied with the state of the health service. The increases in spending announced the previous year had only begun in April, on the eve of the campaign. In a sense the 'tax-and-spend' decisions of 2000 were the manifesto for the election of 2001.

Gordon Brown himself was very much at the forefront of the 2001 campaign. Despite the electorate's dissatisfaction with the state of public services, the Conservatives under William Hague were in complete disarray, finding that, whatever the euro-scepticism of the British public, the 'euro-sceptic card' was an unwanted joker at the election party.

Brown was riding high. As Iron Chancellor he had got the public finances in order – the first Labour Chancellor not to encounter a financial crisis and to have to rein back public spending towards the end of a spell in office – and was widely respected. Economic growth had been impressive and unemployment was still falling. Few people made the obvious connection between the 'iron' quality of his Chancellorship and dissatisfaction with the state of public services, even though exposure to the extraordinary state of the nation's transport system had provoked a correspondent of the *Wall Street Journal* to write an article with the message 'Britain Isn't Working'.

In the atmosphere of the times, nobody seemed to see the real point of Gordon Brown's favourite joke: 'There are two kinds of Chancellor; those who fail and those who get out in time.' Most commentators appeared to have forgotten the way Nigel Lawson had been feted as the greatest Chancellor since Gladstone, only to fall subsequently from grace. Brown might have gratuitously antagonised many of his colleagues, and other departments might complain about the arrogance of his Treasury; the Chancellor's desire to win every argument might have irritated colleagues and officials around Westminster and Whitehall; nevertheless he was widely respected within political circles generally as well as in the City of London and the country at large. He was the obvious successor to Tony Blair should the latter fall under a privatised bus or decide to stand down and back his Chancellor in a leadership election, in accordance with 'the spirit of Granita'.

Time and time again in those days one heard that Gordon Brown was 'a good' or 'an outstanding' Chancellor. Granting independence to the Bank of England was regarded as a stroke of genius. The spending freeze was the necessary condition for putting the fiscal house in order; that was the view from many people's lips. Concern about how manufacturing was suffering from an overvalued pound was the preserve of manufacturers and of one or two 'carping' commentators.

True, the Iron Chancellor had made some obvious errors of judgement. His association with the initial cut in benefit for lone parents rightly caused him a lot of embarrassment, as did one Budget announcement (later rescinded) that the pension would rise by a derisory 75p. His intervention in the 'Laura Spence Affair' was also misguided. He had seized upon a student's rejection by Magdalen College, Oxford, as a classic case of discrimination against applicants from state schools, only to discover that the truth was more complicated. The head of one Oxbridge college commented on this affair: 'We are doing everything we can to fight such discrimination. Gordon Brown is an intelligent man. Why has he done this? He may even have set back the cause he espouses.' This episode was unfortunate. Brown was surely right to question the general bias in favour of the public schools that still dominated the procedures for entrance to Oxbridge. It was just that he plunged into the controversy without knowing the full facts of this particular case.

In this instance he could hardly have chosen a worse case. He seemed to assume that the 'old boy network' was operating and that an outstanding state school pupil from Newcastle had been turned down in favour of someone from a public school. In fact, as the Admissions Tutor for Magdalen pointed out, the College had

had 25 very well qualified applicants to read medicine – all with 'predicted' three As – for five places, and Ms Spence had come tenth in the list after an exhaustive period of interviews and a written test. Three of the five qualifiers were in fact from state schools. Brown said it was a scandal that Ms Spence had had to apply to Harvard, but she in fact applied to Harvard to read a different subject, biochemistry. Ironically, the tutor for admissions at the time, John Stein, Professor of Neurophysiology at the University of Oxford, said that she might well have got in if she had applied to read biochemistry.[11]

The reduction in lone-parent benefit was unforgivable, attributed within the Treasury to a particularly right-wing official and to a rare misjudgement on Brown's part. The 75p pension rise was in accordance with the formula for linking the value of pensions to inflation; the Chancellor was more impressed by the fact that inflation was low, and therefore the associated adjustment small, than by the obvious political implications. In the words of one veteran observer: 'This showed a serious lack of political feel'. Among other things, the episode drew attention to the fact that Labour had abandoned any idea of restoring the link between pensions and average earnings that had been removed by the Thatcher government in the early 1980s. Subsequently the Chancellor made great efforts in successive Budgets to draw attention to the extra help he was providing to poorer pensioners.

Gordon Brown also attracted criticism at the time from some of his colleagues in the Parliamentary Labour Party about the low level of public investment. This was a cause which, as noted, he had promulgated for many years, yet he managed to serve a first term as Chancellor with the worst record for public sector investment in living memory. The criticisms, however, were expressed largely in private. Such colleagues did not wish to rock the boat.

It was a commonplace in Whitehall that Tony Blair and Gordon Brown met and spoke almost every day and had heated discussions on many topics. But it was just taken as a matter of course that this was a political marriage with deep foundations, and that the Prime Minister was tolerant of his once senior colleague's obvious frustrations about not having the top job himself.

The adverse criticisms of his Chancellorship during the first term were minor. Gordon Brown could have chosen, if he so wished, to move to the Foreign Office. James Callaghan before him had gone there, but by a long and tortuous route. Demoted to the Home Office after his resignation from the Treasury in November 1967, Callaghan spent four years in Opposition (1970–74) before becoming Foreign Secretary in 1974 and succeeding Harold Wilson as Prime Minister in 1976.

Callaghan had resigned after the devaluation he fought so long to avoid. Denis Healey, after six years as Secretary for Defence in 1964–70, had been Chancellor throughout the two Labour governments of 1974–79, although his entire political career before that had appeared to be a preparation for the Foreign Office. Nobody seriously expected Healey to resign over the 1976 financial crisis, which was a disaster for Labour but which did not have the dramatic impact of a forced devaluation or a sudden exit from the ERM. Having 'turned back at the airport' in 1976, Healey was still the obvious candidate to try to extricate the Callaghan government from the economic mess of the time.

Brown had consciously striven to avoid the kind of trap that ensnared his predecessor, and perhaps succeeded too well. Both Callaghan and Healey presided over periods of an excessively strong pound that damaged the competitiveness of British industry. In each case, and in several senses, there came a day of reckoning. The pound was once again overvalued in 1997–2001, but this time the day of reckoning was postponed.

The question of the appropriate value of the pound was going to surface more prominently after 2001 in the debate over the possibility of Britain's joining the Eurozone; there was a danger that by staying on at the Treasury Gordon Brown would find that the kind of financial crisis that afflicted previous Labour Chancellors had merely been postponed. But perhaps the most important factor was that Brown felt he had not yet completed his work at the Treasury.

After all, the first term had lasted a mere four years – or four years and one month: the economic news of winter and spring 2001 was overshadowed by the 'foot and mouth' crisis – so much so that the Prime Minister decided to postpone the election from the day he had originally chosen by a month, until things looked reasonably calm on that front. Brown's serious spending programme had been for the second half of a five-year first term *and* a second term. His Chancellorship was nowhere near complete.

But with relatively minor reservations Gordon Brown was considered a resounding success as Chancellor, and his only ambition in 2001 was the Premiership, which Tony Blair was not about to relinquish, whatever he might have said at Granita in April 1994. When asked why Gordon Brown wore his ambition so nakedly on his sleeve, given what a successful Chancellor he was widely perceived to be, someone very close to him said: 'Because it's only when he is the real boss that he can achieve what he wants to achieve for the Labour Party.'

Brown was not terribly interested in the Foreign Office. His interest in foreign affairs seemed to be confined largely to European issues (when they affected the British economy) and to the awesome issue of global poverty, which he made into a major concern of the International Monetary Fund in his capacity as Chairman of the IMF's key political committee. Indeed, in October 1999 some of his fellow Finance Ministers had been surprised to receive telephone calls from the British Chancellor asking them whether, if he put his name forward to be Managing Director of the IMF, they would support his candidature. They were surprised because this was Gordon Brown at the height of his reputation, and the obvious candidate to succeed Blair. Certainly Brown was passionately interested in the problems of the Third World. 'Previous Chancellors were only interested in the subject of debt relief – in Nigel Lawson's case because he knew some countries were so broke that the debt could never be repaid anyway,' said one Treasury official. 'But Gordon Brown believes not only in debt relief but also in active development assistance.' The Chancellor raised the British target for development assistance; worked closely with Clare Short, Secretary for Overseas Development (1997–2003), within the government; and encouraged the IMF in his capacity as Chairman of the International Monetary and Finance Committee

(IMFC) to become what one former IMF Managing Director called 'more of a development assistance agency and less of an IMF.'

Whether the Chancellor was really serious about putting himself forward for the IMF job was not clear. His European counterparts could not really believe he was, and it was their surprise that prompted the leak – which, because the nature of the inquiries was hypothetical and 'off the record', could always have been denied.[12]

It might have been a brief flirtation with the idea by the restless Chancellor or part of some complicated manoeuvre in his dealings with the Prime Minister. At all events, it came to nothing. Brown did not pursue the idea; neither, on the other hand, did he throw his weight behind any other possible British candidate for the job, an omission which bitterly irked senior Treasury officials.

Labour won the election of June 2001 with what was – and still is – misleadingly described as 'another landslide majority'. In fact, the earth did not move and the majority was slightly smaller than in 1997. As Butler and Kavanagh pointed out, the theme of the election campaign was 'apathy', with a 12% drop in turnout to a record low of 59%.

The Chancellor's two great interests – health and education – were also top of the voters' concerns, 73% saying that healthcare would be very important in making them decide which way to vote and 62% citing education. The issue of taxation concerned only 37%, 'managing the economy' and 'public transport' 31%. Gordon Brown's approach to 'tax and spend' appeared, if not to have removed, at least to have pushed some skeletons to the back of the cupboard. Meanwhile it was obvious what had to be done, and the Labour Manifesto for 2001 had one major theme – *Public Services: Investment and Reform*.

Only 26% of voters mentioned Europe as an issue that concerned them. But as far as the man who wished to remain as Chancellor was concerned, the issues of public services *and* Europe were going to loom large in his second term. So was the question of how long he could retain his quite extraordinarily high reputation, as the doubts about his economic strategy began to grow. These issues were of course closely connected with the question of whether he would achieve his overwhelming ambition to succeed Tony Blair. As the second term began, Gordon Brown hoped that his prudence would now be seen to have been exercised for several purposes.

One purpose was the eventual succession. But another was so that he could do the things he believed a 'modern' Labour Chancellor should do. In this respect the 2002 'health' budget – which he had planned for several years – was intended to be the rebirth of a 'prudent' approach to 'tax and spend'.

He himself felt no contradiction between his prudence in 1997–2001 and his 2002 Budget, which prepared the way for the 1p increase in national insurance contributions in 2003. But others would take a different view.

It was not just analysts in the City and independent economic think-tanks – such as the National Institute of Economic and Social Research, and the Institute for Fiscal Studies – who began to show concern about the long-term sustainability of the budgetary position. While Gordon Brown himself felt he had done everything to ensure that the quality of prudence was not strained, old Treasury hands began to wonder too.

These sceptics did not necessarily share the burgeoning popular view that 'prudence is in trouble'. Neither did they argue that it would *necessarily* end in tears. But they had watched public spending as a proportion of GDP rise from 36% in 1998–99 to a planned 41% in 2004–05, and concluded that the 2004 Budget was going to prove the acid test of prudence.

Gordon Brown as Chancellor had enjoyed a long period when debt interest fell and the cost of unemployment and other benefits came down too. This undoubtedly helped the Chancellor to allow spending on health and education to grow at rates considerably higher than public spending as a whole. But he could not confidently expect the trend of debt interest and social security to continue to exert such a benign influence on the total. And health spending was intended to go on rising fast until 2008, to bring British standards up to the European average.

Spending on 'Education, Education, Education' was also rising at well above the long-term growth rate of the economy, but still not satisfying the demand. The Treasury knew full well that surges in spending by these big departments in the past had proved unsustainable. Something had to give.

The big issue had become how well the extra money was spent, and whether the public was satisfied. The Conservative Opposition might be weak, but the media were not short of the drip-drip of stories that money was being wasted or swallowed up by higher pay. True, there were plenty of reports of improved services; but Gordon Brown and his colleagues knew full well in spring 2003 that, at best, judgement about the success of what they believed was a more prudent approach to 'tax and spend' was still suspended. In the hackneyed New Labour phrase, now it was 'all about "delivery"'.

The Attlee government of 1945–50 had run into trouble with its spending plans mid-way through. The Wilson government of 1964–70 was resorting to 'July measures' (to cut back) by 1966. The Wilson/Callaghan governments of 1974–79 had been forced by the markets, via the IMF, to cut spending in 1976. The two-year freeze instituted by Brown in 1997–99 was, in the words of one senior mandarin, 'the second-most important decision Brown made' (after independence for the Bank). In only one two-year period had spending been lower under the Conservatives. The decision aggravated the problems of the public services, but gave the Chancellor a sound fiscal base. The 'good run' with lower debt interest and falling unemployment reinforced his position.

On the revenue side there was concern that the halcyon days of swelling tax receipts during the boom years up to and after the turn of the century would not be repeated (tax receipts from the financial sector had been especially pleasing to the Revenue and the Exchequer). There was also a concern in the Treasury about a middle-class revolt against higher charges. Treasury officials, under Clarke and the early days of Brown, had been tickled pink by the discovery of the tax collector's stone – the 'stealth tax' offered by the so-called 'fuel escalator', a moving tax staircase on which revenues routinely rose each year by several percentage points above the rate of inflation.

But there had been a popular uprising against fuel taxes in the late summer of 2000 – an uprising which undoubtedly took the government and the Treasury by surprise. Gordon Brown understood the politics of this and had no feasible alternative but to walk back down that particular escalator. And the fuss generated by the mere 1% rise in national insurance contributions in 2003 – the financial press was awash with complaints from industry about the impact on costs – showed that Brown was up against a tide of resistance to higher taxes, however hard he had struggled to earn a reputation for prudence.

True, the Treasury could still rely to a certain extent on 'fiscal drag' – the built-in tendency for direct taxation to rise as more and more people qualified either to pay the basic rate of income tax for the first time, or to pay the higher rate for the first time. Thus by 2003, there were five million more income tax payers than five years earlier; and one million more were paying some of their taxes at 40%. The Chancellor also gained when he did not increase tax allowances in line with earnings. Nevertheless, all this was allowed for in the published forecasts. Independent institutes thought prudence was in trouble; this also seemed to be a popular view among the general public; and Treasury old hands were beginning to think that the 2004 Budget would be an important test of their Chancellor's long-term strategy. Would he be able to carry on spending as much as he wished – 'to do the things a Labour Chancellor ought to do' – or would he have to begin planning further rises in taxes for future years? And how would that go down with a nation worried about its pensions?

This was very much a medium-term problem. In the short run there was the Keynesian point that in 2003, at a time of slowdown, the 'automatic stabilisers' should be allowed to work – toleration of lower tax receipts, willing acceptance of higher spending. In this respect, given the long-term planning of the higher public spending recorded in 2003, Brown had been an 'accidental Keynesian'. The question was whether the balance would be right in the medium term, when the economy picked up again.

It was not a good omen for those who believed that better public services required a sustained increase in funding when the Prime

Minister immediately dismissed a suggestion by Peter Hain, the new Leader of the Commons, that consideration should finally be given to increasing the top rate of income tax. On 20 June 2003 Hain was planning to raise the issue in the second Aneurin Bevan Lecture. But following a report of his intention, he was forced by Number 10 to stop speculating about 'those *at the very top of the pay scale contributing more*' (his words to the *Daily Mirror*) and to proclaim instead, 'We will not raise the top rate of tax.' Tony Blair asserted the same day, 'I have not spent the last ten years ensuring the Labour Party is in the position where we say we're not raising the top rate of tax in order to change that position now.'

But Hain had not even put his suggestion in the context of better public services. He was drawing attention to the fact that 'the top 40% rate of tax now catches too many middle-income employees, including teachers and police.'

Gordon Brown was not amused. It was going to be difficult enough to finance bringing up British public services to European standards, without acknowledging that another of his 'stealth taxes' (not increasing tax allowances in line with earnings) was drawing more and more people into the tax net. If Brown had been hoping to persuade Blair to withdraw his veto on a higher top rate of tax, what Roy Hattersley described as the 'hysterical' reaction of the Prime Minister's office did not augur well.

The first Aneurin Bevan Lecture had been delivered at the University of Glamorgan on 23 May 2002 in the presence of Michael Foot by Gordon Brown himself. It contained a paean of praise for Bevan's achievements with the National Health Service. Brown said at the time, 'A free National Health Service at the point of need is now the central dividing line between the political parties in British politics.' The Chancellor also promised: 'The new Britain worthy of Bevan's vision will be built not only around a goal of full employment but around the goal of world class public services.'

These were among what Brown called, 'the social justice priorities of Labour's second term'. It was to achieve such goals that he had exercised his prudence. But the constraints on his financing plans were undoubtedly beginning to show.

CHAPTER TWELVE

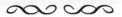

'Euro-wars'

The 'new' Labour government run by the duumvirate of Tony Blair and Gordon Brown began its second term in June 2001 knowing that two major issues were going to dominate the new Parliament – the public services and 'Europe' (there was no mention of Iraq). The Manifesto began with the promise of 'investment and reform' in the public services, stating that 'renewal of our public services is at the centre of new Labour's Manifesto.' There was also a long and rather pious section on Europe – contained in a chapter headed *Britain Strong in the World*.

A government that had spent four years demonstrating its financial probity was rightly embarrassed about how far behind mainland Europe it still was when it came to the provision of public services. It was as if 'New' Labour were coming into office for the first time. But while it was obvious that the electorate wanted European standards, New Labour believed it had something to offer mainland Europe. At the top of the list of 'our ten-year goals' was the statement: 'Europe to have the most competitive knowledge-based economies in the world, *as British ideas lead a reformed and enlarged Europe*' (author's italics). References to the single currency were few and far between, and notably defensive. In his introduction the Prime Minister said: 'We will engage fully in Europe, help enlarge the European Union and make it more effective, and insist that the British people have the final say on any proposal to join the euro.' The body of the Manifesto stated: 'We hold to our promise: no membership of the single currency without the consent of the British people in a referendum.'

'... the final say on *any proposal* ...' – this did not sound like the forcefulness of a Prime Minister who had told a stream of visitors in private that he was determined to join the euro. The very phrase 'any proposal' sounded like a vague preparation for a contingency emanating from elsewhere; it did not exactly accord with the government's stated position that there was no 'constitutional' bar to adopting the euro, or with Gordon Brown's promise, expressed on 27 October 1997, that Britain 'will be in a position to join a single currency, should we wish to, early in the next Parliament.'[1]

For 27 October 1997 was also the day on which Gordon Brown was generally considered to have seized control of the European agenda from the Prime Minister with his announcement of the famous 'five economic tests' which had to be passed:

1. Whether there can be sustainable convergence between Britain and the economies of a single currency;
2. Whether there is sufficient flexibility to cope with economic change;
3. The effect on investment;
4. The impact on our financial services industry, and;
5. Whether it is good for employment.[2]

Of these the Chancellor said: 'the first and most critical is convergence: can we be confident that the UK business cycle has converged with that of other European countries so that the British economy can have stability and prosperity with a common European monetary policy?' In popular parlance, this became known as the question of whether Britain could cope with a 'one-size-fits-all' monetary policy, i.e. with interest rates set by the proposed European Central Bank (in October 1997 the advent of the single currency was still some fourteen months away). Brown pointed out that 'currently Britain's business cycle is out of line with our European partners.' Interest rates in the UK were 7% but the rates were 'close to 3%' in Germany and France.

He blamed the divergence of economic cycles partly on historic 'structural' differences with the Continent, in particular the pattern of the UK's trade and North Sea Oil. But, he said, 'these differences are becoming less distinct as trade with the rest of Europe grows and the single market deepens.' He could not resist the political point that 'divergence is also a legacy of Britain's past susceptibility to boom and bust: the damaging boom of the late 1980s and the severe recession of the early 1990s.'

The Treasury's assessment was that the UK economy was not yet 'convergent' and that the divergence could continue 'for some time'. So what could alter matters? The implication was that trade patterns via closer linkage within the single market might help, and that the terrible 'legacy' could be dealt with via the 'stability' expected from 'continuing toughness on inflation and public borrowing'.

To demonstrate sustainable convergence would take 'a period of years'. While the period was not yet defined, it was narrowed down – or perhaps extended – with the fairly definitive statement that 'barring some fundamental and unforeseen change in economic circumstances', making a decision to join during the current Parliament was 'not realistic'.

One aspect of this important statement that received insufficient attention at the time was that everything was based on the premise that Britain would in due course be deciding on whether to join a *successful* single currency' [author's italics]. This left open objections regarding the constitution of the European Central Bank, or the operation of the Stability and Growth Pact (on fiscal policy); if problems with these were considered to be hampering the workings of the single currency, then behind the word 'successful' could lie a sixth test. It was made clear that the second test – flexibility 'sufficient to cope with economic change' – applied to the flexibility not only of the British economy but also of what was to become known as the Eurozone. The Chancellor also acknowledged that the fifth test – the effect on employment – 'in practice comes back to sustainable convergence', i.e. was subsumed within the first test.

From the publication of the tests onwards, there was great scope for advocates on both the 'pro' and 'anti' sides to cite tests three and four – the impact on investment and on financial services – to support their position. Fears that the City would suffer as a result of

Britain's exclusion from the Eurozone were subsequently contested by the Governor of the Bank of England, Sir Edward George, although at the time the tests were published the Treasury thought it might. The heads of multinationals such as Nissan would frequently raise doubts about their commitment to the UK in the absence of assurances that the decision would eventually be positive; these captains of industry would from time to time receive assurances from the Prime Minister of his good intent.

Industrialists who were in favour of joining the Eurozone often blamed the instability and uncertainty caused by Britain's exclusion as a factor inhibiting new investment. In practice, however, a more tangible explanation was the deleterious impact of an overvalued pound on the profitability of investment.

The 'convergence', or interest rate point, was an obvious difficulty in October 1997. Having inherited the 'Clarke boom' and raised interest rates immediately, Gordon Brown and the Treasury would have been terrified at the thought of a halving of UK interest rates. This would have guaranteed an immediate spending spree by consumers and house buyers. It would have been necessary to offset the impact with quite dramatic rises in taxation of the sort that a Chancellor who was now making a living out of opposing 'tax and spend' could not conceivably have contemplated.

The most glaring omission from the five tests was the exchange rate. The rate of interest may be a very important price in the economy, but so is the exchange rate. Being saddled with the wrong exchange rate had been a central feature of most British governments' problems with the economy during the century that was now drawing to a close. In due course Ed Balls was to deliver an important lecture on that very subject in the autumn of 2003 and the exchange rate was going to figure prominently in the June 2003 'supporting studies'. Yet overt concern for the exchange rate was conspicuous by its formal absence from the list of five tests, although it was implicit in them. Thus, one could question whether an economy that joined the Eurozone at an overvalued exchange rate could remain 'converged'; one could doubt whether such an economy possessed enough flexibility to cope with economic change; investment tends to suffer when companies are unprofitable because of an overvalued exchange rate; and employment is manifestly threatened in such circumstances.

Moreover, the importance of the exchange rate is not just that it should be right 'at the time'. The UK's economy had traditionally suffered from lower productivity than its Continental neighbours and from higher inflation. Both of these problems necessitated periodic devaluations to bring competitiveness back into line: otherwise, exports suffered and imports rose excessively, damaging domestic employment. The need to stabilise the 'real exchange rate' – the exchange rate adjusted for differences in industry's cost and prices – was at the heart of Ed Balls's long-term strategy.

It also seemed decidedly eccentric, on the part of a Chancellor who had shown great concern for the health of manufacturing, that the only 'industry' whose health was singled out as deserving of a special test was 'financial services', more commonly known as the City of London. It was Winston Churchill, when Chancellor in 1925, who had sighed for 'finance' to be 'less proud' and 'industry more content'. True, it was an encouraging sign that the Labour Party had come to terms with the City and no longer regarded it as the class enemy – apart from anything else, the City handled the savings of the nation, including those of the Labour Party's supporters. But manufacturers who were suffering from the strains imposed by the high pound would no doubt have appreciated a nod in their direction from the composer of the five tests.

The reason for the Chancellor's EMU statement of Monday 27 October 1997 – the first day of Parliament after the summer recess – was that press speculation about the government's intentions had got completely out of hand, helped (if that was the word) by some ferocious spinning and counter-spinning by the warring pro- and anti-euro factions at the heart of government.

Gordon Brown's 'position' on Europe had been open to varying interpretations at various times but it was he who was responsible for renewing Labour's commitment to match the Conservative Party's promise of a referendum. Mrs Thatcher, who was of course fiercely hostile to the single currency, had been the first significant political figure to propose a referendum, during a Parliamentary debate on 20 November 1991, just before the fateful European Union (EU) meeting at Maastricht. Neil Kinnock recalls John Smith in 1993 being in favour of a referendum. John Major as Prime Minister picked up the ball – slowly – and it became Conservative Cabinet policy in April 1996, very much against the will of the Chancellor, Kenneth Clarke. Although much of the Blair government's embarrassment over its European policy stemmed from its commitment to a referendum, it was difficult to see how, once the Conservatives had committed themselves, Labour could avoid such a move. Brown, though more 'pro-euro' than Blair in 1996, wanted to retain 'flexibility' and not commit to a referendum. But Blair and Mandelson persuaded him it was essential to prevent the Conservatives making political capital. Geoffrey Robinson was also in favour. Gordon Brown made the announcement during an interview with David Frost on Sunday, 17 November 1996.

Labour was cautious on the single currency during spring 1997, with Blair in particular worried about the Murdoch Press to the point where he himself was prepared to put his name to an article in the *Sun* on the eve of St George's Day, referring to 'another dragon to be slayed: Europe'. It was good enough for Labour to have made its commitment to a referendum and indicate that it was unlikely to be in the 'first wave' of monetary union. But after the election, and especially after such an unexpectedly large victory, the pro-euro camp began to push Blair to capitalise on the size of his majority by 'going for it'.

With policy as yet undecided, and an absurd idea offered to the rest of the EU that it should 'postpone' the launch of the single currency given short shrift, the stage was set for trouble. The most positive step taken by Labour was to end Britain's opt-out from the social chapter of the Maastricht Treaty, thereby giving employers' organisations such as the CBI endless opportunities to complain about 'red tape'. But the 'opt-out' from the single currency remained, despite the fact that at the time the more prominent lobbies of industrialists advocated joining the single currency (just as they had been pro-ERM in 1990). One very prominent industrialist, Sir David Simon, even gave up the prestigious job of Chief Executive of

BP in order to take a junior minister's 'European' portfolio from a seat in the House of Lords. The initial enthusiasm which Simon took to his job suggested that he was one of the many people from 1997 onwards who had been impressed by pro-single currency remarks made by Tony Blair in private, whatever the government's spinning machine might be selling to the Conservative press.

Lord Simon was based in the Foreign Office, where Robin Cook was perceived to be less hostile towards the single currency now that it was becoming evident that most other EU countries were determined to press ahead with monetary union. A report in the *Financial Times* on 26 September 1997 suggested that the government was 'on the point of adopting a much more positive approach to the European economic and monetary union, with a statement shortly that sterling is likely to join at an early opportunity after the 1999 launch'.

This was followed by a similar report in the *Daily Mail* of 13 October 1997, adding the gloss that this was 'a victory for Gordon Brown'. Then on 14 October 1997 the *Independent* reported that Brown had tried to 'bounce Blair into a decision which could lead to the early death of the pound'.

The Treasury had denied the FT report, saying that entry in 1999 or soon after was 'most unlikely'; Gordon Brown hoped the fuss would die down. But his colleague Peter Mandelson, with whom his relations were notoriously difficult, proceeded to fan the flames with a public remark early in October that Britain 'had not ruled out joining EMU in the first wave'.[3]

The *Independent* report was by Anthony Bevins, a journalist close to Alastair Campbell. After all the publicity devoted since October 1997 to Gordon Brown's hostility towards the euro, it may seem surprising that he could have been considered pro-euro at the time. But a Minister close to Brown told me on 29 July 1997: 'The French and Germans are going to do it. There is no future for us outside. Gordon Brown wants to enter at the first opportunity. Robin Cook is the problem.'

Equally, given the public stand taken by Cook over the euro ever since, it may seem surprising that he was considered 'the problem' on the eve of the Parliamentary summer recess in 1997. But in the course of the summer of 1997 Cook became more positive about early entry to the single currency, while Brown developed reservations.

It is important to distinguish between Brown's hostility towards the exchange rate mechanism after 1992 and his position on the single currency itself. By 1991 a Labour Party that had campaigned in 1983 on an anti-European platform was officially in favour of EMU in principle, provided the conditions were right. In December 1994 Cook called for convergence in employment and economic growth, and stated the need for a politically accountable central bank (the Maastricht criteria already required convergence of interest rates, as well as low inflation and strict limits on budget deficits and levels of government debt). On 27 October 1996 Cook saw 'insufficient convergence' for Britain to join 'the first wave' in 1999; but he thought there might come a point when it could be dangerous to remain out of a successful single currency. Cook infuriated Brown by telling the BBC that it could be 'very risky for Britain to give up the option in future of devaluing, if that was necessary'. One of Brown's 'prudent' objectives was to shed the image of Labour as 'the Party of devaluation'.[4]

In November 1996, a month after Cook's dismissal of entry in the first wave, Brown told a City of London audience that there would be 'genuine and active consideration' of the merits of the euro, and made no attempt to rule out entry in the first wave. Cook proceeded to give the strong impression in subsequent months that Labour had more or less ruled out joining in the first wave but that this did not apply to 2002, when euro notes and coins would come into circulation. But on 26 February 1997, just two months before the general election, Brown stated: 'If the economic conditions are right, we will retain the option of joining the single currency in the next Parliament and in the first wave.'[5]

One of the key influences on the FT report of 25 September was an indication to its political editor, Robert Peston, by David Clark, Cook's political adviser, that Cook was now being more positive about the single currency. This was part of the background to Peston's report that the government was considering entry 'around the turn of the century', partly because of 'a growing convergence of views between Robin Cook, the Foreign Secretary, and Gordon Brown, the Chancellor, who had previously been seen at loggerheads.'

An informed source described Tony Blair's position as 'euro-sceptical' about a year before the 1997 general election, but it seemed to become more positive after 1 May, notwithstanding the sceptical 'spin' directed at the Murdoch press during the campaign. Blair himself, for example, assumed rather a high profile at the June 1997 Amsterdam Summit, and began to see the attractions of 'engaging' with Europe. Blair's prominent position in the impromptu bicycle ride taken by EU leaders during an interval from the Amsterdam Summit was symbolic of the way he took effortlessly to the European stage, and soon became a star attraction.

Despite the perceived hardening of his position during his Chancellorship, Gordon Brown had given the impression to Lord Paul and others that he was enthusiastic about the proposed single currency before the 1997 election. Some of the Treasury officials working closely with him, while noting that his real interest in European meetings was not kindled until he fought and defeated a proposal (for a withholding tax) which he feared would damage the City's comparative advantage, nevertheless deduced that the ever-cautious Brown was not at all dismissive of the single currency in the early months of his Chancellorship. Within weeks he gave a speech to the CBI on *The British Genius*, in which he was very positive about Europe: 'Let me put the government's position on Europe beyond doubt,' he said. 'We are in for the long term; we are in to stay. And it is in Britain's essential interests that we now play a leading role in shaping Europe's future.' Neil Kinnock, observing from his post in Brussels, thought the man he had considered for Chancellor in 1992 was a lot keener in May 1997 on the single currency than he subsequently appeared. And an official who worked closely with the new Chancellor maintained: 'For much of 1997 Gordon Brown was more pro-Europe than Tony Blair – at least until the Charlie Whelan announcement. Whether I was duped I don't know. Perhaps the change was related to the success of the MPC, because the real fear was that it was not going to work, that the pound would go through the floor and therefore we would need Europe to support it. I don't know at what point Brown became anti, but am sure Ed Balls was the influence.' As Ian Hargreaves and Steve Richards observed at the time (*New Statesman*, 24 October 1997): 'For Brown, the austere formalities of European monetary union coincide precisely with his view of the prudent management of the national economy, and the euro offers the prospect of a life free of sterling crises and the wild swings thereby caused in investment, output and jobs.'

But so far Brown's new fiscal and monetary orthodoxy had proved popular beyond his wildest dreams. As the above Treasury official observed, the real fear had not materialised. And there were other considerations.

Lord Simon, the euro-enthusiast who worked closely with the Treasury on 'Reform in Europe', tried to square the circle of spin surrounding the Chancellor's position on Europe by saying that 'Gordon is strategically pro the euro but tactically anti.'[6] Even Simon, who was horrified by the lack of any contingency planning or serious preparation for the single currency under the Conservatives, agreed that in October 1997 the UK was not ready to join the first wave of entrants in 1999. Other industrialists who were basically in favour shared his view. Quite irrespective of what the 1997 assessment of the 'tests' had shown – and the verdict was negative – industry and the financial sector could not have got its act together by 1999, whereas the future founder members of the Eurozone were well advanced with their preparations.

Some observers of the scene concluded that Brown's manifest dislike of meetings in Brussels and Luxembourg turned him against the euro – 'he arrives late, leaves early and is impatient while he's there,' said one senior official. Another said: 'Of course, the problem with these European meetings is that the Chancellor can't control them the way he likes to control meetings in London.' The 'tactically anti' point was closely related to Brown's extreme caution in not wanting to offer the Conservatives, or their press, 'a chink' with which to damage Labour by exploiting the predominantly anti-euro feeling in the country at large.

As far as Simon was concerned, the problem was that after the 1997 'five tests' had been laid down, things just 'drifted'. Once the 'Lisbon Agenda' on supply side reform in Europe had been agreed, Simon was 'not prepared to hang around'. Meanwhile Ed Balls had plenty of opportunity to hammer away at the Chancellor with his view that the euro decision could not be made merely for 'political' reasons and that the economics had to be right.

Ed Balls had set out his stall on Europe in his Fabian pamphlet of 1992 – as he had on his advocacy of an independent central bank. Yet Gordon Brown tended to take a long time to be persuaded about anything. He would listen and consult endlessly; he would nod; he would ask questions; he would mull ideas over; he would ponder; he would brood. Rupert Pennant-Rea recalled that, when he was Editor of the *Economist*, he had a hand in arranging first for John Smith and later for Gordon Brown, as Shadow Chancellors, to go to conferences organised by the Aspen Institute of Colorado, and be exposed to American ideas. These trips used to take place in August, and had an impact on Brown, who used the opportunity of the trips to visit Washington and Harvard as well, where he became acquainted with American ideas and developed his enthusiasm (most certainly not associated with Old Labour) for entrepreneurship and various workfare schemes that had first been tried out in places such as Wisconsin. Pennant-Rea recalled a conversation at Aspen in August 1994 in which he urged the idea of an independent central bank upon Brown. Brown seemed hostile and asked lots of questions. This was when Pennant-Rea was Deputy Governor of the Bank of England. The following summer the two had lunch in London and Pennant-Rea had another go.[7] This time there was no hostility and there were fewer questions. As noted earlier, Brown finally decided upon an independent Bank the weekend before the 1997 election, although Balls had been working on him for years. Similarly, also dating from the 1992 pamphlet and that first meeting between Brown and Balls, Balls had been hostile towards the single currency. But Brown certainly gave the impression that he was more sympathetic towards the single currency than Balls during his early months at the Treasury. Of Balls's strategy for approaching the single currency (if necessary) from a position of strength, Brown had accepted the fiscal advice first, the monetary advice second, and the formal postponement of the single currency option itself last of all. After that, despite many false alarms – usually emanating from the pro-euro courtiers at Number Ten – the euro was effectively off the British agenda for the rest of the first term and much of the second.

Before being forced into their definitive statement on 27 October, Blair and Brown tried to kick the euro ball into touch via a press interview. Blair agreed to a suggestion from Brown that the latter should give an interview to a reliable *Times* Lobby Correspondent, Philip Webster. Unfortunately this interview itself got 'spun' – both by the headline and by Charlie Whelan, who was overheard doing so on his portable 'phone in a Whitehall pub. Moreover the Prime Minister, having failed to track down anyone else, was reduced to calling Whelan at the Red Lion to find out what was going on.[8]

The text agreed between the Blair and Brown camps had been innocuous enough: 'We said in our Manifesto, and it remains true today, that it is highly unlikely that Britain can join in the first wave. If we do not join in 1999, our task will be to deliver a period of sustainable growth, tackle the long-term weaknesses of the UK economy and to continue to press for reform in Europe.'

The headline was 'Brown Rules Out Single Currency for Lifetime of This Parliament' – stronger than the text, but in the spirit of what the interviewer had been given to understand by Brown, Balls and Campbell.[9] In this case Campbell, himself euro-sceptical at the time, did not succeed in pleasing his master and all hell broke loose. Blair held Brown ultimately responsible and, to cut a long story short, everybody was told to behave better.

And so the five tests came to be published alongside an initial Treasury assessment making it clear that the time was not yet ripe. Although Balls's caution towards the euro had been noted earlier in this book, it is important to emphasise that this was fully endorsed in the negotiations preceding the 27 October statement by the senior

Treasury official on European monetary affairs, Sir Nigel Wicks. Although Wicks became keen on British membership of the euro later, and at the time was Chairman of the key EU committee of officials preparing for Euro Day, Sir Nigel in October 1997 was firmly of the view that the UK and the Eurozone would not have converged by 1999. (Wicks had helped to draw up the 'Maastricht Criteria'!)

The importance of the October 1997 statement was that it was a policy for the euro that lasted for the duration of the 1997–2001 Parliament and beyond. It was an agreed policy, although the atmosphere between the Blair and Brown camps was such that at one stage the Prime Minister threatened to deliver the statement himself. Before the 'agreement' there was disagreement over whether Brown should apologise for the way the policy had been unveiled in the press first; over whether Brown should accept a rewritten draft of his speech – 'in better English' – from the Prime Minister's private secretary; and about just how much emphasis to put on the remote possibility that a positive decision could still be taken later in the Parliament.

In the end, the Chancellor finalised his own speech and delivered it, but his desire (backed by Wicks) to eliminate all uncertainty for the 1997–2001 Parliament was thwarted by Number Ten, at whose insistence the words 'barring some fundamental and unforeseen change in economic circumstances' had been added to the assertion that: 'Making a decision, during this Parliament, to join is not realistic.' This strong assertion did not prevent sporadic bursts of speculation, the most prominent one being a series of 'positive' statements on the euro from some of the Chancellor's Cabinet colleagues in spring 2000. But these were scotched by a fairly definitive restatement of the policy at the annual Mansion House speech on 15 June that year. The policy was essentially one of 'carry on preparing, but decide after the next election'. Brown officially declared the Treasury, in a speech agreed with the Prime Minister, to be 'the guardian of the policy'.

If the words 'barring some fundamental and unforeseen change in economic circumstances' had been regarded by the Treasury as an unnecessary (but as it turned out, unused) loophole to mollify enthusiasts for the single currency, Brown also considered it the one loophole available to the Conservatives. But it was hardly worth making a meal of this 'concession'. The whole tone of the announcement was negative about the chances of entry before the next Parliament. 'It is,' said Brown, 'sensible for business and the country to plan on the basis that, in this Parliament, we do *not* propose to enter a single currency.' Government and business must start preparing for the possibility of entry in the next Parliament, but 'at present, with no preparation, it is not a practical option'. While emphasising that what was at issue was Britain's membership of 'a successful single currency', Brown stated unequivocally, 'It is in the British national interest for it to work.'

Interestingly, the five tests were not quite as new or spontaneously dreamt up as many observers have suggested. They had been put into the public domain when Labour was still in Opposition. The only difference was the order in which the tests were presented. For on 26 February 1997, Gordon Brown had announced: 'Whenever a decision is considered, we will want to apply the following British economic tests. First, what is the likely impact on investment by British firms in Britain and Europe and on inward investment to Britain? Second, what will be the effect on our financial services? Third, whether business cycles are compatible. Fourth, whether there is sufficient flexibility to respond to any problems that may arise. Fifth, what will be the employment impact?'[10]

These tests were put forward as being specifically British 'extras', on top of the requirements laid down in the Maastricht Treaty of 1992 about convergence of interest rates, strict limits on budget deficits, and exchange rate stability within the ERM for two years before adoption of the euro.

Brown was to be criticised for dragging his feet on the euro when he came into office, but he had certainly hedged his bets in advance. In February 1997 he added: 'keeping the option open does not mean ignoring the real obstacles facing Britain and other countries, which are increasingly difficult to overcome by 1999.'

When asked by the US Treasury Secretary on a visit to Washington on 20 February 1997 what the British position was, he was still not certain that the single currency *would* go ahead in 1999, but said there were 'formidable obstacles' to Britain's participating immediately. He listed the five tests – which would get a public hearing in London the following week – and talked of a 'triple lock: the British opt-out, a vote of the British Parliament and a vote of the British people.'

It is important to remember that, even during the April 1997 election campaign, Labour was half-hoping that the single currency issue would be postponed anyway: thus Blair could not understand why the Conservatives were so obsessed by the issue, observing that 'the thing might not happen anyway'.[11] The Brown camp, which has been much criticised since for being anti-European, was itself concerned in the run-up to the May 1997 general election that Labour would end up in an anti-European position. Even at the Amsterdam European Council of June 1997, there were some doubts as to whether the 1999 deadline would still be met (the original options having been 1997 or 1999 'at the latest').

Nevertheless, Brown and Balls were shocked at what they regarded as the paucity of work that had been done at the Treasury on preparations for the single currency – despite the fact that the outgoing Chancellor, Kenneth Clarke, was such a prominent pro-European. Equally, as noted earlier in the chapter on the granting of independence to the Bank of England, Sir Terence Burns at the Treasury and Sir Howard Davies at the Bank were taken aback by the fact the Bank was being made independent for what Balls called 'entirely British reasons', not as part of a route to the Eurozone.

Despite this, Treasury officials were surprised from 2 May 1997 onwards by the way in which the incoming Labour Ministers were far more interested in 'Europe' than the outgoing Major government. 'They were far more engaged in Europe, to an extent that the department generally had not anticipated,' said one official. 'There was a step change in the nature of our engagement with Europe.' This official regarded the definitive statement of the government's position on the euro in October 1997 as 'pro-euro and essentially positive'. With regard to the more widespread view that, by definitively ruling out membership in the first wave (1999) and probably for the rest of the Parliament, Brown was being anti-European, this official said: 'Ask Charlie Whelan about that.'

How to reconcile the kicking into touch of the euro question in October 1997 with Brown's positive position as recently that year as July? This was a classic example of Dow's Dictum: Christopher Dow, the British economist who spent a long time as Economics Director of the Bank of England, would shake his head sagely at the end of a July meeting about the economic outlook and say: 'Things will look very different in September.'

Brown reflected on the euro question while on holiday in Cape Cod that August, and he and Balls had a series of meetings with Sir Nigel Wicks and other key Treasury officials in mid-September. They were planning to devote a Chancellorial speech to the CBI in November to the issue of the single currency but were overtaken by events, in the shape of the press speculation. It was obvious at that stage that the British and Continental economies were a long way from the convergence that would make the same monetary policy appropriate for all: the British economy was expanding far faster than what became known as the Eurozone, and the exchange rate was too strong for medium-term comfort. Meanwhile the newly independent Bank of England was widely considered a success and any fears that the Treasury's new economic team might need to seek refuge in 'Europe' had receded.

Faced with the economic analysis, Brown now had no doubt that Britain could not possibly join in the first wave. The next question was whether to rule it out for the entire Parliament. On this question Wicks, who had lived through the destabilising period of the run-up to ERM entry in the 1990s, was firmly of the view that uncertainty would be best eliminated by ruling it out for the Parliament. Wicks's view was embodied in Brown's October 1997 statement on EMU: to 'leave the options open ... would be politically cosy but wrong. There would be instability, perpetual speculation about "in or out", "sooner or later".'

Perhaps the funniest aspect of the press reports at the time was the suggestion that Brown was attempting to 'bounce' the government into the single currency in the first wave. This was apparently based on a misinterpretation of a routine report about the performance of Britain's economy *vis-à-vis* the rest of the EU. It was called a 'convergence report' but was a long way from suggesting that the British economy had 'converged' with the prospective Eurozone.

While Brown and his colleagues were devising their policy towards the euro in October 1997 they were amazed to learn that the Conservative Shadow Cabinet under William Hague was effectively ruling out membership for ten years. There was a great difference between this and preserving options should the single currency prove a success and the British economy become more obviously ready for entry.

Meanwhile, although Brown was embarrassed by the formation of an inner group of Eurozone finance ministers who would meet separately, he successfully fought an attempt by the French to make this group a more formal body, so that the wider EU group of finance ministers remained the key decision-making body. The essential position on the euro in Downing Street after October 1997 was epitomised by Geoffrey Robinson: 'Though, as agreed between them, each would talk with different emphasis on the issue, they were essentially united on the policy. Tony did not want a running debate on the euro or a referendum to spoil the build-up for the second election and Gordon did not want to see early entry put at risk the sound economic strategy he was putting into place to win that election.'[12] Robinson's judgement was that of a man who had some experience of smoothing relations between the Downing Street neighbours.

Having kicked the euro question into touch during October 1997, Gordon Brown had to do the same all over again within weeks of the 7 June 2001 general election. There was a renewed burst of speculation that, with another large majority, Labour might spring the kind of surprise it did after 1 May 1997, when it announced its plans for the Bank of England. But the parallels were far-fetched. Sir Edward George pointed out that the pound was far too high – at DM 3.15–3.20 (in 'old money') – for entry to the Eurozone (which had of course been functioning since 1999). He said a general decline in the pound would boost inflationary pressures and interest rates would have to rise, which would take British interest rates further away from European rates. 'That,' he pointed out, 'would be an obstacle to early entry'.[13]

Ed Balls himself made a rare public intervention (he was always assiduous in trying to keep journalists well informed with background briefings). In a lecture on the MPC he made it clear that the Chancellor's priority was not the euro but his plans 'to close the productivity gap, to promote full employment and to invest in public services'.

Other countries had conducted economic policies directed at achieving an appropriate long-run exchange rate in the run-up to joining the single currency. But Balls emphasised: 'there is no short-term exchange rate target competing with the inflation target'. He echoed George by saying that any attempt to manipulate the exchange rate would put both the inflation target and 'wider stability' at risk. This was a strong response to suggestions in the foreign exchange markets that the government might be adjusting its economic policy towards exchange rate convergence with the euro.[14]

The stage was set for another major attempt by Gordon Brown to dampen speculation about the euro. But the speculation was understandable in the light of the way that, in October 1997, the Chancellor had left the door open for entry 'early in the next Parliament'. Moreover, he had also urged 'government and business (to) prepare intensively' for such a contingency.

Much to his chagrin, Brown was eventually tied down. Towards the end of that first term the Leader of the Opposition, William Hague asked Blair, during Prime Minister's questions (7 February 2001): 'Does "early" mean the first two years of that Parliament?' The reply was: '"Early in the next Parliament" means exactly what it says. It would of course be within two years.'

One does not have to be a linguistic philosopher to regard this reply as a somewhat loose definition of 'early'; but when challenged by a fellow Cabinet Minister about another commitment he gave, Blair replied, 'It's just words.' The 'words' may have been a loose definition of 'early in the next Parliament', but they were not loose enough for Gordon Brown, who was furious at not having been consulted about Blair's answer. However, the Prime Minister himself had been taken by surprise. If the question had come from a Blairite Labour back-bencher, conspiracy theorists could have been forgiven for inferring that this was a 'planted' question. But it had come from the Leader of Her Majesty's Opposition, who was later to observe that this was the only 'straight reply' he ever received from Tony Blair. And it presented the Chancellor with enough of a deadline to offend a man who liked to keep his cards close to his chest and choose his own deadlines. But Brown would not have been Brown, and the Treasury not the Treasury, if between them they had failed to seize the maximum room for manoeuvre. The Chancellor, angry and unconsulted though he had been, was in effect to redefine 'within two years' to mean 'half way through' (assuming another four-year term). He did so on the occasion of the annual Mansion House speech, which took place on 20 June 2001, a few weeks after the beginning of that much-prized second term.

The Mansion House speech was traditionally devoted to monetary policy, but under Brown became an occasion for pronouncing on Europe. Ed Balls in his lecture earlier in the year had offered scope to those who thought he was more sceptical than Brown about the euro by saying, rather lukewarmly, 'euro membership could be an alternative and valid route to stability for Britain.'

Some Treasury officials regarded Brown's 2001 Mansion House speech as a strong restatement of the principle of Britain's joining the euro, even if once again the wedding was being postponed. The phrase Brown alighted on was 'pro-euro stability'. Another economic assessment would take place, but he was determined not to 'short-cut or fudge' that assessment. The Treasury's 'guidance' at this stage was that the assessment would take place at the 'back end of two years' – the first half of 2003. Some commentators thought the policy was hardened by Brown's insistence, in a speech to the CBI on 5 November 2001, that the tests would be 'comprehensive and rigorous'. Yet he had used precisely the same phrase in the Mansion House speech in June.

Asked about the euro that summer, one of Tony Blair's associates said: 'I think we'll go for it.'

Tony Blair talked, at the Labour Party annual conference on 2 October 2001, about 'having the courage of our argument' with regard to the euro. This was taken in some 'pro-euro' quarters as a sign of another assault on the Chancellor. The commitment to conduct a 'full' assessment within two years of the beginning of the Parliament, i.e. by 5 June 2003, had been the result of the competing forces of the Chancellor's procrastination and the Prime Minister's desire 'to go for it'. But Blair was up against the fact that it was a publicly-agreed policy to wait for the results of the five tests; these were in the hands of the Chancellor and a Treasury that increasingly regarded its own economic stewardship as superior to that of the Eurozone; and during the panic of October 1997 it had been Blair himself who had insisted on the statement that the results of the five economic tests should be 'clear and unambiguous'.

It was not difficult to predict that the Treasury would make full use of the scope afforded by the 5 June 2003 (two years after the 2001 general election) deadline for the results of the tests. But in the course of 2002 the press and airwaves were seldom free of speculation; pro-euro members of the Cabinet – or, in Peter Mandelson's case, former members of the Cabinet – were continually arguing the case for a more positive approach. The advent of euro notes and coins in January 2002 was an occasion for hope that the euro might capture the imagination of a largely sceptical British public.

On one occasion, at the end of February 2002, there were reports that Blair's advisers were urging 1 May 2003 as a date for the referendum – i.e. around the Treasury's self-chosen deadline for the three assessments. But Ed Balls told a Chatham House seminar 'Too often in the past, over the last hundred years, decisions have been made because of a political imperative, which was seen to override what was right from an economic point of view.' That week Sir Edward George told the Treasury Committee that 'the current level of the exchange rate is an immediate obstacle to euro entry'. And for good measure Brown himself told the Commons 'I'll be the person who will present the economic assessment'. The Treasury was in no hurry, but nevertheless, the Chancellor could not resist goading the Conservatives: for, while he was forever kicking the euro into touch, he was in favour in principle, while the Conservatives were dogmatically ruling out entry to the Eurozone 'even if it is in the national interest to join.'

In the Mansion House speech of 26 June 2002 Brown insisted that 'Britain's future for a pro-European like me is at the centre of Europe not isolated on its fringes.' Brown delivered a passionate defence of the need for the tests, and unveiled the news of the many 'supporting analyses' that would accompany them.

He emphasised that this was 'perhaps the biggest peacetime economic decision we as a nation have to make' and that 'to join without a proper, full assessment of the five tests could, in my view, prejudice our stability, risk repeating past failures of exchange rate management, and could return us to the days of stop-go at the expense of our ambition for high investment, full employment and high and sustained levels of growth.'

This did not prevent his more passionate pro-euro colleagues from keeping up the pressure. The next theory was that exposure to the new currency on their summer holidays might sway important sections of the electorate. But the polls remained stubbornly resistant to the wishes of such Ministers.

Then Neil Kinnock, the European Commission Vice President, was reported as holding out hopes that if Britain did apply for membership of the Eurozone it could negotiate changes in the operation of the Stability and Growth Pact before joining. It would need a devaluation of the pound, but otherwise 'Britain will be pushing at an open door, but it is a door that needs pushing.' (*Guardian* 18 September 2002.) Kinnock tried to persuade Brown to be more positive about the euro. This might have been part of a deal whereby Brown could present changes in the Stability Pact as evidence that he had converted Brussels. Brown and Balls both rejected this idea. John Monks, retiring General Secretary of the TUC, was party to this and jokingly described it as 'the conspiracy that failed'. Neil Kinnock insisted: I was never aware of being part of any conspiracy.

This was on the eve of the TUC 2002 annual conference. Within weeks Brown was attacking the European Commission after the Commissioner for European and Monetary Affairs, Pedro Solbes, had called for Eurozone member countries to reduce their budget deficits by 0.5% a year. 'I don't think the British public want the European Commission to cut £5 billion a year from spending, as is implied by these proposals,' he said. 'The British public has a clear idea that the schools and hospitals which are financed by our plans should go ahead.' And, just to ram the message home: 'My plans are prudent.'

The Treasury did a lot of preparatory work for the Cairncross Lecture delivered by Ed Balls on 4 December 2002. Entitled *Why the Five Economic Tests?* the lecture was intended as a riposte to those who argued that the tests were a mere figleaf – even Gus O'Donnell, by now the Permanent Secretary to the Treasury, had said on a private occasion a year earlier (in his capacity as head of the Government Economic Service) that the results of an economic assessment could never be 'clear and unambiguous' and that in the end the judgement would be 'political'.

Developing his theme at Chatham House earlier in the year that it would be a mistake to let political considerations override economic ones, Balls now expatiated on how disastrous the consequences had been when this had occurred in the past. He went into detail about such disastrous episodes as the return to the gold standard in 1925, concluding that 'the government of 1925 did not ensure that economics, not politics, was the deciding factor on the timing and manner of the decision ... (and) they did not base the decisions on a proper economic assessment of the long run consequences.' Balls also cited ruling out the option to devalue in 1946 and 1964 as examples of ill thought-out economic policies. He was especially scathing about the ERM experience, calling in evidence the words of Tony Blair during the 2001 election campaign: 'In principle, I believe it [the euro] is the right thing for Britain. But in practice, we must not repeat the mistakes of the Exchange Rate Mechanism and join under the wrong economic conditions.'[15]

To those in the pro-euro lobby who were urging haste, Balls repeated the Chancellor's words of October 1997 'convergence must be capable of being sustained and likely to be sustained – in other words we must demonstrate a settled period of convergence.'

With the Treasury's exercise well under way, Martin Wolf of the *Financial Times* had written 'Never can the British government have made a comparably detailed analysis of any policy decision.' The Treasury was fond of saying that, for all the continual spin and speculation, the policy towards the euro had not altered since October 1997. But the pro-euro lobby felt that Pelion was being piled upon Ossa, during 2002, as the news of the extra 'supporting studies' was unveiled, the tone of the Chancellor's approach to Brussels became notably assertive, and Balls in the Cairncross Lecture casually threw in that the economic analysis would include the consequences of 'any short-term transitional issues.' This was seized upon by some commentators as 'a sixth test' – or even 'seventh' if one allows for Brown's unhappiness with the workings of the ECB and the Stability and Growth Pact.

The assessment exercise may have been serious, and the Chancellor's longer term intentions towards the euro honourable, but he kept up his anti-euro tone early in 2003. In January, a participant at one of the occasional 'Keynes Seminars' held by Brown at Number 11 Downing Street, while sharing the Chancellor's concerns about the workings of the European Central Bank, was horrified by the virulence of Brown's private assault on the institution. 'I could hardly believe what I was hearing,' he said.

Then came the Budget, on 9 April 2003, which was notable for a two-edged approach to Europe. On the one hand Brown made gestures in the direction of eventual entry to the euro: he commissioned a study 'to examine the case for, and how, Britain can develop a market for long-term fixed rate mortgages – something that is important to the UK in or out of the euro, and more important in a single currency area.' He also said there was a case 'in principle' for Britain to adopt the 'harmonised' index of consumer prices (HICP) used by the Eurozone. The Treasury would continue to examine the detailed implications of such a change.' The Budget Report contained a section which stated: 'Were the UK to join EMU, these flexibilities [in the markets for labour, capital and products] would be even more essential, as the ability to adjust interest rates and exchange rates would no longer be available at a national level. In such circumstances, the labour, product and capital markets would need to respond dynamically so as to enhance the economy's resilience to shocks without putting at risk high and stable levels of growth and employment.'

On the other hand the Budget speech contained a section that might have been considered to tempt providence in the way it contrasted the wonders of British economic performance with the condition of the Eurozone. This was at a time when the foundations of the Chancellor's confident forecasts for growth were being questioned, as was the viability of his 'tax and spend' plans for the following few years, as borrowing rose rapidly above earlier forecasts. But despite the adverse criticisms from City analysts, the press and independent economic institutes about his Budgetary arithmetic, Brown still felt able to claim that borrowing and net debt over the years to 2008 would be kept well within the bounds of his own 'golden' and 'sustainable investment' rules.

The 2003 Budget was delayed because of the uncertainty caused by the invasion of Iraq, and the Budget itself was rather over-shadowed by the news that the war had just ended. The economic assessment of the euro question had been completed; there was talk of releasing it on Budget Day itself; the official line was that it was too big an issue to be unveiled while Iraq dominated the news. It was evident that the references to the Eurozone in the Budget Report reflected the work done on the assessment. But the fact was that, although Brown had presented his draft economic assessment to the Prime Minister, the two of them could not agree on an acceptable formula for interpreting the results of the tests in time for the Budget speech.

On 15 May the government announced the 'countdown' to the announcement of the decision on the euro. Members of the Cabinet were given 19 volumes of 'technical studies', collectively totalling 6000 pages. The areas covered included: analysis of European and business cycles and 'shocks'; estimates for the equilibrium exchange rates for sterling against the euro; housing, consumption and EMU;

modelling the transition to EMU; and the workings of monetary and fiscal policy.

After reading, scanning or perhaps just weighing these volumes, other Cabinet Ministers met the Prime Minister and Chancellor for 'trilateral' discussions, before receiving the Chancellor's official 'assessment'. The next stage was a Cabinet discussion early in June, to be followed by the official announcement on 9 June.

Despite this elaborate 'consultative' procedure, everyone knew that Gordon Brown had decided the time was not yet ripe, and that in an ideal world he would have liked to rule out a referendum for the rest of the Parliament. The essential truth was that neither he nor Blair thought they could win a referendum;[16] the difference between them was that the Prime Minister wished to have a form of announcement that kept the door ajar and accentuated the positive. In this sense it was almost a re-run of October 1997, with the Treasury wishing to rule out any uncertainty, but the Prime Minister feeling he had to show willing to the pro-euro lobby (many in the Cabinet) and to his European counterparts.

Inevitably the press and airwaves were dominated by reports of 'splits' and, equally inevitably, Blair and Brown did their best to make a public show of unity. Gordon Brown told David Frost on 18 May 2003 that 'nobody has ruled out a referendum as an act of dogma during the Parliament' and firmly stated his (very) long-term view that 'it is possible, in fact it's necessary in this country, to build a pro-European consensus.' Two days later he was interpreted by the pro-euro lobby as being negative again in a speech to the CBI. Yet many of the things he said about the Eurozone's need for reform echoed what he had been arguing consistently in earlier speeches.

For Brown the economics had to be right, and it was in the national interest to wait. The exchange rate might by this time have come down towards a more realistic level *vis-à-vis* the euro but there were many other areas, including different methods of housing finance, that caused him concern. And he still believed the economic policies of the Eurozone left a lot to be desired. In the opinion of Mandelson, who had resumed his sniping activities, and of many others, further delay would reinforce the anti-European lobby and damage future investment.

The veteran political commentator Alan Watkins likened the true position of Blair and Brown on the euro to the way Spenlow and Jorkins, to whom David Copperfield was articled, dealt with difficult decisions. Spenlow would indicate that he was sympathetic, but emphasise that his partner, Mr Jorkins, had reservations. One close observer of both Blair and Brown characterised the differences between them on the euro thus: 'Gordon has obsessively concentrated on taking an economic decision for economic reasons, Tony on taking an economic decision for more political reasons. But this not to say that Gordon ignores the political realities. The differences lie in the balance.'

Indeed, Brown never ignores the political realities. He always has his eye on what possible advantage there might be to the Opposition if Labour makes a false move on the issue. As Hugo Young, himself a fervent supporter of entry to the euro, has observed: 'For one of them the euro-glass may be half-full and for the other half-empty, but they share a desire, ultimately, to make the historic change. Knowing all that, if they run away from a referendum, we'll know what their reasons are. These will all be to do with the fear of losing.'[17]

In fact in Brown's case, the longer he remained at the Treasury, the more he became genuinely concerned about the economic aspect of the decision, and with the danger of making an historic mistake. Blair might wish to go down in history as the Prime Minister who finally took Britain into the euro. But for Brown wanting to go down in history is not a good enough reason, and the Treasury's study of previous historical adventures with the exchange rate during the last century, outlined in Balls's December 2002 lecture, and detailed in the June 2003 economic assessment, only served to strengthen his reserve.

While the fashionable 'pro euro' line in Westminster and Whitehall was that Britain should join in order to exercise greater influence over the debate about the evolving shape and governance of the Eurozone, Ed Balls's view was: 'Will it matter to those looking back from the perspective of 2080 if Britain joined in 2010 or 2015?'

As for shaping the Eurozone from within, the determined Gordon Brown was obviously hoping to exert a reasonable degree of influence from outside.

In the summer of 2000 someone who was for a time very close to Brown's thinking, said: 'It is sad, but the euro decision raises too many difficulties. It may be 2015 before we can join.'

It is clear to me and to many others I have spoken to, including Brown himself, that he has always felt a great weight of responsibility on his substantial shoulders with regard to the question of the euro. He was both affronted and hurt by suggestions, before the Prime Minister accepted the negative verdict of the Treasury in May 2003, that he should somehow relent as part of a deal whereby he would give the go-ahead for joining the euro and his succession to Blair would be assured.[18]

Brown took the opportunity with Frost (on whose programme he had first committed Labour to a referendum in November 1996) to put on record what he had previously indicated to others only privately: 'David, I would never make some sort of private arrangement when the national interest is at stake.' In the event, the interesting thing was the relative smoothness with which the euro exercise proceeded in spring 2003. 'Perhaps it was Iraq, but it was less disruptive than we feared at the beginning of the year,' one official observed.

The results of what Sir Edward George called 'the Treasury's exhausting – I mean exhaustive' economic assessment duly appeared on Monday 9 June. There was a 246 page report entitled *UK Membership in the Single Currency – An Assessment of the Five Economic Tests*, and this was accompanied by 19 supporting documents, covering issues such as 'Fiscal Stabilisation and the EMU' and 'Estimates of Equilibrium Exchange Rates for Sterling Against the Euro'.

It was the biggest such economic exercise the Treasury had ever undertaken, and drew heavily on assistance from distinguished outside economists as well. There was something for everyone, in that the 'pro euro' camp could point to microeconomic benefits from greater competition, a lower cost of capital and closer trading links. The gain from lower transactions' costs did not bulk large in the overall calculations, but microeconomic considerations taken together could, according to the assessment, lead to a small increase in the economy's long term growth rate.

On the other hand, the Treasury's reservations about subjecting the British economy to the 'one-size-fits-all' monetary policy were loud and clear, and, although the exchange rate had recently fallen towards more realistic levels, it concluded that the economy was some way from 'sustainable convergence'.

Blair and Brown talked long and hard about the issue before doing their best to put on a united front. Brown's concession to Blair was that the Treasury would have another look at the euro question around the time of the 2004 Budget, and that, if the situation had dramatically changed, there could still be a referendum in the current Parliament. But it was obvious that the Treasury retained grave reservations about the Stability Pact. Meanwhile its trump card was a calculation indicating that if interest rates were reduced to European levels during the current Parliament, the impact would have to be offset by large increases in taxation and/or reductions in public spending. This did not look a promising platform for a general election.

The Treasury also highlighted the way that changes in interest rates had a bigger impact on the behaviour of consumers in Britain because of the impact on the housing market. There was talk of persuading Britons to behave more like Continentals and make greater use of long term fixed rate mortgages, and various studies to this effect were set in train. Brown made other gestures towards the 'euro' such as firming up his indication in the Budget that the government would adopt the Eurozone's 'harmonised' index for consumer prices.

But the general impression was that with regard to the euro, the Chancellor was playing a very long game.

Conclusion – 'it's a long game'

*A*s the longest-serving Labour Chancellor, Gordon Brown has already earned his place in the history books. But such a record is incidental to the aspirations of this most ambitious and driven politician.

From an early age Brown has been concerned about poverty, unemployment and inequality. His more youthful work – his juvenilia – reflected the beliefs and values of the left of the time. But by the time Brown entered Parliament in 1983, the kind of policies connoted by such beliefs – nationalisation, high rates of taxation, wholesale redistribution of income – were proving unpopular with the electorate. Even more modest versions of Old Labour policies, such as John Smith's 'Shadow Budget' of 1992, proved an electoral liability.

At the same time, for all the 'Thatcherite Agenda' of lower marginal income tax rates, privatisation and strict limits on the powers and privileges of trade unions, the Conservative Party and the British economic establishment were failing in the central task of economic management. The traditional Keynesian polices of the postwar era ran into trouble in the 1970s, as inflation proved extraordinarily difficult to control in the face of powerful domestic (escalating wage demands from trade unions) and world forces (the latter being induced mainly by the oil price shocks of 1974–75 and 1979–80).

This made life difficult for traditional Keynesians, while monetarism (the attempt to master inflation by controlling the money supply) seemed to offer a simple solution. However, monetarism proved more complicated in practice and, long after the event, was even disowned by its godfather, Professor Milton Friedman. The failure of attempts to control the money supply led the Conservative government of the 1980s to resort to the European exchange rate mechanism as a discipline, but this expedient, too, ended in tears.

British politicians, whether in power or vying for it, began not to trust themselves. Nigel Lawson's Chancellorship was a search for rules by which to steer the economy. While disavowing the Conservative approach, Gordon Brown, in Opposition, also spent much of his time seeking a formula which would provide him with a 'stable' economic background, in order the better to pursue his political aims.

Brown and Tony Blair worked in close harness from shortly after they entered the Commons in 1983, under the Leadership of Neil Kinnock, with John Smith as an active 'mentor'. They played an important role in the process by which the Labour Leadership moved from advocating withdrawal from the European Economic Community in 1983 to becoming more passionate advocates than the Thatcher government of the ERM, which Britain finally joined in 1990, and the single currency.

The failure of the ERM experiment left Brown, by now Shadow Chancellor, without the stable economic anchor he sought to enable him to concentrate on his 'fairness agenda' when he should eventually gain office. The young man who supplied him with his new anchor – the fiscal and monetary framework of which he was to make so much from 1997 onwards – was Ed Balls, then a 24 year-old leader writer on the *Financial Times* and author of a Fabian pamphlet (1992) which gave many clues to the progression of Brown's future policies. Brown felt on the defensive because Labour had lost three elections in a row, two of them at least in part because the Conservatives had been able to exploit what became known as the 'tax-and-spend' issue.

The death of John Smith was a shattering blow to Brown, who was a closer friend of Smith's than was Tony Blair. The modernisation of Labour had begun under Neil Kinnock but paused under John Smith, who thought the Conservatives stood a good chance of losing the next election by themselves. But Blair and Brown had been impatient, and after Smith's death the two of them reinforced their efforts to produce what became known as 'New Labour' policies.

In effect, the duumvirate that was going to run the New Labour government after 1 May 1997 was formed in the weeks following Smith's death, and the well-publicised, chronic tensions within the duumvirate were the consequence of Brown's frustrated ambition when he agreed not to challenge Blair for the Leadership, in return for assurances about the 'fairness agenda', a much enlarged role for the Treasury after the election, and Blair's backing in a subsequent election 'for the leadership'.

Unlike John Smith, however, Blair and Brown were so nervous about the outcome of the election that they felt it necessary to make remarkable pledges: to freeze public spending for two years and not to raise the basic or higher rate of tax during the lifetime of the next Parliament. Brown only decided on granting independence to the Bank of England the weekend before the election, but did not reveal his hand until the week after.

The 'fiscal rules' and the independent Bank of England became Gordon Brown's lodestars – his substitute for the ERM. They were offered to him by Ed Balls as an alternative policy to 'Europe'. The Balls argument was that joining the European economic and monetary union (EMU) should not be seen as a desirable means of imposing discipline on the British economy, and might actually sink it. No, the British economy had to be made fit enough to join EMU.

For Gordon Brown this strategy became an integral part of a very long game. There was a brief period, in the first few months of the new government, when Brown was sufficiently nervous about whether the new strategy would work to keep open the option of joining the embryonic Eurozone. By September 1997, however, the Monetary Policy Committee was already considered a success, and the fiscal rules had impressed the financial markets. Brown was conscious of the way past Labour governments had been too ambitious and eventually encountered a financial crisis. He was determined to avoid that fate. And in the first term at least (1997–2001) he succeeded.

The *quid pro quo* for the two-year freeze on public spending was that a Labour government that was elected to 'do something' about the state of the nation's infrastructure and public services ended up investing less in these areas than the Conservatives had done in any comparable four-year period going back to the 1970s. And the *quid pro quo* for the '2.5% inflation' brief given to the Monetary Policy Committee was that manufacturing industry suffered from a chronically overvalued pound from 1997 until the second half of 2002, when sterling finally began to descend towards more competitive levels.

The damage done to British manufacturing was disguised to a considerable extent by the success the government and the MPC enjoyed in bringing unemployment down, and in continuing to oversee an impressive rate of expansion in non-manufacturing sectors of the economy. The MPC became more and more conscious of 'imbalances' in the economy – between manufacturing and services, for example – and of the way a familiar, old-fashioned British consumer boom was encouraged by low interest rates and rising house prices. But in effect the MPC's brief was to try to keep the economy on 'automatic pilot' (provided that inflation was under control), not to bother itself about the imbalances to which it drew attention and for which the Chancellor's policies and its own actions were partly responsible. Industrial production was 2.5% lower in 2002 than in 1997 in the UK, whereas it was 9.25% higher in the European Union, largely reflecting the deleterious impact of the overvalued pound on British industry's exports, and on its ability to compete with exports. Between 1995 and 2002 imports rose by 66.2% but exports by only 39.9%, an indication that all was not well beneath the generally rather complacent claims that the UK had fared better than other leading industrial economies.

But on the surface the Brown Chancellorship between 1997 and the first half of 2003 was associated with a reasonably rapid overall growth rate, falling unemployment and a serious attempt to alleviate poverty on the part of a Chancellor who tried to 'redistribute by stealth' in the face of market forces that were tending to make the rich richer and the poor (relatively) poorer.

One of the principal forces maintaining employment in the face of the world economic slowdown of 2002–03 was the 'unintended Keynesianism' in the way Gordon Brown had approached the public sector. First there was a famine; then a feast, with public spending rising fast and the newspaper advertisements replete with job opportunities in the public sector. But the early years of prudence had served to make the problems of the public sector either worse than the inheritance or, at the very least, to have delayed improvements in, for example, the Health Service and the rail network. A Labour government elected with an enormous majority was pusillanimous in its approach.

As I have attempted to demonstrate in this book, the big influences on Gordon Brown were the 'three Ms': the strong social conscience he inherited as a 'Son of the Manse'; the lesson he drew from his study of his hero James Maxton, that political principles were not enough if rigid adherence to them kept the aspiring politician from attaining office; and the loss of the 1983 election under Michael Foot – with whom Brown maintained a good relationship, but the lessons of whose defeat were not lost and were compounded by Labour's subsequent defeats in the elections of 1987 and (especially) 1992.

The result was the adoption by Brown of a cautious approach to fiscal and monetary policy – but it was always 'Prudence for a Purpose'. By 2003 the viability of the carefully laid plans for future expansion of public spending – bringing the UK up to European standards – was being questioned. But Gordon Brown himself was riding high, and speculation about his future was soon laid to rest when he and John Prescott rode to the rescue of the Prime Minister when Blair's position was briefly threatened after the resignation of Robin Cook and Clare Short during the Iraq War.

In everything he does – from domestic economic policy to its relation to Europe and the thorny question of the euro – Gordon Brown plays a long game. At the time of writing it seems far from over.

Notes and references

Introduction

1. David Reisman, *Anthony Crosland: The Mixed Economy*. Macmillan: London, 1977; p. 1.
2. Gordon Brown, Speech to Labour Finance and Industry Group, 17 August 1993.

Chapter one

1. *The Times*, 15 May 1993
2. Paul Routledge, *Gordon Brown – The Biography*. Pocket Books, Simon and Schuster: Hemel Hempstead, 1998; p. 7.
3. *Ibid*: p. 26.
4. *Ibid*: p. 30.
5. *Ibid*: p. 30.
6. *Ibid*: p. 30.
7. *Ibid*: p. 37.
8. *Ibid*: p. 36.
9. *Ibid*: p. 39.
10. James Naughtie, *The Rivals*. Fourth Estate: London, 2001; p. 8.
11. Paul Routledge, *op. cit*. p. 43.
12. *Ibid*: p. 43.
13. *Ibid*: p. 62.
14. *Ibid*: p. 62.
15. *The Times*, 15 May 1993.
16. Roy Jenkins, *A Life at the Centre*. Macmillan: London, 1991; pp. 296–7.
17. *Student* (Edinburgh), 20 October 1971.
18. James Naughtie, *op. cit*. p. 20.
19. *Ibid*: p. 22.
20. *Ibid*: p. 23.
21. Paul Routledge, *op. cit*. p. 79.

22. Conversation with the Rt. Hon. Neil Kinnock, 10 May 2002.
23. Alf Young, 8 July 1997; quoted in Paul Routledge, *op. cit.* p. 80.
24. *Edinburgh Evening News*, 17 April 1979.
25. *Edinburgh Evening News*, 26 March 1979.
26. Tony Benn, 'Conflicts of interest'. In *Diaries 1977–1990*. Hutchinson: London; p. 499.
27. *Glasgow Herald*, 28 February 1983.
28. Paul Routledge, *op. cit.* p. 96.

Chapter two

1. Declaration by the 'Gang of Four' (Roy Jenkins, David Owen, Shirley Williams and William Rodgers), Limehouse, 25 January 1981.
2. Giles Radice, *Labour's Path to Power – The New Revisionism*. Macmillan: London, 1989; p. 25.
3. *Ibid.* p. 24.
4. Martin Westlake, *Kinnock – The Biography*. Little, Brown: London, 2001 (see Chapters 9–11 on Kinnock's road to the Leadership; see also Robert Harris, *The Making of Neil Kinnock*. Faber: London, 1984).
5. Martin Westlake, *op. cit.* p. 168.
6. Neil Kinnock, speech at Birkenhead, 31 January 1981.
7. Martin Westlake, *op. cit.* p. 176.
8. *Ibid.* p. 232.
9. Neil Kinnock, speech at Wandsworth Town Hall, 8 September 1983.
10. Martin Westlake, *op. cit.* p. 234.
11. James Naughtie, *op. cit.* p. 26.
12. *Ibid.* p. 28.
13. *Hansard*, **50**: cols 141–2.
14. Gordon Brown and Robin Cook, 'Scotland: the real divide'. In *Poverty and Deprivation in Scotland*. Mainstream: Edinburgh, 1983; p. 10.
15. *Ibid.*
16. Paul Routledge, *op. cit.* p. 124.
17. Gordon Brown, *Maxton*. Mainstream: Edinburgh, 1986; p. 9.
18. *Ibid.* p. 126.
19. *Ibid.* p. 18.
20. *Ibid.* pp. 18, 21.
21. *Ibid.* p. 251.
22. *Ibid.* p. 253.

23. *Ibid.* p. 250.
24. *Ibid.* p. 309.

Chapter three

1. Conversation with the Rt. Hon. Neil Kinnock, 10 May 2002.
2. Paul Routledge, *op. cit.* p. 140.
3. Henry Neuberger, 'Productive and competitive economy'. Discussion paper for Labour Party policy review, 1989; p. 8.
4. Mark Wickham-Jones, 'Making economic policy in the Labour Party, 1980–1990: bringing economists back in'. In *Public Policy for the Twenty-first Century* (social and economic essays in memory of Henry Neuberger), Neil Fraser and John Mills (eds). The Policy Press: Bristol, 1990; p. 242.
5. *Ibid.* p. 244.
6. *Ibid.* p. 240.
7. Roy Hattersley, 'Government borrowing: what Labour would do'. ECSTRA working paper, 1985.
8. Andy McSmith, *John Smith.* Verso: London, 1993; p. 105.
9. *Ibid.* p. 147.
10. Paul Anderson. In *Safety First*, Paul Anderson and Nyta Mann (eds). Granta: Cambridge, 1997; p. 67.
11. *Hansard*, 14 January 1988, col. 542.
12. *Ibid.*
13. Paul Anderson, *op. cit.* p. 68.
14. Andy McSmith, *op. cit.* p. 120.
15. *Hansard*, 12 January 1989, cols 1005–8.
16. *Ibid.*
17. *Ibid.*
18. David Butler and Dennis Kavanagh, *The British General Election of 1992.* Macmillan: London, 1992; p. 268.

Chapter four

1. Edmund Dell, 'Britain and the origins of the European Monetary System'. *Contemporary European History*, March 1994; **3**(1).

2. Nigel Lawson, *The View from No. 11*. Bantam Press: London, 1992; William Keegan, *Mr Lawson's Gamble*. Hodder and Stoughton: London, 1989.
3. Charles Grant, *Delors – Inside the House that Jacques Built*. Nicholas Brealey: London, 1994.
4. Martin Westlake, *op. cit.*
5. Lord Eatwell, conversation with author, 17 June 2002.
6. Lord Eatwell. In *The Economic Legacy 1979–1992*, Jonathan Michie (ed.). Academic Press: London, 1992.
7. Lord Eatwell, lecture to South Bank University, 1995.
8. Bryan Gould, *Goodbye to All That*. Macmillan, London, 1995.
9. *Ibid.*
10. *Ibid.*
11. Andy McSmith, *op. cit.*; Bryan Gould, *op. cit.*
12. *Ibid.*
13. *Ibid.*
14. Philip Stephens, *Politics and the Pound*. Macmillan: London, 1996.
15. Conversation with European Commission official, 27 February 1995.
16. Martin Westlake, *op. cit.*
17. Bryan Gould, *op. cit.*
18. *Ibid.*
19. European Commission official, 27 February 1995.
20. Conversation with the Rt. Hon. Neil Kinnock, 24 June 2002.

Chapter five

1. Norman Lamont, *In Office*. Little, Brown: London, 1999.
2. Press conference, H. M. Treasury, 6 May 1997, and on frequent subsequent occasions.
3. Gordon Brown, *Tribune*, 25 September 1992.
4. *Fabian Review*, September 1992; **104**(5).
5. Conversation with the Rt. Hon Neil Kinnock, 10 May 2002.
6. James Naughtie, *op. cit.*
7. *see* Note 5.
8. *see* Note 5.
9. A senior and respected Labour back-bencher in conversation with the author, 1 May 2002.
10. Gordon Brown's 'fairness agenda' had appeared as a Fabian pamphlet

(No. 563, 'Fair Is Efficient – A Socialist Agenda for Fairness') in April 1994, a few weeks before John Smith's death.
11. Conversation with the then proprietress of Granita, 18 January 2002.

Chapter six

1. Paul Routledge, *op. cit.*
2. *Ibid.*
3. Conversation with the Rt. Hon. Neil Kinnock, 10 May 2002.
4. Gordon Brown, text of speech, 'New Policies for the Global Economy', 27 September 1994.
5. Michael Heseltine, speech to Conservative Party Annual Conference in Bournemouth, 12 October 1994.
6. Swraj Paul, *Beyond Boundaries*. Penguin: Harmondsworth, 1999.
7. The author has had numerous conversations with Gordon Brown and Ed Balls over the years. He sees no point in listing every occasion. Some have been public and some are based on what my good friend and colleague Andrew Rawnsley has immortalised in the phrase 'private information'.
8. Edward Balls, 'Euro-monetarism: why Britain was ensnared and how it should escape'. Fabian Society Discussion Paper No. 14, 1992.
9. *Ibid.*
10. *Ibid.*
11. *Ibid.*
12. *Ibid.*
13. *Ibid.*
14. *Ibid.*
15. *Ibid.*
16. *Ibid.*
17. *Ibid.*
18. *Ibid.*
19. *Ibid.*
20. Paul Routledge, *op. cit.*
21. Gordon Brown, 'The Choices Facing the Country', speech to the Labour Finance and Industry Group, 17 August 1993.
22. *Ibid.*
23. *see* Geoffrey Robinson, *The Unconventional Minister*. Michael Joseph: London, 2000.
24. Gavyn Davies, *The Independent*, 22 May 1995.
25. Gordon Brown, 'Labour's Macroeconomic Framework', speech to the Labour Finance and Industry Group, 17 May 1995.

Chapter seven

1. 'New Labour' appeared as the heading of a section of Gordon Brown's speech, 'Labour's Macroeconomic Framework', delivered to the Labour Finance and Industry Group, 17 May 1995.
2. Matthew d'Ancona, 2002.
3. Conversation with the author, late 1980s.
4. Gordon Brown, speech at the official opening of the new Treasury building, 25 September 2002.
5. Geoffrey Robinson, *op. cit.*
6. Edward Balls, 1992, *op. cit.*
7. *Ibid.*
8. Gordon Brown, 'Labour's Economic Approach', speech on 17 August 1993.
9. *Ibid.*
10. *Ibid.*
11. The MPC evolved from eight to nine members to accommodate the additional 'deputy governor' appointed for banking supervision. Supervision was removed but the extra 'deputy' remained.
12. Edward Balls, 1992, *op. cit.*
13. Gordon Brown, 'Labour's Macroeconomic Framework', speech to the Labour Finance and Industry Group, 17 May 1995.
14. *Ibid.*
15. *Ibid.*
16. *Ibid.*
17. Gordon Brown, 'Building a Recovery that Lasts', speech at the Centre for Economic Performance, Economist Business Forum, 26 February 1997.
18. Sir Edward George, *The Observer*, 8 June 2003. The author has also drawn on many helpful conversations with Sir Edward over the years.
19. Gordon Brown, speech at the official opening of the new Treasury building, 25 September 2002.
20. Ed Balls and Gus O'Donnell (eds), *Reforming Britain's Economic and Financial Policy*. H. M. Treasury: London, 2002.

Chapter eight

1. The author, *The Observer*, 28 January 1996.
2. Geoffrey Robinson, *op. cit.*

3. *Ibid.*
4. This and a number of subsequent quotations from officials come from interviews and conversations which were conducted on the basis of anonymity.
5. *The Observer*, 25 January 1998.

Chapter nine

1. Gordon Brown, 'Building a Recovery that Lasts', speech at the Centre for Economic Performance, Economist Business Forum, 26 February 1997.
2. *see* DeAnne Julius, 'Back to the Future of Low Global Inflation', The Maxwell Fry Global Finance Lecture, University of Birmingham, 20 October 1999.
3. *see* Dr Sushil Wadhwani, 'British Unemployment and Monetary Policy', speech to the Society of Business Economists, 2 December 1999; *and* 'The Stock Market Capacity Uncertainties and the Outlook for UK Inflation', speech to Edinburgh University Economics Society, 21 November 2001.
4. Mervyn King, 'The MPC Two Years On', lecture at Queen's University, Belfast, 17 May 1999.
5. *Ibid.*
6. Bank of England, *Minutes of Monetary Policy Committee Meeting, 6 and 7 August 1997*, published 17 September 1997.
7. *Ibid.*
8. *see* Mervyn King, 'A Tale of Two Cities', speech to Cardiff Business School, Cardiff University, 18 June 2001.
9. Bank of England, *Minutes of MPC Meeting*, November 1997.
10. Bank of England, *Minutes of MPC Meeting*, January 1998.
11. Mervyn King, 'The MPC Two Years On', lecture at Queen's University, Belfast, 17 May 1999.
12. *Ibid.*
13. Ed Balls and Gus O'Donnell, *op. cit.*
14. Mervyn King, 'The Inflation Target Ten Years On', speech at the London School of Economics, 19 November 2002.
15. *Ibid.*
16. Sir Edward George, House of Commons Session 2000–2001, Treasury Committee Ninth Report, *The Monetary Policy Committee – An End of Term Report*, 22 March 2001.

17. *Ibid.*
18. Sir Edward George, speech to the Royal Society for the Encouragement of Arts, Manufacture and Commerce (RSA), Birmingham, 11 April 2002.
19. *Ibid.*
20. Interview with Willem Buiter, *The Observer*, 20 February 2000.
21. *Ibid.*
22. *see* Dr Sushil Wadhwani, 'The Impact of the US Slowdown on the UK Economy', speech in Newcastle, 22 February 2001.
23. Bank of England, *Minutes of MPC Meeting*, 7–8 February 2001.
24. Mervyn King, speech to Plymouth Chamber of Commerce and Industry, 14 April 2000.
25. Mervyn King, speech to CBI North East Region, Newcastle upon Tyne, 22 November 2001.
26. *Ibid.*
27. Wynne Godley and Alex Izurieta, 'The Wrong Set-up? A Critique of British Economic Policy Under Labour', April 2003; and 'Coasting on the Lending Bubble both in the UK and the US', June 2003. Working papers, Cambridge Endowment for Research in Finance, Judge Institute of Management Studies.
28. Mervyn King, Inflation Report Press Conference, Bank of England, 12 February 2003.
29. *Ibid.*
30. Edward Balls, 1992, *op. cit.*

Chapter ten

1. *Effects of Taxes and Benefits on Household Income*, Government Statistical Service, 2003.
2. Nigel Lawson, conversation with author, 8 January 1991.
3. *see* Speeches of Sir Edward George and Mervyn King, 1997–2003 *passim* (some quoted in Chapter Nine).
4. David Butler and Dennis Kavanagh, *The British General Election of 2001.* Palgrave: Basingstoke, 2002.
5. *2002 Spending Review – New Public Spending Plans 2003–2006.* HM Treasury (cmd5570), July 2002. The planned rise in public spending between 2000–01 and 2005–06 was £144.36 billion, or £90.2 billion in real terms (i.e. after adjusting for public sector inflation), taking 'total managed expenditure' by the public sector from 38.2% to 41.9% of GDP.

6. Lord Healey, quoted in 'In My View', *The Observer*, 29 June 2003.
7. Lord Lawson, *Financial Times*, 5 October 2001.
8. John Hills, 'Following or Leading Public Opinion? Social Security Policy and Public Attitudes Since 1997'. Pamphlet, Institute for Fiscal Studies, 2002.
9. John Hills, 'The Blair Government and Child Poverty'. Working paper, 2003, for future US publication, '1% For the Kids'.
10. Smeeding, Rainwater and Burtless (2001), quoted in Hills, 2003, *op. cit.*
11. John Hills, 2003, *op. cit.*
12. *Ibid.*
13. *Ibid.*
14. *Ibid.*
15. David Piachaud and Holly Sutherland, 'Child poverty'. In *Understanding Social Exclusion*. Oxford University Press: Oxford, 2002; and 'Changing Poverty Post-1997'. CASE: Paper 63, London School of Economics, 2002.
16. Edmund Dell, *A Strange Eventful History – Democratic Socialism in Britain*. Harper Collins: London, 2000.
17. 'Deregulation' became a code-word for the redressing of the balance of power between employers and Labour under the Conservatives.

Chapter eleven

1. The quotations in this and other paragraphs are from anonymous officials, not official spokesmen.
2. Conversation with Paul Maltby, PFI expert at IPPR, 30 May 2003.
3. A detailed account and explanation of the fiscal rules is contained in Ed Balls and Gus O'Donnell, 2002, *op. cit.*
4. House of Commons, Session 1999–2000, Treasury Committee Fourth Report, 'The Private Finance Initiative', March 2000.
5. John Grieve Smith, *There Is A Better Way*. Anthem: Wimbledon, 2001.
6. Nick Cohen, *The Observer*, April 2003.
7. But 'transport' accounted for two-thirds of 'signed PFI deals' in 2003–04. 'Budget 2003', H. M. Treasury, March 2002.
8. 'Budget 2003', H. M. Treasury, March 2002.
9. *Ibid.*
10. *Ibid.*
11. Conversation with Professor John Stein, 30 May 2003.
12. *The Observer*, October 1999.

Chapter twelve

1. Gordon Brown, 'Statement on Economic and Monetary Union', 27 October 1997.
2. *Ibid.*
3. *see* Andrew Rawnsley, *Servants of the People*. Penguin: Harmondsworth, 2001.
4. *see* John Kampfner, *Robin Cook*. Gollancz: London, 1998.
5. Gordon Brown, 'Building a Recovery that Lasts', speech at the Centre for Economic Performance, Economist Business Forum, 26 February 1997.
6. Lord Simon, conversation with author, 4 March 2003.
7. Conversation with Rupert Pennant-Rae, 24 February 2003.
8. Andrew Rawnsley, *op. cit.*
9. *The Times*, 18 October 1997.
10. Gordon Brown, 'Building a Recovery that Lasts', speech at the Centre for Economic Performance, Economist Business Forum, 26 February 1997.
11. Tony Blair to Robert Harris, April 1997.
12. Geoffrey Robinson, *op. cit.*
13. *The Observer*, 17 June 2001.
14. *Ibid.*
15. Ed Balls, Caircross Lecture, Oxford, 4 December 2002.
16. One euro-sceptical Treasury official commented, 'Is this a referendum you want to win?'
17. Hugo Young, *Supping with the Devils*. Atlantic Books: London, 2003.
18. Such suggestions are also authoritatively dismissed by John Rentoul in his book, *Tony Blair, Prime Minister*. Little, Brown: London, 2001.

Index